I0819696

BEATING HEART OF THE WORLD

BEATING HEART OF THE WORLD

The Taos Art Colony, the Pueblo Resistance, and the Battle for Indigenous America

STEVEN L. DAVIS

HIGH ROAD BOOKS | ALBUQUERQUE

High Road Books is an imprint of the University of New Mexico Press

Printed in the United States of America

ISBN 978-0-8263-6966-6 (cloth)
ISBN 978-0-8263-6967-3 (ePub)

Library of Congress Control Number: 2025054188

Founded in 1889, the University of New Mexico sits on the traditional homelands of the Pueblo of Sandia. The original peoples of New Mexico—Pueblo, Navajo, and Apache—since time immemorial have deep connections to the land and have made significant contributions to the broader community statewide. We honor the land itself and those who remain stewards of this land throughout the generations and also acknowledge our committed relationship to Indigenous peoples. We gratefully recognize our history.

Cover illustration: *Going East* by Walter Ufer, courtesy of
the Fred Jones Jr. Museum of Art at the University of Oklahoma
Designed by Felicia Cedillos
Composed in Adobe Caslon Pro

for Georgia Ruiz Davis

The actinic rays of the solar spectrum draws many people to Taos. Some of them are born strange, some achieve strangeness, and some have strangeness thrust upon them.

—T. M. PEARCE

The Indians must conform to the white man's ways, peaceably if they will, forcibly if they must. . . . They must conform to it or be crushed by it.

—T. J. MORGAN, COMMISSIONER OF INDIAN AFFAIRS (1889–1893)

They told us that Indian ways were bad. They said we must get civilized. I remember that word, too. It means "be like the white man."

—LORENZO MARTÍNEZ, TAOS PUEBLO

Your god is the god of greed. We want you to come and breathe the same pure air that we breathe. Why don't you live like the Indians?

—PABLO ABEITA, ISLETA PUEBLO

Contents

Author's Note

I've long been intrigued by the odd ranks of artists, writers, and scattered freethinkers who gravitated to Taos in the early twentieth century. These spirited renegades established a world-famous artist colony while leaving behind a celebrated yet also controversial legacy.

For years I devoured the plentiful books, articles, and scholarly studies on this topic. But as the readings piled up, I felt something was missing. While many writers and scholars presented illuminating material, the art colony seemed to exist as a self-contained island, notable chiefly for its assemblage of celebrity. I kept thinking the convergence of so many prominent people should have amounted to something more consequential than insular self-regard. But I could never detect a narrative thread connecting Taos to a world beyond itself.

Then I encountered R. C. Gordon-McCutchan's book about Taos Pueblo's long fight to regain its sacred Blue Lake (*The Taos Indians and the Battle for Blue Lake*, 1995.) This study provides a comprehensive legal history, detailing the sustained efforts of tribal leaders and others over many decades to win justice for Taos Pueblo. Yet what also caught my attention was the author's reference to Bert Phillips, a local man who aided the Pueblo's early efforts to protect its homeland from white encroachment. Gordon-McCutchan described Phillips as, simply, a "Taos old-timer." Yet I knew Phillips as far more. He was the painter who founded the Taos art colony.

At that moment, the idea for this book was born. For I finally understood the broader historical context missing from my view of the art colony: At the same time Taos was attracting world-famous artists and writers, the US government was moving to exterminate New Mexico's Pueblo People by stripping away their lands and attacking their cultures.

This same scenario had played out countless times before in American history. The resilient Pueblos, who had defied conquest for centuries, had become some of America's last holdouts. The Puebloans had once unleashed a fierce revolt against Spain in 1680, but in this new century they found a different way to resist. Recognizing the political value of the high-profile whites gathering in Taos, Pueblo leaders actively courted receptive members of the artist colony as supporters. The painter Bert Phillips may have been the first to take up the Pueblos' cause, but he was hardly the last.

These outsiders were never regarded as "white saviors." Instead, they were considered useful allies to help the Pueblos achieve their own strategic aims—primarily protecting their lands and cultures. None of these supporters were perfect, and some—including Phillips—would prove deeply flawed. Yet at a pivotal moment in history, these advocates rose to challenge their own culture's prevailing genocidal policies.

When the Taos art colony and the Pueblo People joined together, they created a remarkable new resistance movement, one that swelled into a national campaign for Indigenous justice. Ultimately, this crusade from Taos would finally break America's fever for conquest, setting the nation's relations with Indigenous people on a new course by restoring lost lands, empowering tribal self-government, and securing protections of Native cultures, languages, and religions that exist to this day. While this peaceful, decades-in-the-making revolution may not have manifested the sharp, stunning violence of the 1680 Pueblo Revolt, its ultimate impact is just as consequential. That such a fascinating and important story has gone largely untold is astonishing to me—and it's why I've written this book.

While I have assembled the various pieces of this epic battle into a cohesive narrative for the first time, it is important to recognize that many dozens of previously published works contain key elements of this history. Among those sources are several creditable books on the Taos art colony, Indigenous history, environmental history, and federal Native policy. I also consulted numerous academic studies and books on the individual artists, writers, politicians, naturalists, anthropologists, and others represented in this volume.

Those secondary readings were supplemented by my firsthand research in several important archival repositories. These include Princeton's Taos Blue Lake archive, Yale University's extensive collections on Mabel Dodge

Luhan and John Collier, many vital papers at the New Mexico State Records and Archives Center, the University of New Mexico's Center for Southwest Research, and more. While working on *Beating Heart of the World*, I was able to view personal letters and firsthand reports that put me as close to the action as possible. These rich and revealing archival treasures were supplemented by government records, transcripts of congressional hearings, official correspondence, bulletins, newsletters, speeches, and other materials. In reviewing the many often conflicting accounts that make up the raw resources of this history, I have tried to select those facts that provide the best approximation of reality as I understand it.

A Note on Terminology

Hispano. Refers to Spanish-speaking New Mexicans who identify as descendants of Spanish or Mexican settlers.

Anglo. An imprecise but convenient umbrella term to describe "white people."

Indian. For the time period of this book (1898–1934), the word *Indian* was commonly used to designate "Indigenous people." Yet that term, originally imposed by misinformed outsiders, is increasingly viewed as problematic. For this narrative, I've avoided its use beyond direct quotations or existing designations, such as the Bureau of Indian Affairs and the Indian New Deal.

Taos. For those unfamiliar with Taos, it can be confusing to distinguish between Taos Pueblo and the city known as Taos. The Pueblo, anchored by two multistory adobe compounds, was founded around 1000 CE. Three miles south of the grand Pueblo lies the city of Taos, officially known as Don Fernando de Taos and established under Spanish rule in the seventeenth century. In using *Taos* throughout this book, I've tried to provide appropriate context so that the reader can discern whether I'm referring to the Hispano-founded town or Taos Pueblo.

Prologue

JANUARY 10, 1933
UPPER EAST SIDE, MANHATTAN

On this bright afternoon in the bleakest winter of the Great Depression, two men who'd journeyed two thousand miles from Taos Pueblo stepped out of a taxicab near Central Park. Draped in sky-blue tribal blankets and wearing beaded deerskin moccasins, their long black hair was neatly arranged into twin braids. Ignoring gawking bystanders, the pair strode toward a palatial five-story brownstone on East 65th Street, its entrance guarded by Secret Service agents. There, Tony Luján and Antonio Mirabal announced themselves. They were quickly ushered inside, for President-Elect Franklin D. Roosevelt was expecting them.

Nine weeks had passed since Roosevelt's landslide victory over Herbert Hoover, yet another two months remained before he would be sworn in. Given the ominous economic crisis he stood to inherit, nobody expected Native policy reform to be high on his agenda. Yet the president-elect had readily cleared space in his jammed schedule to meet with the Taos men.

Luján and Mirabal were both experienced at statecraft, emerging as key resistance leaders over the past decade when the US government tried to seize Taos Pueblo's land and smother its nature-worshipping religion. Tony Luján, six feet tall and broad-shouldered, spoke little English but radiated a serene majesty with his granite-solid good looks. He'd married a wealthy New York heiress and had parleyed with writers D. H. Lawrence and Willa Cather. He'd posed for the photographer Ansel Adams and he'd gotten lost in the woods on a frolic with Georgia O'Keeffe, much to his wife's dismay. Luján had proved vital in helping Taos and New Mexico's other Pueblos defeat the notorious Bursum Bill in the 1920s, which aimed to strip away the Pueblos' remaining lands. As part of that campaign, he'd led a contingent of feather-clad Puebloans into the New York Stock

Exchange, where they sang and performed a tribal dance to rally opposition to the bill.

Luján's companion, Antonio Mirabal, was a small, slightly built man whose large round eyes burned with intensity. He had once posed for a painting by the artist Maynard Dixon. Mirabal only received two years of schooling as a child but went on to use a cast-off dictionary to become proficient in English. He'd since become Taos Pueblo's leading intellectual and its chief diplomat. He subscribed to several publications including the *Congressional Record*. Mirabal had once spent a day with Carl Jung atop Taos Pueblo, debating the nature of reality. He was among the tribal leaders who defied the US government during its attacks on Taos Pueblo's religion, saying, "They have taken our lands, but they can shoot us down before they do this other thing to us."[1] He and the others were denounced as "half-animals" and thrown in jail.

Both Luján and Mirabal had seen many changes in Taos since the first white artists arrived in a horse-drawn wagon in 1898. The early painters believed the Natives to be a "Vanishing Race" and sought to capture their final images in a series of sentimental portraits. The founder of the art colony, Bert Geer Phillips, appeared well intentioned but was also capable of betrayal and incited two riots in Taos. The hapless Phillips tried to aid Taos Pueblo in protecting its sacred Blue Lake from white encroachment, though his efforts backfired in 1906 when President Theodore Roosevelt instead commandeered the area for a national forest named after Kit Carson.

While Taos Pueblo suffered, the new artist colony's fame spread far and wide. It ultimately attracted the "Queen of Bohemia," a New York socialite who dabbled in peyote while directing the American avant-garde from her Greenwich Village salon. Soon after her arrival in Taos, Mabel Dodge Sterne began a scandalous affair with tribal leader Tony Luján. She became captivated by the Taos People's peaceful, communal lifeways and their holy regard for the natural world. She saw a stark contrast to her own culture's record of endless war, hyperindividualism, and environmental destruction.

Mabel eventually divorced her artist husband and married Luján, becoming Mabel Dodge Luhan. Viewing Taos Pueblo as "the beating heart of the world," she began summoning those she considered "Great

Souls" to join her in Taos, where she hoped to spark a new, utopian American civilization based on Native values.

Just as Mabel launched her crusade, the US government marshalled its final assault against the Pueblo People. Native religious rites and ceremonial dances were banned, and the US Senate unanimously passed a new bill to confiscate Pueblo lands. This same scenario, a slow-motion genocide, had played out countless times before. It seemed that nothing could stop the brutal crush of conquest.

Yet the arc of American history made a sharp turn at Taos, bending at last toward justice. Mabel and Tony Luján became the unlikely catalysts, bringing the bohemians and Pueblos together to spark a new resistance movement—the most vigorous mass campaign for Indigenous rights the United States had ever seen.

Emerging from the bohemian ranks to take charge was a renowned social reformer and minor poet named John Collier. One of the luminaries drawn to Taos by Mabel, Collier hardly looked the part of an insurrectionist leader. A scholarly-minded mystic by nature, he was a small, rumpled man who wore oversized wire-rim glasses. Yet Collier burned with a passion for justice and he proved an indefatigable warrior. For a decade he battled the corrupt US Indian Bureau, scorching the establishment with longshot victories. Denounced as a radical, a communist, and a bad poet, Collier was targeted by government investigations and even hanged in effigy on the Santa Fe Plaza. His zealotry alienated moderates, but his standing among the Pueblos remained solid. Tony Luján and Antonio Mirabal regarded him as the one white person they could trust to carry on their fight.

Working with the Pueblo People, Collier developed a monumental vision: Against impossible odds, the resistance aimed to reverse centuries of dispossession and cultural extinction. They would turn back the tide of European conquest, empowering and revitalizing Indigenous America.

For this revolution to have a chance, they needed to gain a seat at the table of power. With Franklin Roosevelt's election, the insurgency saw its chance.

Inside Roosevelt's townhome, Luján and Mirabal were led through a boisterous entry hall packed with cops, reporters, and politicians. Coats and hats and briefcases were piled everywhere, and cigarette smoke clouded the air. The Taos men were guided up a flight of stairs to a quiet second-floor reception area. A few moments later they were ushered into Roosevelt's private study, a book-lined room with sunlight pouring in through floor-to-ceiling windows. Roosevelt, seated before a crackling fireplace, greeted his visitors warmly with firm handshakes. The Taos men took seats across from him and began making their case.

Antonio Mirabal did most of the talking. "We have had trouble for many years," he said, explaining how the US government's Indian Bureau had long persecuted the Taos People and other Native Americans. Roosevelt listened attentively, nodding when Mirabal told him, "Now is the time to change." Then Mirabal came to his point. He told Roosevelt there was only one white man the Natives wanted to head the Bureau: "The people sent us to get John Collier for commissioner."[2]

Roosevelt made no promises, but he assured both men that he would do all possible to help Native people. More handshakes were exchanged, and Luján and Mirabal made their way back to the first floor. Mirabal spoke to the press about the incoming president. He described Roosevelt as "very friendly" and added, "He is a kind and a fine man."[3]

Over the next few months, Roosevelt delayed taking any action. Various moderates emerged as favorites for Indian Commissioner, each with strong senate support. Yet the president never moved to nominate any of them. Whenever Collier's name came up, howls of protest arose. No one believed him a serious candidate, and Collier himself judged that he had no chance. Then, on April 15, 1933, Franklin Roosevelt announced his stunning decision. He chose the "radical" John Collier for his Commissioner of Indian Affairs. From the small sparks in Taos, a spreading revolution now seemed poised to change America forever.

PART I

A VANISHING RACE?

CHAPTER 1

WE DIDN'T KNOW TAOS

1898

DECEMBER 13, 1898

Bert Phillips had gained his first glimpse of the local Catholics' religious passions, yet the artist was feeling anything but holy as he clutched a .44 revolver and barricaded himself inside Gusdorf's General Store. With him were most of the other Anglo-Americans in Taos, about twenty men and women in all. They had frantically rounded up every bit of ammunition they could find before retreating to this imposing building on the main plaza.

It was almost midnight, and the temperature outside had fallen to zero. In the dim glow of the kerosene lanterns, Phillips could see the Gusdorf brothers' orderly shelves lined with rows of canned cabbage and Arbuckle's Coffee. At the rear of the store, near the bolts of cloth, the women were clumped together for safety behind a bulky counter. Phillips and several other men were spread out along the floor, guns ready. Others took turns as lookouts posted at the front and back doors.

A rampaging mob had already destroyed two other Anglo-owned businesses in town. One of those places, a local saloon where Phillips had sought refuge earlier, was now pockmarked with fresh bullet holes. A single telegraph wire, thirty miles away, offered Taos's lone connection to the outside world. The General Store's co-owner, Albert Gusdorf, was out there somewhere in the freezing darkness. He had vowed to get word to

Santa Fe to send reinforcements. But local vigilantes had set up blockades on every road. No one knew if Gusdorf would make it.

From inside the store, they heard angry shouts on the plaza, where a swarming throng carried torches, axes, and guns. Their battle cries pierced the air: "*Remember '47!*"

A chill ran through Phillips. He knew of the horrific Taos Revolt of 1847, which erupted shortly after the United States occupied New Mexico during its war against Mexico. Hispano and Pueblo rebels had attacked the Anglos in Taos, including the first US governor, Charles Bent, who was shot full of arrows and scalped alive in front of his family.

It seemed unbelievable that Bert Phillips, the mild-mannered painter who until recently had been living a cosmopolitan life in New York City, could find himself in this dire situation. Yet there was no denying that he'd helped start all this trouble.

Phillips's father back east had warned him against going to New Mexico, exclaiming, "You will lose your scalp!"[1] But it wasn't the Natives who concerned Phillips. He'd already made friends at Taos Pueblo, the venerable Native settlement three miles north of town. Instead, Phillips had inflamed local Hispanos, who were now massing for battle.

While Phillips and the others tensed inside the store, the crowd's shouts began to move down the street. Perhaps the mob didn't realize where the Anglos were hiding. Or maybe they'd chosen another target for the time being. Everyone remained on alert, ready to defend themselves. Until the shooting started, there was nothing to do but wait. As the hours slowly crept toward dawn, Phillips set down his pistol. He picked up some stationery and a fountain pen from Gusdorf's stock. If he was going to die inside this store, he wanted to leave some record of what happened.

In the flickering light, he dipped the pen into an inkwell and began composing a hurried letter to his best friend, Ernest Blumenschein, a fellow artist who had journeyed with him to Taos over the summer. Blumenschein had since gone back to New York. Phillips had kidded his pal at the time about leaving, accusing him of "a bad case of nostalgia for the sights and sounds of Broadway."[2] Now the time for joking had passed. Phillips wrote:

Dear Blumy:
You will be interested to know that we, the Americans, are armed to the teeth and expecting an attack from a mob of Mexicans at any moment . . ."[3]

Phillips kept writing, explaining to his friend how he had been arrested at gunpoint, how he had escaped from jail, and how the local sheriff, Luciano Trujillo, now lay dying "with three bullets through his damned head" as people filled the streets, shouting "Kill all the Americans!"

"You can't imagine what this is like," Phillips wrote. "We didn't know Taos."[4]

At age thirty, Bert Geer Phillips could hardly be considered a worldly success. A bantam-sized man, he'd grown up in Hudson, New York, where he gained local fame as a child artist. He went on to spend most of his adult life in elite art academies, studying under various masters. Over the years he developed into a technically proficient yet thoroughly bland painter. Now balding and terminally broke, Phillips often relied on his indulgent parents to help keep him afloat with small loans.

Despite his meager circumstances, Phillips carried himself with cocky bravado. He wore a stylish fedora and sported a fat moustache that bristled like an overgrown paintbrush. In Paris, studying at the Académie Julian, Phillips had befriended Ernest Blumenschein, a younger painter with dazzling potential. An intense, bespectacled twenty-four-year-old, Blumenschein was a virtuoso violinist and the son of a respected orchestra conductor. To his father's dismay, Blumenschein had turned his back on professional music career. Instead, he swelled with ambition to become a great American painter. In the meantime, Blumenschein scratched out a living by selling his drawings to newspapers and magazines.

After the two friends graduated from Académie Julian, they decided to open an art studio together in New York. They offered the usual fare of the day: genteel portraits of the bourgeoise along with moody landscapes topped by Dutch windmills. Sales were slow and the artists uninspired. Far more excitement could be found a few blocks away at Madison Square Garden, where the legendary Buffalo Bill packed in crowds with his old-time Wild West show. Phillips had grown up reading adventure stories of Buffalo Bill, and he'd been obsessed by Natives for as long as he could remember. Like many Americans, he felt growing nostalgia for the vanishing Old West—and for the Indigenous people who seemed to be exiting the national stage.

Both Phillips and Blumenschein dreamed of painting Natives, confident that such poignant subjects would help set them apart from the crowded ranks of New York artists. They recruited actors from Buffalo Bill's show to pose, but the resulting portraits, executed in midtown Manhattan, lacked the desired verisimilitude.

An older artist in Paris had told them about Taos, speaking reverently of the magnificent mountain scenery and the crisp, high-desert air. He said they would find traditional Natives living there, people in an ancient village at least a thousand years old. Phillips and Blumenschein began to dream of making the long journey to see Taos for themselves.

In May 1898, after months of saving and planning, the two painters boarded a train west. They departed New York just as the United States declared war on Spain—"in the cause of humanity" as President McKinley put it."[5] The nation raged with patriotic fever, and hundreds lined up to volunteer for Teddy Roosevelt's Rough Riders.

When Phillips and Blumenschein arrived at Denver, war was the furthest thing from their minds. Instead, they were awed by the views of the Rocky Mountains. The men purchased a brand-new buckboard wagon along with a team of horses. Though they barely knew how to ride, the two tenderfeet headed for the mountains, sleeping under the stars and stopping to sketch and paint wherever the spirit moved them. Blumenschein could handle a shotgun and kept them supplied in fresh meat from doves and rabbits. A friendly dog joined their expedition, and they named him Tip. They lost a horse one night when it fell over a cliff, hanging itself on its stakeout rope. Another time a flash flood nearly swept away their entire outfit. Just beyond Pike's Peak, a gang of gun-toting bandits raided their camp, looking for valuables. The outlaws left in disgust after finding nothing but art.

It was late summer when the two men finally approached Taos. The New Yorkers were hungry and dirty, and they'd spent their last three dollars getting a broken wagon wheel repaired. But at seven thousand feet, the crisp air felt invigorating and the high-desert light was dazzling. At the edge of the sagebrush plain, a wall of blue mountains erupted, rising to a nest of clouds. "The mountains are aglow," Phillips exclaimed, "with golden lights and blue and purple shadows."[6]

The artists entered the small Hispano village of Taos, its flat-roofed, mud-colored adobe homes huddled around the church and central plaza. They found a wagon road leading to the old Pueblo village they'd heard about. The route was shaded by fat cottonwoods and water sluiced through a nearby irrigation canal. Up ahead loomed a bulky peak that seemed to command the entire setting. Sunlight and shadows played across its jagged heights.

Figure 1. Taos Pueblo, ca. 1880s. Photograph by Cunningham & Co. (1880–1889). Library of Congress Prints and Photographs Division, LC-DIG-ppmsca-39909.

They rounded a bend and caught their first sight of Taos Pueblo. Two massive adobe buildings rose like terraced pyramids, each several stories high and accessed by ladders. The twin structures were engineering marvels, capable of housing hundreds of people. Yet for all their imposing splendor, each compound flowed with gentle curves, softly sculpted by human hands.

An ice-blue mountain stream glided through the Pueblo, its banks lined with bushy red willow. Above everything was Taos Mountain, the big peak they'd noticed earlier. Its wide flanks seemed to cradle the village within its protective arms. Phillips stared at the mountain. It seemed "like a sentinel,"[7] watching over everything.

The two men drew closer and stopped to survey the scene. It was harvest season, and the entire village buzzed with activity. Taos men, blankets wrapped around their waists, brought fresh wheat in from nearby fields. Women in knee-high moccasins baked bread in beehive-shaped outdoor

Figure 2. Taos Water Girls. Photograph by Edward S. Curtis, 1905. Library of Congress Prints and Photographs Division.

ovens. Grain was being threshed the old-fashioned way, by driving a band of horses around a corral. Phillips could hear men singing to the animals as they worked. The artists watched as a young woman retrieved water from the river, balancing a large clay jar on her head and smoothly ascending a ladder to an upper floor. Then came another sound and they listened carefully. Somewhere in the Pueblo a man was beating a drum and singing a soft song that sounded like a prayer.

Bert Phillips had not expected this. Like most Americans, he'd been raised to believe that Indigenous people were warlike savages who'd been defeated and subdued by superior American might. Their depleted remnants were supposed to be living out their final days on barren reservations. Yet here at Taos was a peaceful culture that seemed to exist unbroken—and seemingly miraculously untouched by modern America. Gazing in wonder at Taos Pueblo, Phillips realized that this was the vision he'd been seeking ever since he'd picked up his first paintbrush.

The artists found an enticing campsite, just downstream from the Pueblo in a grove of sheltering cottonwoods. They unpacked their tent and began setting it up along the riverbank. Within minutes a group of armed men on horseback arrived from Taos Pueblo. Their leader was the war chief, in charge of protecting the Pueblo's lands from trespassers. He spoke to them in Spanish, but they did not understand. Yet the war chief made himself very clear: they were on Pueblo territory and needed to clear out. Sadly, the artists reloaded their wagon.

They retreated to the nearby Hispano village of Taos, but they had no intention of leaving this area. They cashed out, selling off their horses, wagon, and most of their supplies. They rented an old home near the plaza for a couple of dollars. The building was next door to where Governor Bent had been scalped during the Taos Rebellion fifty years earlier. The hole in the adobe wall—which Bent's family had dug trying to escape—had never been repaired.

The two strangers from New York, both armed with sketchbooks, became a curious new sight in Taos. Phillips put word out that he wanted to paint

Figure 3. Bert Geer Phillips, Portrait of Tudl-Tur (Sun Elk, or Manual Mondragón), ca. 1910, oil on board, 12 × 9 1/4 in. (30.48 × 23.5 cm); The San Diego Museum of Art: Gift of Frank R. Phillips, 1979.39. www.SDMArt.org.

Natives, and soon an impressive-looking man from Taos Pueblo presented himself at his door. He was in his early thirties, close to Phillips's age, but much taller, with chiseled features and sharp, intelligent eyes. Like other Pueblo men, he was draped in a blanket and wore his hair in two long braids. English was his third language after Tiwa and Spanish, but he spoke it well, having attended an American-style school as a child. He told Phillips that his name was Manuel Mondragón. Along with nearly everyone else at Taos Pueblo, he made his living as a farmer.

The excited Phillips showed the visitor his paintings, and Mondragón soon agreed to sit for a portrait. The artist quickly set up a makeshift studio at his rented adobe and got to work. As he studied his blanket-clad subject, he realized that, while Mondragón looked suitably noble, the composition lacked drama. So Phillips asked around until he located something more

Figure 4. Founding artists of the Taos art colony, ca. 1910s. Left to right: Ernest Blumenschein, Oscar Berninghaus, Eanger Irving Couse, Bert Geer Phillips, Joseph Henry Sharp. Seated at front is W. Herbert "Buck" Dunton. Photograph by K. W. Couse. Courtesy of the Palace of the Governors Photo Archives (NMHM/DCA), Negative Number: 028820.

fitting for him to wear. Eventually, his model posed in buckskin, complemented by a vintage bone breastplate. Phillips also placed an eagle feather behind his subject's head. The finished portrait resembled a Sioux warrior more than a peaceful farmer from Taos Pueblo. Yet there was no denying Mondragón was presented in a very flattering manner: a confident man, deep in thought but ready for action. Phillips, excited at breaking new ground, regarded this new work as his best. Even his hard-to-impress friend, Ernest Blumenschein, admired it.

Blumenschein also found Taos to be a revelation, calling it "the first great unforgettable inspiration of my life."[8] Along with Phillips, he attended Taos Pueblo's San Geronimo Festival, a big trade fair held to celebrate the annual harvest. Striding around with his sketchbook,

Blumenschein furiously captured several scenes, from ceremonial dances and relay races to the Pueblo's anarchic trickster clowns, whose bodies were painted in brown and white bands. A few weeks later, his Taos portfolio bulging, Blumenschein decided to return to New York, anxious to show off his work to magazine editors. He took along some of Phillips's paintings, promising to try and interest gallery dealers.

After Blumenschein left, Phillips began spending more time with Manuel Mondragón. His model, seeing that Phillips had displayed a lively interest in old Native artifacts, presented him with a beaded Cheyenne tobacco bag as a gift. He also explained to Phillips that Mondragón was his Christian name, but that everyone at the Pueblo also had a true Native name, given by their family and inspired by nature. His was Tudl-Tur: Sun Elk.

Phillips didn't know much about the Pueblo's religious practices, but it was becoming obvious to him that "their whole life is keyed to the rhythm of nature." Sun Elk explained that the ceremonial dances performed by the Taos People were a form of prayer, "so that we may get plenty of water and rain for our crops not only for this place but for all over the world, for the benefit of every living thing."[9]

Sun Elk became a regular lunchtime companion at Phillips's home, often bringing others from the Pueblo. "There is scarcely a day but at least two or three of the Indians are here," Phillips wrote to Blumenschein. "I really like them and enjoy having them around. . . . Their friendship is sincere and they appreciate the way we treat them as equals."[10]

The Taos men reciprocated, inviting Phillips to visit the Pueblo. No matter what time of day he arrived, food was always offered: fresh-baked wheat bread along with boiled corn and beans. For Phillips, the encounters were a revelation. "The Indian is more hospitable than the white man," he observed. He made it a point to invite more Pueblo men to his home, noting, "Eating the same food at the same table has a magic of its own for overcoming misunderstandings."[11] Before long, Sun Elk told him that the Taos People had given him a complimentary Native name, Tzu-bar-tú-na—White Eagle Feather.

Phillips knew from the beginning that many of the Hispanos in Taos resented his presence. He'd only been in town a few days when somebody poisoned his dog, Tip.

Though only a painter, he was part of a swelling tide of Anglo-American men streaming into northern New Mexico to make their fortunes. Miners, ranchers, loggers, bankers, speculators and grifters were everywhere. Anglos had taken charge of many of Taos's commercial establishments, and they owned and operated the saloons and gambling dens on the plaza. At the bars, the favored drink was a rough local whiskey called "Taos Lightning." A holdover from the frontier days, it was rumored to be flavored with gunpowder. After downing a shot, it was customary for a man to shout at the top of his lungs.

As the US war against Spain raged, anti-Spanish propaganda flooded the country. The Anglo men drinking in the Taos bars spoke darkly of the local Hispanos, many of whom proudly identified with their Spanish heritage. Rumors spread that some Taoseños were flying the Spanish flag, though no one had ever seen such a thing. Territorial Governor Miguel Otero protested, "I am getting tired of hearing that the New Mexican people are not loyal to the stars and stripes." Nevertheless, the *New York Times* reported that in New Mexico, "as a rule, the Spanish-speaking part of the population has given all its sympathy to Spain [with] a deep hostility to American ideas and American policies."[12]

Bert Phillips soon gained a new friend in the Taos saloons: Lester Myers, a small man who was a big talker. In his mid-thirties, Myers claimed to have been a boxer and a professional baseball player back in Ohio. He said that he'd volunteered for Teddy Roosevelt's Rough Riders, only to be rejected on account of his height. He told Phillips that he came west for his health—and to get rich.

A natural schemer, Myers spoke endlessly of gold mines and future business empires. He'd worked as an accountant back east and brought a substantial grubstake with him to Taos. He'd purchased an interest in a toll bridge across the Río Grande but was already feuding with his business partner. From what Phillips could tell, Myers seemed to be carrying on a half-dozen disputes. Yet there was something appealing about the man's plucky spirit.

Myers and Phillips, like many newly arriving Anglos in New Mexico, scorned the Hispanos' Catholic religion. Taos was a stronghold of the Penitente Brotherhood, a relic sect from medieval Spain known for expressing devotion through self-flagellation. In secretive Holy Week processions, the Penitentes lashed themselves with whips made of cactus and barbed wire, leaving trails of bloody footprints. Some even carried crosses into the nearby Sangre de Cristo Mountains to re-enact the crucifixion. For centuries the Catholic Church had tried to snuff out the practice, yet it lived on in northern New Mexico.

Phillips didn't speak Spanish, and he didn't realize that the Penitentes embodied far more than controversial rituals. The Brotherhood also comprised a civic mutual aid society that knitted Taos's Hispano community together. Phillips, ignorant and contemptuous, made his opinion known: "Bloody, fanatic, barbaric, disgusting, repulsive, pitiful and yet fascinating as blood & cruelty is always fascinating."[13]

In Taos, Anglo arrogance and Hispano resentment were a combustible mix waiting for the right spark. Relations between the two groups were tense but not violent—not until Bert Phillips and his new pal Lester Myers decided to attend a religious parade.

On December 12 came the Feast Day in honor of the Virgen de Guadalupe. On that same morning, newspapers reported that Spain had just signed a humiliating peace treaty, surrendering much of its remaining empire to the United States: Cuba, Guam, Puerto Rico, and the Philippines. The United States also annexed Hawaii. The American media gloated: "While the Spaniard has been sinking into impotence, the Anglo-Saxon has augmented his power until it fills the earth."[14]

As evening descended on the holy day, fat snowflakes fell and a bitter cold descended. Phillips joined Myers as they went to watch the Catholics' religious procession. Nearly everyone in town had turned out. Bonfires were lit along the parade route, and onlookers huddled near them for warmth. Phillips observed as local Hispanos, men and women and children, walked piously through the snow and ice behind an image of venerated saint. Local men took off their hats and placed them on their chests as a gesture of respect.

Phillips and Myers decided to keep their own hats on. A constable approached. Speaking in Spanish, he pointed at the offending headgear. Myers jawed back at him in English. As the argument escalated locals began crowding around the two outsiders. Someone reached out and snatched Myers's hat from his head. Shoves were exchanged, and suddenly the two Americans were sprinting away, a parade of people now chasing after them.

Phillips and Myers got caught at the central plaza. Amid the shouting and jostling, Anglo locals and miners charged out of the nearby saloons. Taos County Sheriff Luciano Trujillo pushed his way through the crowd. When Trujillo heard what had happened, he moved to arrest Myers and Phillips. The Anglos roared in protest, arguing there was no law requiring a man to remove his hat. More shoving ensued. In the confusion, Phillips managed to slip away. The sheriff hauled Myers off to the courthouse and locked him in the prison cell. Then he came back to the plaza, looking for the fugitive artist.

Phillips had taken refuge in a saloon owned by Long John Dunn, an outlaw who'd come to Taos after killing a man in Texas. Sheriff Trujillo entered the packed bar, flanked by two deputies. He strode up to Phillips and pulled out his revolver, pushing it into the painter's face. Phillips stared down the barrel for a long moment. "He seemed undecided whether to shoot or not," he wrote to Blumenschein later. "My mind was clear and calm, in a sort of a pause waiting for him to shoot."[15]

A burly young miner named Al Gifford, who'd been standing near Phillips, stepped toward the sheriff. Trujillo turned his gun on Gifford and cocked the hammer. Across the room, other men reached for their own guns.

Phillips slowly raised his hands, saying he'd go peaceably to jail and that there was no need for any shooting. As he was led away, many of his hard-drinking supporters in the saloon were angry and let the sheriff know it.

Trujillo and his men hustled Phillips across the plaza to the courthouse. The sheriff locked the artist in the iron cage alongside Lester Myers and pointed his gun at the men through the bars, enjoying the prisoners' discomfort. Then Trujillo returned to the saloon with his men.

Inside the bar, he went straight to Al Gifford, the man who'd tried to protect Phillips earlier. "You pushed me," the sheriff said, drawing his revolver as one of the deputies reached for Gifford to arrest him. Gifford drew his own gun in response. Suddenly the room was ablaze with gunshots. Men dove under tables and others crawled out the door. When the smoke cleared, bullet holes pocked the walls. The sheriff had fired four shots, Gifford got off two, and at least another dozen rounds came from other men in the room.

Incredibly, only one person had been hit by gunfire. Sheriff Trujillo had been shot three times. One through the temple and one behind his ear. Another bullet went through his chest, severing his trachea and windpipe.

Gingerly, his deputies picked the man up and carried him to a nearby home. The doctor in town was summoned. This was T. P. Martin, the only licensed physician within five hundred square miles.

Hurrying through the darkness to treat the fallen sheriff, Dr. Martin saw dozens of angry Hispanos gathering in the narrow streets. The local priest fell in beside him. "Have you got a gun?" the cleric asked him. "No," said Martin, beginning to worry what might happen if his patient didn't survive.

"Well, I've got two," the priest assured him, showing the doctor his bulging pockets.

Inside the house, Martin bent to examine the sheriff. He knew that Phillips and Myers were locked in the jail. They would be sitting ducks if a lynch mob went after them. Thinking quickly, Dr. Martin felt around the sheriff's body until he located the keys. Quietly, he slipped them to an understanding man, who stepped out of the room and strode briskly toward the courthouse.

Word spread that Sheriff Trujillo was in critical condition and would probably die. The lawman was surrounded by his praying family, including his wife and two young children. While Dr. Martin dressed the wounds, vigilante groups formed to hunt down Al Gifford. First, they went to the homes nearest the plaza, banging on doors and demanding entry. At Sabino Espinosa's, where Gifford had rented a room, they forced their way inside and tore apart the furniture. Continuing on, they searched house after house yet found no sign of their quarry.

Nervous Anglos began gathering ammunition and retreating to Gusdorf's General Store, hoping for safety in numbers. Bert Phillips, freshly sprung from jail, rushed to join them.

As news of the shooting spread, Hispanos from outlying areas came to Taos to aid the pursuit of Gifford. The separate packs merged into a huge, howling mob of over a hundred people. They broke into the locked saloon where the shooting had taken place. They ransacked the building, destroying furniture and smashing liquor bottles. Then they stormed the Anglo-owned gambling house next door, chopping at the gaming tables with axes and tossing a broken roulette wheel into the street.

Inside the general store, Phillips and the others had no idea where Gifford could be. They just hoped that their man who made a run for the telegraph station had managed to get through. In fact, a telegram did reach Santa Fe in the early morning hours:

> TAOS UNDER ARMS. SHERIFF KILLED . . .
> EVERY AMERICAN IS IN DANGER.

In his letter to Blumenschein, Phillips saluted the courage of his comrades inside the store: "I made up my mind that the crowd we have is as good a body of men to die with, if necessary, as a fellow could ask."[16]

Outside Phillips could hear a growing rumble. The mob had returned and was now approaching Gusdorf's store. Fresh shouts of "Kill all the Americans!" filled the air. Phillips and the other men cocked their guns, ready to fire. A lookout, Harold Cobb, opened the front door a crack and aimed his rifle into the darkness. He turned and whispered, "Shall I shoot?"[17]

"No, you damn fool," said another man. He grabbed Cobb and pulled him back inside, quietly latching the door.

More shouts were heard from outside, but these were in a different key. Someone was urging for calm. Phillips listened carefully. The man speaking was Malaquias Martínez, the local political leader. It was Martínez who had taken the sheriff's key from the doctor and freed Phillips and Myers from the courthouse jail. Now he was interceding with his fellow citizens, proclaiming there had already been enough bloodshed during this holy time. He spoke of the rule of law and pleaded for men to think of their families and homes. Martínez came from a prominent family and was one of the richest men in town. Everyone respected him. Men began drifting away from the mob. The fever broke.

Bert Phillips and the others could finally exhale. But no one dared go outside. Things remained very tense in Taos until military reinforcements arrived the next day to restore order. Al Gifford was located and duly arrested and transported to Santa Fe. While there was evidence against the miner, it was also known that Sheriff Trujillo was no angel—he was under three existing criminal indictments for assault with a deadly weapon. A deal was struck: Gifford agreed to leave New Mexico and never return.

Bert Phillips also had every reason to depart. He had survived the adventure of a lifetime, a story he could regale people with for years. He could return to New York and rejoin his pal Ernest Blumenschein. There, he could paint his impressions of the Wild West from the safety of his studio in midtown Manhattan.

Only Phillips decided to stay in Taos.

CHAPTER 2

THE TREASURE AT BLUE LAKE

1899–1902

While Phillips was pinned down by a vigilante mob, his friend Ernest Blumenschein's artwork depicting Taos Pueblo appeared in *Harper's Weekly*, one of the nation's leading magazines. Eleven of Blumy's drawings from the San Geronimo Festival were featured in an extravagant two-page spread. It was a spectacular coup for the young artist, still only twenty-four. Other magazine editors noticed, and Blumenschein's career began taking off.

Back in Taos, it was easy enough for Phillips to feel overlooked. But Blumenschein had not neglected his pal. On his way back to New York, he'd stopped in Chicago and shown Phillips's paintings to Martin O'Brien, who owned a flourishing art gallery. The dealer agreed to accept Phillips's work on consignment. After some prodding, O'Brien even consented to advance Phillips a few dollars, allowing him to continue to scrape by in Taos.

Phillips kept his rental adobe and signed up for Spanish lessons. Relations with local Hispanos were hardly warm, but open conflict was avoided. It helped Phillips immensely that the Honorable Malaquias Martínez, who had quelled the mob and represented Taos as a senator in the territorial legislature, took a friendly interest in him. Martínez's grandfather had been the revered frontier priest, Antonio José Martínez,[1] who in 1834 set up the first printing press in New Mexico and championed Hispano rights. The grandson, Senator Malaquias Martínez, was

Figure 5. Bert Phillips with a model from Taos Pueblo, ca. 1910s. Photograph by George L. Beam. Courtesy of the Palace of the Governors Photo Archives (NMHM/DCA), Negative Number: 086269.

now one of the largest landowners in Taos. An urbane man with a carefully styled handlebar moustache, Martínez lived with his family in a stately Victorian-style home. Active in several business ventures, he ranched more than four thousand sheep along with hundreds of cattle. At age forty, he'd distinguished himself as an up-and-comer in the legislature, pledging loyalty to his fellow Hispanos while simultaneously accommodating the Anglo powerbrokers. Many saw a bright political future ahead for him.

Phillips continued painting portraits of Sun Elk and soon gained other Pueblo models, including Sun Elk's younger sister, Crucita. The busy artist became a familiar sight at Taos Pueblo, where he attended every ceremonial dance open to outsiders. Phillips also became known for his keen interest in old Native artifacts. He bargained endlessly with tribal members, trying to persuade people to part with arrows, pottery, rugs, drums, animal skins, and even ceremonial clothing. He told Sun Elk he needed the items as props for staging his paintings, but it was clear his passion extended far beyond set decor.

Phillips's aggressive collecting could be off-putting, but he listened respectfully whenever Sun Elk told stories of his people's history. Phillips heard about the great Pueblo Revolt of 1680, which began in Taos and drove the Spanish from New Mexico for a dozen years. The artist also learned of the Taos People's stable, prosperous agricultural society—and how the Pueblo had been repeatedly raided over the centuries. The worst attack of all came in 1847, when the US Army stormed the Pueblo after the bloody Taos uprising that killed seventeen Anglos including Governor Charles Bent. Vengeful soldiers bombarded the Pueblo's mission church with mountain howitzers and slaughtered nearly two hundred people. Surviving Pueblo leaders were shackled and put on trial. Malaquias Martínez's grandfather, the famous priest, offered Taos Pueblo a deal: He would defend the Native captives in exchange for Pueblo land. The desperate survivors agreed. In the end, the Taos men were all hanged and the padre kept the property.[2]

Bert Phillips's eyes were often drawn to the commanding presence of Taos Mountain, which summoned clouds and played with light from its craggy heights. Sun Elk regarded the peak as a living force and spoke of its sacred relationship with Taos Pueblo. "I, too, felt it was alive," Phillips said. "I knew I could never leave it. That I would live out my life within the shadow of this mountain."[3]

Sun Elk began guiding Phillips into the alpine forests above Taos to scout for paintings. The artist, riding a borrowed Pueblo horse, found

Figure 6. Sun Elk (Manual Mondragón). Photograph by Vernon Bailey, 1903. National Anthropological Archives, Smithsonian Institution, BAE GN 01910C1 06327200.

endless inspiration, "always new messages of beauty . . . like lyrical and symphonic music coming to my mind through my eyes rather than my ears."[4] In the evenings, the two men camped alongside small streams filled with cutthroat trout. Occasionally they encountered other men from Taos Pueblo, who would join them around the campfire. Sun Elk played his flute, and the music floated through the forest like a soft wind.

Spending time in the mountains with Sun Elk and others, Phillips became awed by the Puebloans' deep understanding of their land. They seemed to know every plant and animal in their domain while also comprehending how each related to the others as part of a vast web of life. "Their knowledge of the flora and fauna of the surrounding country seems marvelous to those to whom it has been revealed," Phillips observed. "On such knowledge plus something else, their power depends."[5]

Rather than asserting mankind's dominion over all things, Sun Elk and the others viewed humans as full partners in nature's cooperative relationships. The Taos People saw everything as holy and interrelated—and they made it clear to Phillips that their religion was based on honoring and maintaining this natural life force.

In town, Phillips began spending time with a pleasant woman named Rose Martin. A year younger than him, she was almost a head taller, with a trim figure and bright blue eyes. She admired Phillips's paintings and helped him set up art lessons for locals as a means to earn a bit of income. She liked Sun Elk and became friendly with his family, often joining Phillips on visits to the Pueblo. In the spring of 1899, as temperatures warmed and the snow melted, Phillips and Rose began taking long horseback rides together. Their courtship blossomed, and Phillips soon proposed. She said yes, but her family objected. They did not want their daughter marrying a starving artist. Yet a few months later, the couple defiantly wed in a small private ceremony in Taos, attended by a handful of friends including Sun Elk.

Now that Phillips was married, the necessity of earning a regular income became crucial. His pal Lester Myers, co-instigator of the Taos riot, offered a solution. Myers pointed to the mountains overlooking Taos, where prospectors had found gold, silver, copper and coal. At least ten commercial mines were operating, and New York speculators had moved in. Myers suggested that great treasures lay buried, awaiting only the right man to uncover them. Phillips agreed that Myers was onto something. He'd seen prospectors use gold dust to pay for their purchases at Gusdorf's General Store. The action was nothing on the scale of the great California Gold Rush, but it was enough to fire a man's imagination. Together with Myers, Phillips staked a claim on a nearby mountain called Gold Hill.

Phillips and Myers spent much of the summer of 1899 at an elevation of eleven thousand feet, digging into the side of the mountain. Soon they came across faint traces of gold threading through the rock. With growing excitement, they kept tunneling, bracing the ever-lengthening shaft with fresh-cut timber. Deeper and deeper they shoveled, spreading word in Taos that they were on the verge of a major strike. Finally, Gerson Gusdorf set them straight. Yes, they'd found gold, but only in trace quantities. The two men would have to excavate several tons of rock and somehow transport everything to a faraway smelter in Colorado for processing. Even if that were possible, the costs would far outweigh whatever bit of money the ore produced.

Phillips and Myers had struck out. In this they were not alone. The Taos saloons were full of men with broken dreams. The surrounding mountains were so powerfully majestic that it seemed impossible they didn't also hoard spectacular riches. Old-timers claimed that the Spanish had once operated a valuable mine back in the 1600s, but the Natives had destroyed it during the Pueblo Revolt. Phillips also heard stories that the Taos People owned a sacred lake, high in the mountains, where they hid their silver and gold. The Puebloans patrolled their territory with armed guards, Phillips was told, to keep anyone from stealing their treasure.

In September 1899, as Phillips marked the one-year anniversary of his arrival in Taos, good news arrived from Chicago. The *Tribune* carried a rave review of his work at O'Brien's Gallery, calling two of his Sun Elk portraits "unquestionably the best paintings of this class . . . that have been shown in Chicago."[6] Phillips, at long last, seemed on the cusp of commercial success.

A small avalanche of publicity followed, as other newspapers began publishing reproductions of his work alongside glowing write-ups. O'Brien notified him that a major collector bought one of his paintings and more sales were expected. Now the dealer needed more art. Phillips was offered a contract to supply two paintings a month for the next year, for which he would be advanced fifty dollars each. This $1,200 annually was not quite like striking gold. But it did amount to a marginal middle-class income. Given the low cost of living in Taos, he had finally achieved a measure of financial security.

Getting the paintings to Chicago was no easy matter. Phillips carefully packed the canvases into a wooden crate, which was loaded on to a stagecoach that rolled west across the desert plateau until it reached the Río Grande Gorge. There it made the corkscrew descent eight hundred feet to the foaming river. After crossing a rickety toll bridge and a steep climb up the other side, it was another twenty-five miles to the tiny settlement of Servilleta—home of the closest rail line to Taos, a narrow-gauge spur from Colorado called "The Chili Line." The crate was packed on to the train alongside produce and livestock, then hauled across the mountains to Denver. There the paintings were transferred to another train for the final thousand miles of their journey.

While Phillips scratched out a modest living from his art, his friend Ernest Blumenschein continued his dazzling ascendency in New York. In 1900 Blumenschein, still only twenty-five, was elected to an elite club of leading artists and feted with a one-man exhibition. He also won a major art prize with a large cash award—more money than Phillips would see in a year. With the windfall, Blumenschein decided to return to Paris, where many of the world's greatest painters lived and worked.

Blumenschein vowed to Phillips that he would eventually come back to Taos, where the two friends dreamed of establishing an artist colony. Phillips encouraged his friend to help him recruit others: "For heaven's sake tell people what we have found! Send some artists out here. There is a lifetime's work for twenty men."[7]

Phillips's first catch was a commercial artist from St. Louis, Oscar Berninghaus, who had been hired by the Denver and Río Grande Railroad to create illustrations of Western landscapes. On a whim, Berninghaus detoured for a side trip to Taos. He ended up staying for eight days, painting portraits of Taos Pueblo people and becoming fast friends with Bert Phillips. Berninghaus soon became a regular summer resident.

Other artists drifted in. In November 1900, the renowned Western painter, Frederic Remington, arrived for a week's stay. Remington was an old friend of Theodore Roosevelt's and had painted the famous Rough Rider charge up San Juan Hill. Now Roosevelt had just been elected vice president, and Remington was in high spirits. Phillips escorted the stocky artist out to Taos Pueblo, where he made sketches and praised the mountain scenery. Before leaving town, Remington graciously purchased one of Phillips's Pueblo portraits. He also promised to help spread the word about Taos.

More artists arrived: Joseph Henry Sharp and Eanger Irving Couse, each already renowned for their paintings of Native people. Both had trained at Académie Julian in Paris alongside Phillips and Blumenschein. Sharp, an older man in his forties, had prospered painting the Crow People in Montana, selling dozens of portraits to the Smithsonian. He'd briefly visited New Mexico several years earlier, and he'd been the one to suggest to Phillips and Blumenschein that they should see Taos. Now that Phillips was settled there, Sharp made a return visit. Liking what he saw, he decided to make Taos his permanent summer home.

E. Irving Couse gained prominence painting Native peoples along the Columbia River in Oregon. He presented gentle images of domestic life, rather than the Wild West stereotypes of marauding Natives on the warpath. Couse explained, "The Indian is just as human as the white man and has many qualities which to my mind might well be imitated."[8] But his Oregon models had begun pressing for better pay, and Couse was ready for a change. In New York, he ran into Blumenschein, who sold him on Taos with his descriptions of its natural beauty and accommodating Pueblo models.

Couse journeyed to Taos with his family in 1902, arriving during a summer snowstorm. The Couses were not impressed by the local amenities. Indoor plumbing was nonexistent and canned food was ubiquitous. Mrs. Couse noted that the lone butcher in town also doubled as the undertaker. She had trouble acclimating herself to the sight of slabs of beef strung up alongside the wood coffins. Nevertheless, the artist found local Puebloans willing to model, and to work cheap. The Taos People, observing that Couse was a portly man who favored green sweaters, soon dubbed him "Green Mountain."

These painters arriving in Taos were family men, not avant-garde bohemians. Trained in the academic salon tradition, they were worlds away from cutting-edge innovators of modern art. They had barely acclimated themselves to impressionism, much less the radical new paths blazed by Van Gogh and Cézanne. Yet they were exceedingly talented craftsmen. Their artistic ambition was to present dignified portraits of Native

Americans from an idyllic past. They often posed their models in picturesque contemplation: thumping a drum alongside a waterfall or kneeling before a fire to decorate a clay pot. Ethnographic accuracy was rarely a consideration. These painters were perfectly happy to plop a feathered Plains Native's war bonnet onto a Pueblo model's head and dress him in Apache buckskin if it made for a better picture.

While the art colony took root in Taos, the subjects of its sentimental paintings faced mounting threats from outside forces. Rapid change had descended on New Mexico with the arrival of so many Anglo-Americans in recent years. The newcomers were scooping up vast amounts of land, bringing radical changes. In the old days, both Natives and Hispanos remained closely tied to the land as a means of sustenance. Now, as Anglos gained increasing control, land became treated as a commodity for short-term profit.

Much of the mountain range surrounding Taos Pueblo had already been ravaged. Overgrazing by sheep and goats had decimated once-abundant grasslands, leaving barren slopes behind. Forests had been cleared all the way to the edges of mountain streams, turning waterways into bone-dry scars. In a thicket of woods near Taos, people had sawed the branches off every tree for firewood, leaving the standing trunks to rot.

The contrast between this widespread destruction and Taos Pueblo's own domain was striking. The Taos People farmed the same high-desert land their ancestors had worked for centuries—and it remained productive. The Puebloans limited their grazing stock and rotated the animals among different meadows throughout the year to conserve pasturage. They patiently gathered firewood from scattered pieces of deadfall, even though it meant more work. Everyone at the Pueblo knew to never cut down a tree within two hundred yards of any stream.

Thanks to its wise conservation practices, Taos Pueblo possessed northern New Mexico's richest forests and grasslands. Their bountiful, well-watered holdings encompassed nearly a hundred thousand acres—and sat adjacent to a wealth of mineral riches. While the Taos People considered their territory a sacred homeland, the newly arriving Anglos viewed the Pueblo's holdings in far different terms. To them, it was a resource ripe for plunder.

In recent years, outside stockmen had begun trespassing, driving their sheep and cattle on to Pueblo lands to graze. Would-be homesteaders set up cabins on Native territory, hoping to win government approval for extravagant land claims. In the mountains above Taos Pueblo, rogue prospectors dug fresh mines and timbermen conducted illegal logging operations.

Few of these intruders worried about the law—and in some cases they *were* the law. In one instance, outsiders exploded dynamite on Pueblo land for a new silver mine. When tribal leaders filed a complaint, a squad of armed men rode into the Pueblo and shot one of the Natives' cows as a warning. Pueblo defenders managed to capture one of the attacker's horses. It turned out to belong to the deputy sheriff in Taos.

In the old days, the Taos People had posted sentinels to watch mountain passes for approaching enemies. Now, the Pueblo's war chief and his men were even more vigilant in patrolling the tribe's lands. Armed with rifles and six-shooters, they were constantly finding and evicting invaders. Yet more invaders kept coming.

In truth, an open conspiracy existed to dispossess American Natives, and the plot extended far beyond Taos. Centuries of warfare had come to an end, but Indigenous people remained under attack—now by way of laws rather than guns.

The chief weapon in this ongoing war of conquest had become the 1887 Dawes Act. Hailed at the time as "just and kind for the Indian,"[9] the law called for assimilating the remaining Indigenous people and then "liberating" them from their reservations. The program forcibly removed Native children from their families and sent them to faraway boarding schools. There, tribal languages, cultures, and religions were stripped away while lessons on Christianity and the holy profit motive were drilled in.

Lorenzo Martinez, the first child from Taos Pueblo sent to Carlisle

Indian School in Pennsylvania, recalled: "We all wore white man's clothes and ate white man's food and went to white man's churches and spoke white man's talk. And so after a while we also began to say Indians were bad. We laughed at our own people and their blankets and cooking pots and sacred societies and dances."[10] By the time Martínez graduated from Carlisle, he'd lost the ability to speak his native language.

Once enough Natives from a given tribe were deemed "civilized," the US government moved to dissolve the reservation. Individual families were allotted modest bits of acreage to consider their own property while vast swaths of their people's former communal homelands were opened to outsiders. Since passage of the Dawes Act, tens of millions of acres of Indigenous lands had been legally transferred to whites, all without the US Army having to fire a shot.

The nineteen Pueblo tribes in New Mexico had become some of the country's last holdouts, stubbornly preserving their communal lands and their traditional ways of life. No Pueblo was more resolute than Taos, yet it was clear that powerful interests were now aligning against them. How could a tribe of some four hundred souls hope to stave off a rapidly expanding nation of seventy-six million people?

From the perspective of Sun Elk and others at Taos Pueblo, the nearby artist colony represented more than the opportunity to earn marginal wages. While the artists' paintings displayed little interest in the Taos People's actual lives, the Puebloans knew that the images were commanding widespread attention and winning high-profile sales. Sun Elk had seen with his own eyes how portraits of himself and his younger sister, painted by Bert Phillips, had been reprinted in full color by Chicago newspapers.

Clearly, the artists settling in Taos were doing more than just selling paintings. They were also becoming some of the most nationally prominent people in New Mexico. To Sun Elk and others, this ascendant public status spurred a corresponding political calculation. Given the array of rapacious forces gathering against the Pueblo, it made sense to cultivate such luminaries as potential allies.

The most obvious candidate was Bert Phillips. He may not have been the best-known member of the art colony, but he lived in Taos year-round and had developed the closest relationships with the people at Taos Pueblo. Phillips was hardly perfect. He possessed more than his share of swashbuckling Anglo arrogance, and he'd been known to loot archeological sites for Native artifacts. Still, of all the painters working in Taos, Phillips seemed to possess the most sympathy for the Pueblo People.

One day, Sun Elk promised to show Phillips a special place in the mountains, an area sacred to the Taos People. Loaded with camping gear, the two men set off on horseback, following the small blue river upstream from the Pueblo. But this time, instead of seeking out beautiful places to paint, Sun Elk led Phillips on a tour of the Pueblos' broader territory. He showed Phillips damaged meadows where local stockmen had brought their animals on to Pueblo lands. He pointed out the rogue logging cuts, the pits dug by outlaw miners, and the ruins of squatters' cabins. He spoke of the difficulties his people faced in beating back the growing waves of invaders.

Then Sun Elk turned his horse on to a steep trail and the men climbed through ranks of dark pine into groves of sunlit aspen. At last they reached the high realm of blue spruce and Douglas fir. These serene forest giants had been alive since before Columbus. To Sun Elk, the ancient evergreens were symbols of life. He spoke of them as living saints, explaining to Phillips that many religious shrines were about. He and many others from the Pueblo visited this area frequently, making their way to holy destinations—sacred natural places where they performed religious rituals, praying for the health of the entire living world.

The two men emerged from the forest into bright sunlight. Now they were above the timberline, surrounded by frozen peaks. They followed a high ridge carpeted with sunny wildflowers and soon came to an overlook. A thousand feet below, nestled in a natural bowl, was a round alpine lake ringed by trees. The clear water appeared emerald in the shallows, merging to deep blue in the center. From above, it looked like a giant piece of polished turquoise. This was Ba Whyea, Sun Elk told Phillips. Blue Lake.

Blue Lake was the headwaters of the small river, the Río Pueblo de Taos, that splashed twenty-five miles through mountain cañons until it reached Taos Pueblo. The stream irrigated fields where the Taos People grew the crops that had nourished their way of life for a thousand years.

In the evening, camped along Blue Lake's peaceful shore, Sun Elk explained to Phillips that the lake was more than the source of life-giving waters. He described how the Taos Peoples' ancestors had first emerged into the world from this very body of water a long time ago. When people at the Pueblo died, their souls returned to dwell in this lake. Each August, almost everyone at Taos Pueblo came together for a pilgrimage to this shrine. Blue Lake was Taos Pueblo's vision of heaven; the crowning glory of its nature-based religion.

Speaking darkly about the threats posed by outsiders, Sun Elk told Phillips that if Blue Lake were ever lost, it would mean the end of Taos Pueblo's religion—and its people.

Phillips had heard the stories in town: the tales of Taos Pueblo hoarding riches at the bottom of a sacred lake. Now he understood that Blue Lake was a treasure, but not in the way white people thought. Few of them could comprehend that the real wealth at Blue Lake was spiritual.

CHAPTER 3

THE NATURALISTS

1903–1904

Upon taking office as president, Theodore Roosevelt hurled himself into the nation's affairs as forcefully as he had once charged up San Juan Hill. He broke up monopolies, won bold progressive reforms, and took charge of building the Panama Canal while holding two press conferences daily. The youngest chief executive in US history, he was massively popular, seeming the perfect human embodiment of his nation's restless vigor.

In the spring of 1903, Roosevelt decided to launch an unprecedented presidential adventure: a sixty-six-day barnstorming tour through twenty-two states and territories. New Mexico leaders were jubilant. Though the president would only visit a single day, this would be their big chance to create a favorable impression and persuade him to support their long-denied quest for statehood. The territorial legislature quickly carved out a brand-new county, naming it Roosevelt in the president's honor. An extravagant gift was commissioned for Roosevelt, a mammoth-sized book extolling New Mexico's virtues, adorned with gold filigree and turquoise stones. For this offering, the artist Bert Phillips gained the ultimate commission: one of his Pueblo portraits was laid in as the book's frontispiece.

As Roosevelt rolled across the country in his six-car presidential train, he gave speeches from the rear platform at hundreds of railway stops. He opened the World's Fair in St. Louis, and he spent sixteen days at Yellowstone. A month into his journey, a farm girl in western Kansas handed him a baby badger, just two weeks old, that her brother had trapped. Roosevelt kept the animal as a pet, feeding it milk and cut-up potatoes.

A few days later, on May 5, 1903, his train arrived in Santa Fe, where he was greeted by jubilant crowds and a twenty-one-gun salute. Wearing a top hat, Roosevelt paraded through the streets in a carriage bedecked with white roses. At the capitol, he bounded onto the stage, where he was presented with gifts including the ornate book with Phillips's painting. Once the boisterous audience finally quieted, Roosevelt began speaking, drawing wild applause as he complimented the many Rough Riders who had come from New Mexico. More cheers came when he spoke of New Mexico as "this territory of the present" that "shall be a great state in the American union."[1]

But Roosevelt had more in mind than simply flattering the locals. As president, he was increasingly preoccupied by an escalating environmental crisis. Even as his fellow Americans slashed and burned their way across the continent, industrial conglomerates and robber barons had leapfrogged ahead, pillaging natural resources and leaving shattered landscapes behind. Americans had long viewed nature as an inexhaustible resource, but Roosevelt saw the need to push his country to evolve in a new direction.

He had earlier declared, "The conservation of our natural resources is the most weighty question now before the people of the United States."[2] In his first months in office, Roosevelt had already created seven new national forests—and he was just getting warmed up.

In Santa Fe, Roosevelt had come to promote his environmental agenda. He appealed to the crowd, "I wish to bespeak your support [for] the forest reserves." He described how his new national forests would safeguard future timber supplies while also protecting grasslands for the benefit of sheepmen and cattle ranchers. "I want the land preserved," the president urged, "not the exploiting of the land for a year or two at the cost of its future impoverishment." Raising a clenched fist, he argued: "That is the way to use the resources of the land."[3]

After his rousing appearance, Roosevelt continued his journey, leaving behind an enthralled citizenry and a deeply wary political establishment. New Mexico was dominated by fellow members of Roosevelt's Republican Party, but these men were not progressives like the president. Instead, they constituted a notoriously corrupt, loose-knit cabal known as the Santa Fe Ring. They stewed about Roosevelt's misguided zealotry: his calls for environmental protection and government ethics. Roosevelt's ideas about conserving mountain forests struck them as dangerously radical, undermining the very freedoms that had made America exceptional—and made them rich. Many of those in the Santa Fe Ring had spent years amassing vast land empires in New Mexico—and they were hungry for more.

Two days after Roosevelt left Santa Fe, a small band of travelers on horseback entered New Mexico from the east. Among them was a middle-aged woman who continually scanned the sky with a set of field glasses. Her husband, the group's leader, shot various birds and mammals during the day and then set out traps each night to catch more. Carefully retrieving each kill, he cut open the animals' stomachs to examine the contents and log their diets. Then he directed an aide to prepare the specimens for shipment to Washington, DC, where the corpses would be duly measured and cataloged. This man was Vernon Bailey, Chief Naturalist of the US Biological Survey (now known as the US Fish and Wildlife Service).

Bailey, who'd grown up barefoot trapping gophers on his parents' small farm in Minnesota, never had much schooling, but he was a genius at understanding animal behavior. He'd become one of the country's leading experts at catching and killing them. President Roosevelt, who marveled at his ability to exterminate the despised wolf, bestowed him with the nickname "Wolf" Bailey.

A lean, round-eyed man who resembled a hungry owl, Bailey had been mentored by one of America's leading naturalists, C. Hart Merriam, head of the US Biological Survey. Bailey not only worked for Dr. Merriam, he had also married the boss's younger sister, Florence, a Smith College graduate and well-known ornithologist.

Florence Merriam Bailey joined her husband on these expeditions, although she brought a very different approach to studying her beloved birds. "In these days we have not the excuse that it is necessary to shoot a bird to find out what it is,"[4] she maintained. She had developed the radical

Figure 7. Florence Merriam Bailey and Vernon Bailey. Florence Merriam Bailey from *The Condor: A Magazine of Western Ornithology*, 1904. Vernon Bailey in 1905 from Library of Congress Prints and Photographs division, cph.3b06625

idea that one could learn a great deal more about birds by observing them, alive, in their natural habitats. She published her firsthand accounts of bird behavior in popular articles and books, but the scientific establishment remained dismissive of her "subjective" approach.

At age forty, the dignified-looking Florence was never known to openly criticize her husband's brutal "objective" methods. After all, collecting and cataloging specimens was long-standing practice among naturalists. She couldn't even vote, much less hope to overthrow scientific convention.

In this summer of 1903, the Baileys, accompanied by two Biological Survey employees, patiently worked their way across New Mexico's eastern plains. They rode horseback during the day and camped at night in canvas tents, sometimes lashed by rain and pummeled by hailstones. Near Santa Rosa their horses disappeared. The animals were quickly returned once a suitable reward was posted. At remote outposts, they waited in vain for government checks that would allow them to resupply their grub and reshoe their horses. Congress bristled at funding nature studies, and monies from the federal government were notoriously erratic. Vernon Bailey, like other Biological Survey employees, often had to dip into his own funds to keep working.

By September, Bailey's team was exploring the timbered heights of the Sangre de Cristo Mountains. On this trip, Bailey had been given a special mission: to report on the state of the forests, a matter of increasing urgency for President Roosevelt. The group followed a bumpy wagon road up the east side of the mountains, setting up camp at 8,700 feet, just below Taos Pass. When they awoke the next morning, the surrounding peaks were dusted in fresh snow. They searched for the snow grouse, also known as the ptarmigan, a rare bird known to range in alpine zones. Earlier travelers had documented the bird, but the Baileys found no trace of it. Instead, they saw that bands of sheep had overgrazed much of the area, destroying the habitat for the ptarmigan and scores of other animals. The naturalist's overnight traps remained empty.

They crossed the divide and began descending toward Taos. Unlike the artists and other visitors who were awestruck by the region's beauty, Vernon Bailey, with his practiced eyes, was underwhelmed. Scrutinizing the local mountains, he realized the range was dominated by cattle and sheep ranching and much of the original forest had been destroyed.

"Apparently the country has been burned to make more grass," he wrote in his journal, "but not enough soil was left to raise grass and the burned slopes are mainly worthless." Bailey also encountered numerous played-out mining claims, which he observed were "full of prospect holes and washed out places."[5]

Finally, the Baileys' small party came out of the mountains and rode into Taos, following the narrow, crooked streets to the bustling central plaza. After months of camp life, they relished the opportunity to be in an actual town and see other people. They visited the post office so that Bailey could mail his specimens to Washington. They ate at a restaurant and they strolled around the plaza, resupplying their outfit at Gusdorf's General Store. Then they noticed a small adobe home with a sign in English: Taos Indian Curio Shop.

Bert Phillips, now married four years and the father of two young children, had tasted tantalizing success as an artist, but his sales remained modest, especially when measured against his better-known peers. Summertime Taos resident Joseph Henry Sharp had sold 155 of his Native paintings to the millionaire Phoebe Hearst, mother of newspaper tycoon William Randolph Hearst. Sharp was now financially set for life. Another Taos painter, E. Irving Couse—Green Mountain to the Taos Puebloans—routinely won major prizes in New York, where his works fetched up to $500—five times the value of Phillips's own paintings. Phillips's younger friend Ernest Blumenschein, who'd journeyed with him to Taos in 1898, was now enjoying a glamorous life in Paris. Blumenschein made a splendid living as a top commercial artist, illustrating works by promising young writers Jack London and Willa Cather.

Phillips, meanwhile, was trying to feed his family. His art alone wasn't getting the job done. He'd seen a successful curio shop in Santa Fe and decided to go into business for himself. Already a relentless artifact collector, he devoted a corner of the family home to his new enterprise, filling it with pottery, beadwork, blankets, baskets, and more.

When Vernon and Florence Bailey entered the Taos Indian Curio Shop, the artist greeted them warmly. Learning of Bailey's work with the Biological Survey, he became even more attentive. When the couple asked about the local Natives, Phillips became rhapsodic, describing the Taos People's high intelligence and deep regard for nature. He spoke of their lovely music and the spiritual significance of their ceremonial dances. "The Indians worship all things beautiful,"[6] Phillips told them. He showed the Baileys a photograph of Sun Elk, explaining that his friend's name had been inspired by a band of elk emerging from a dark forest into the golden sunlight.

The Baileys were charmed by Phillips's enthusiasm. They purchased a Navajo blanket along with some smaller items. They asked about a good place to camp, somewhere with wood, fresh water, and pasturage for their horses. Phillips reached for a pencil and drew them a map indicating a site on Taos Pueblo land. He promised to talk to tribal leaders about allowing the Baileys to stay.

Vernon and Florence Bailey followed a small stream, the quietly rippling Río Lucero, into a mountain cañon sheltered by gold-leafed cottonwoods. Soon they found the riverside campground Phillips had directed them to. Green grass beckoned their horses and crisp autumn leaves rustled pleasantly in the breeze. In the mountain heights above, fiery yellow aspens blazed against the cool blue spruce. Florence heard the bright song of a Lazuli bunting and exclaimed, "This is the richest, most beautiful camp of the whole season."[7] Another bird flitted overhead, and Florence reached for her binoculars, quickly locating a pair of Rocky Mountain sapsuckers feeding their young.

The Baileys had just set up their camp when three scowling Taos Pueblo men arrived on horseback. Their leader was the war chief, Segundo Romero. All three men carried rifles. Asked to explain their presence on Pueblo land, Vernon Bailey introduced himself as an agent of the US government with orders to collect information about local flora and fauna. The youngest man interpreted for the others and the war chief's expression hardened. Then Bailey mentioned that the artist Bert Phillips had directed them to this spot. At the mention of Phillips's name, the Taos men immediately softened. The artist, as it turned out, had painted a portrait of the war chief's son, titling it, "A Prince of Royal Blood." The men agreed to let the Baileys remain overnight, although they had to pay a fee for the privilege.

Phillips soon interceded with Pueblo leaders, who granted the couple permission to stay longer. The Baileys were also invited to tour Taos Pueblo. When they arrived the next morning, they were welcomed by the governor himself, who shook hands warmly.

It was harvest season, and everyone was engaged in the time-honored rituals of milling wheat and replastering the Pueblo's thick adobe walls. "We were particularly impressed by the health and vigor of the people," Florence Bailey observed. Their guide led them up a series of ladders all the way to the crowning story of the Pueblo. Taking in the view, Florence could see how Taos Mountain overlooked the Pueblo community and its neatly tended agricultural fields. "What color! What a setting!" she enthused.[8]

For their biological survey, Phillips arranged for Sun Elk to be their guide. As Vernon Bailey began exploring the land controlled by Taos Pueblo, his initial negative impressions of the Taos Mountains began to shift. He encountered sparkling streams and lush, healthy, forests. Earlier, Baily had dismissed aspens as a nuisance "brush" because the wood held no commercial value. But now, as the trees burst into fall color, he changed his mind. "Aspens have come up in dense masses that now cover the upper middle slopes of the mountains with a yellow robe," he noted. "A road cut through these groves is wonderfully beautiful."[9]

As Sun Elk led the Baileys through the mountains, he provided detailed natural histories for several animals, greatly impressing the couple with his knowledge. With his guidance, Florence Bailey encountered birds she had only been able to imagine—including songbirds that nested exclusively in standing dead trees. Near the timberline, she saw the red and gold rufous hummingbird sipping from red flowers. Up on a wintry peak, they came across a brown-capped rosy finch, the first-ever documented in New Mexico. After a blast from Vernon Bailey's gun, the bird became property of the US government. Sun Elk also led the Baileys to the biggest ornithological prize of all—a pair of the vanishingly rare white ptarmigan. Those birds, too, were shot and claimed as federal property.

While Taos Pueblo's abundant forests appeared to be thriving, the relative lack of large game animals concerned Bailey. They came across a few mule deer tracks but saw no deer. Sun Elk found trees marked by black bears, but the animals remained elusive. There was no sign of any grizzly. From Sun Elk, Bailey learned that the antelope, once so plentiful, had vanished. No bighorn sheep had been seen in years. All the elk, including the Merriam's elk (*Cervus canadensis merriami*), named for Florence's brother, had completely disappeared. Sun Elk explained that dramatic losses of these animals had occurred over the past ten years—coinciding with the arrival of hordes of Anglo-Americans to the region.

Sun Elk did more than simply guide the Baileys. Just as he had done with Bert Phillips, he led them to the Pueblo's sacred Blue Lake, explaining its religious significance and its source as the Pueblo's life-sustaining water. Florence Bailey, clearly moved by the encounter, wrote in her journal, "May it always be kept sacred to the religion of the Indians and . . . never profaned by the eye of the white man."[10]

Sun Elk also showed the couple evidence of numerous incursions on to Taos Pueblo's lands. He pointed out places where overgrazing damage had occurred and where prospectors had dynamited the land. He told the Baileys that their campsite on the Río Lucero was in an area much coveted by local Hispanos because of its rich pasturage. Shortly before the couple's arrival, the war chief and his men had driven out a large flock of intruding sheep.

Soon more snow blanketed the higher elevations. The end of the season was fast approaching, and the Baileys would need to depart for Washington. Vernon Bailey met with Bert Phillips and discussed his desire to return to Taos the next summer and continue his biological survey work. Phillips helped arrange for the couple to store their camp gear and overwinter their horses at Malaquias Martínez's nearby ranch. The territorial senator charged only a nominal fee, happy to oblige the prominent official from Washington.

The Baileys joined the Phillips family for a farewell dinner at the artist's small home. The couple was full of praise for Sun Elk, and they spoke glowingly of the Taos People—their rich culture, their communal work, their wise conservation ethics. Vernon Bailey addressed Phillips. "I would like to do something for the people," he said. "Could you suggest something?"[11]

The next day, Phillips and the Baileys descended into the Pueblo's council chamber through a "skyhole"—the door on the roof with a ladder leading down. The governor welcomed them, and they took seats on a blanket-covered bench. As their eyes adjusted to the dim light, they could see a gunrack on the whitewashed walls, along with an image of the Virgin de Guadalupe. Also on the wall were two silver-tipped canes. One had been given to Taos Pueblo by King Philip of Spain in 1620; the other was presented by Abraham Lincoln in 1864. The canes, carefully preserved over the years, symbolized the Taos People's sovereignty over their ancestral lands.

Within moments, the room began to fill with members of Taos Pueblo's tribal council, each man shaking hands with the visitors as he entered. An interpreter placed a box in front of Vernon Bailey for him to use as a table. He also handed the naturalist a pencil and a pad of paper. For the next few hours, the Taos men took turns speaking. They produced an old map showing the full extent of their territory, and they pointed out all the places now claimed by outsiders. They talked of the powerful interests aligned against them: cattlemen, sheep raisers, loggers, prospectors, water thieves, land-hungry newcomers, all of them backed by politicians, public opinion, law enforcement, and the courts. They expressed worry—"fearful" is the word the interpreter used—that their Blue Lake watershed, with its rich forests, inviting grasslands, and bountiful water, would be stolen away. They asked Bailey, *Can you help us hold our land?*[12]

Vernon Bailey made a solemn pledge. Upon his return to Washington, he would propose that the Taos Mountains be set aside as a special forest reserve by the US government so that the land would be permanently protected for the benefit of Taos Pueblo. He would see that the matter was taken up personally with President Theodore Roosevelt.

In Washington, the Baileys approached Florence's brother, C. Hart Merriam, the prominent naturalist who directed the US Biological Survey. Merriam was a close friend of Roosevelt's and a long-time conservation ally. Moved by the Baileys' descriptions of the situation in Taos, Merriam immediately agreed to the plan.

Vernon Bailey typed up a report on the state of the forests in the Taos area. He described the ragged condition of most of the range but complimented the Taos Puebloans for their "beautiful dark stretches of forest."[13] He suggested that a suitable forest reserve could be established in the Taos Mountains if immediate steps were taken to protect what remained. Hart Merriam notified Roosevelt and gained the president's approval.

Within two months of Bailey's report—lightning speed in the bureaucracy—Agriculture Secretary James Wilson sent a letter to his colleague at Interior:

> It appears that the region adjoining the Taos Pueblo Indian

> Reservation . . . is largely timber and wood land and that the forest cover is of great importance in the regulation of the water flow. I have the honor to request, therefore, that the following described lands be temporarily withdrawn from settlement, pending an examination as to their suitability for the purposes of a forest reserve.[14]

Two weeks later, on December 5, 1903, Interior Secretary Ethan A. Hitchcock responded: "There appears to be no reason why the vacant, unappropriated public lands . . . should not be withdrawn as requested by the Secretary of Agriculture, and I have the honor to recommend that I be directed to make the temporary withdrawal."[15]

A week later, an order was issued barring homesteading any of the land in question. This development appeared to be excellent news for Taos Pueblo, except for a calamitous misunderstanding. The area the US government had defined as "vacant, unappropriated public lands" was Blue Lake and its surrounding watershed, which the Taos People had considered their own since time immemorial.

Theodore Roosevelt occasionally showed flashes of regard for individual Native people, but the president had little respect for their cultures. "In dealing with the Indians," Roosevelt said, "our aim should be their ultimate absorption into the body of our people." The president was a fierce proponent of the 1887 Dawes Act, which directed the government to assimilate Native Americans and dismantle their communally held lands. Roosevelt praised the law as "a mighty pulverizing engine to break up the tribal mass."[16]

Yet Roosevelt's old friend C. Hart Merriam had steadily gained greater appreciation for Native peoples. As head of the US Biological Survey, Merriam had frequently encountered Indigenous people whose knowledge of the natural world struck him as extraordinary. He became increasingly dismayed by the government's treatment of Natives. He began publicly criticizing "the aggressive selfishness of the whites" and the "gradual but progressive and relentless confiscation of [Native] lands and homes."[17]

In March 1904, after Merriam learned that no dispensation had been made for the Taos People in preparing the new forest reserve, he pressed Roosevelt on the issue of Indigenous rights. He told the president that America's treatment of Natives "has been so unjust and cruel that it is a national disgrace."[18]

His plea did not go over well, and Roosevelt snapped at his old friend. A contrite Merriam wrote a few days later: "It is a long time since any act of mine has brought down on my head such a blow. . . . The fact that you are the only man in the world having the power to help the Indian situation is my excuse for troubling you. If I annoy you too much, tell me to quit, but don't charge me with unfaithfulness."[19]

In the summer of 1904, Florence and Vernon Bailey returned to New Mexico, arriving on the Chili Line from Denver and taking an overland stage to Taos. They enjoyed a warm reunion with Bert Phillips and retrieved their horses from Malaquias Martínez's ranch. They were pleased to see the animals in fine condition.

Accompanied by Phillips, the Baileys went to the Pueblo to discuss developments in Washington. Inside the council chambers, Vernon Bailey wanted very much to share good news, but he also was acutely aware that complications had arisen. Addressing the assembled men through an interpreter, he said that a new national forest reserve was quite likely and that every effort was being made to ensure that the Taos Puebloans would retain exclusive use of their land. When the meeting concluded, everyone seemed pleased and handshakes were exchanged all around.

The Baileys were given an even more favored campsite on Pueblo land, this one nestled in a grove of cottonwoods along the Río Pueblo de Taos, the mother stream that flowed down from Blue Lake. They were soon joined by Sun Elk, who they had hired to again guide their field work in the mountains. The three would spend the next six weeks roaming the countryside. This was really what the Baileys had come for. After all, they were naturalists, not politicians.

Theodore Roosevelt's conservation drive kept picking up steam. After a visit to Yosemite and a campout with John Muir, the president became more determined than ever to protect the land and the animals on it. One of the most disturbing issues of the day was the widespread slaughter of birds—and much of the killing was being done in the name of fashion, for ladies' hats. Florence Merriam Bailey had been protesting this brutal practice since her days as a student at Smith College twenty years before. Untold millions of birds across America had perished, plume hunters sweeping down on entire rookeries to seize the parents and leaving the hatchlings to die. The figures were staggering. A monthly auction of egret feathers accounted for 24,000 birds. In one week 500,000 hummingbird bodies were delivered to London milliners.

Knowing that the reactionary US Congress would not budge in the face of the growing conservation crisis, Roosevelt swept aside the legislative branch and acted on his own. In 1903 he issued an executive order declaring the first-ever wildlife refuge in the United States—a three-acre island in the Everglades where egrets raised their young. The president would eventually create fifty more federal bird sanctuaries.

Figure 8. Theodore Roosevelt, 1904. Photograph by the Pach Brothers © Wikimedia/Creative Commons.

Roosevelt also took advantage of a new law allowing the president to designate certain areas as national monuments. When Congress refused to make the Grand Canyon a national park, Roosevelt moved to secure the area by declaring 800,000 acres to be a national monument, which offered lesser status but similar protection. In doing so, the president included 185,000 acres belonging to the Havasupai People. Roosevelt told the Natives, whose ancestors had been living in the area for at least 700 years, that it was time for them to move on.

Roosevelt adopted the same approach in creating national forests. In many cases, he simply folded lands belonging to Native Americans into his new federal reserves. Conservationists cheered the president's actions, but they overlooked the dirty secret at the heart of his crusade. For all his professed love of the environment, Roosevelt had no patience for the original Americans who had the most experience and arguably the deepest understanding of how to coexist with nature. Instead, Roosevelt viewed conservation as the white man's domain; a rational, scientific, progressive policy to be directed by Anglo-Americans, who alone had demonstrated their superiority in mastering nature.

"The continent had to be won," Roosevelt maintained. "We need not waste our time in dealing with any sentimentalist who believes that, on account of any abstract principle, it would have been right to leave this continent to the domain, the hunting ground of squalid savages. It had to be taken by the white race."

"The truth is," Roosevelt argued, "the Indians never had any real title to the soil."[20]

Before the Taos Mountains could be made a national forest, an official government inspection was required. In late summer 1904, Theodore F. Rixon, a Special Field Assistant for the US Geological Survey, was dispatched to investigate whether the region truly merited federal protection.

Like Vernon Bailey before him, Rixon was troubled by overgrazing damage, which had left "barren and dusty mountains." Yet when he entered Taos Pueblo's lands he was very favorably impressed. "Considerable credit is due to the intelligence of the Indians," Rixon reported. Taos Pueblo, he observed, "is the only spot throughout this territory where conservation principles have been adopted and enforced."[21]

In an age when Native American values were routinely dismissed as unworthy, Rixon made a bracing recommendation. He suggested that the US government could learn a great deal from the Pueblo's holistic approach to land and water management: "The result warrants its similar adoption and enforcement by the Government on all its forest reserves in New Mexico."[22]

As Roosevelt moved forward to declare a Taos Forest Reserve—and thereby claim the Pueblo's Blue Lake area as its own—Vernon Bailey became increasingly apprehensive. He knew the Taos People and his friend Bert Phillips were counting on him and he did not want to let them down without a fight. Bailey, who had come from such humble circumstances, had gained a notable professional career. He was widely regarded as an expert within a narrow range of abilities, but he remained acutely aware of his social and educational shortcomings. He hadn't even finished high school, whereas Theodore Roosevelt, Hart Merriam, and Roosevelt's forestry adviser Gifford Pinchot had all come from wealthy families and attended Ivy League colleges. Bailey knew his place, and he never attempted to interject himself into policy or politics. But as he saw Taos Pueblo's needs were being ignored, he was moved to action.

He penned an appeal to President Roosevelt and Forester Pinchot. Bailey presented his plea as a businesslike "Memorandum," but there was no mistaking its persuasive intent. The naturalist described the Taos Puebloans as "industrious, self-supporting people." He wrote of their nature worship, pointing out that "their religion is an essential part of their life and happiness." He told the men about the Pueblo's Blue Lake, where the tribe made its annual religious pilgrimage. "Parts of this land have been taken from the Indians by fraudulent means," he explained. And with the US government now set to claim the rest of the Blue Lake watershed, Bailey asked that the government respect Taos Pueblo's long history and current use: "While the boundaries of the Taos Forest Reservation are being decided, I would like to keep before you the importance of this reservation to the Taos Indians."[23]

Bailey also wrote to Bert Phillips, asking him to alert Taos Pueblo to send its own appeal. On October 21, 1904, Governor Domingo Gonzales, along with the tribal council, sent a carefully worded letter to Interior Secretary Hitchcock:

> Hearing that it is the intent of your Department to create a "Forest Reserve" embracing the Taos Mountains, and that said area contains the watershed of the Pueblo Creek [Río Pueblo de Taos] which flows through our residency, [We] petition your honorable Department, in the event of the creation of this Reserve, to set aside the watershed of said Pueblo Creek contained within the confines of said Reserve for the exclusive use of our tribe.

In its letter, Taos leaders pointed out, "We have heretofore for innumerable years enjoyed the exclusive use of said district. . . . We have already taken the greatest of attention in preserving the timber along the streams."

Summing up its appeal, the letter concluded: "We therefore most respectfully petition your Honorable Department to give this matter your most careful consideration and when the proper time arrives to issue to us an exclusive permit to the use of the said area."[24]

The Taos leaders never received a reply.

CHAPTER 4

AMERICAN DEVILS

1905–1909

JUNE 13, 1905

As his carriage rattled along the high road to Santa Fe on this brilliant spring day, the Honorable Malaquias Martínez admired the view of the glistening snowpack on the nearby mountains. It had been a brutal winter, and many sheep had died on the ranges, but those punishing blizzards now promised abundant summer water. Perhaps, for once, enough water for all.

Rushing snowmelt filled rivers and streams, the runoff so heavy that it washed out several bridges across the Río Grande. Martínez was unable to take his usual road to the territorial capital. Instead, he set out on what locals called the inside route, which threaded through several high-altitude Hispano villages hugging the western edge of the Sangre de Cristos.

This detour was fine with Senator Martínez. He enjoyed the opportunity to make firsthand observations and see how his constituents' lands were doing. Martínez liked to present himself as a simple farmer and stockman, but in truth this forty-four-year-old with carefully appraising eyes and a drooping handlebar moustache had much larger ambitions. When he arrived at the capital, he would attend a private party at the governor's mansion, joined by all the leading men of the territory. Many of those power brokers viewed Martínez as someone who might one day capably serve their interests in a higher office.

Figure 9. Malaquias Martínez, ca. 1910s. From Ralph Emerson Twitchell, *The Leading Facts of New Mexico History*, vol. 4 (Torch Press, 1917).

Martínez enjoyed renown for his eloquent oratory, just like his famous grandfather, the revered Taos priest, Antonio José Martínez. When the first Anglo-Americans began streaming into New Mexico in the 1830s, Padre Martínez had thundered against their drinking, gambling, and schemes to turn devout women into prostitutes. He decried their wholesale killing of buffalo and deer, predicting the animals would soon go extinct. When the United States occupied New Mexico in 1846, Padre Martínez remained defiant. Some believed he had orchestrated the bloody 1847 insurrection in Taos. Inscribed on his tombstone in Taos was the motto "La Honra de su País" (The Honor of his Homeland.)

Senator Malaquias Martínez was hardly the firebrand his grandfather had been. These were different times, and Martínez saw the need to adapt. Loyal to his Hispano heritage, he also understood that engaging the Anglos was necessary to retain a healthy measure of political and economic power for his own people. Yet as he traveled along the road from Taos to

Santa Fe, it was easy enough for him to see how his fellow Hispanos were suffering under the Anglo order.

South of Taos, Martínez's carriage rolled into the village of Peñasco, where the Rio Santa Barbara tumbled out of the mountains, irrigating fields of corn and wheat. Hispano people in this area had family roots dating back to the 1700s, but their land was under attack. Peñasco, like all Spanish land grant settlements, included a large area held in common, known as an ejido. Often tens of thousands of acres, these ejidos were meant to provide communal grazing, timber, and hunting resources for everyone in the village. In recent years, this idea of communal land stewardship became undermined by invading Anglos. Sympathetic courts in New Mexico, presided over by judges with vested interests in the outcomes, ruled time after time that ejidos must be broken up and subdivided into individual parcels. Each land grant heir, the law dictated, should have the freedom as an American citizen to sell his or her individual share. In some instances, judges ruled that if a single heir wanted to sell a small piece of an ejido, then the entire grant must be put up for auction.

Anglo attorneys and land speculators descended on Peñasco and other villages, intent on dispossessing the locals. Sometimes the tactics were as crude as handing out silver dollars in exchange for signatures on English-language documents that people couldn't read. At other times, attorneys pretended to represent Hispanos while secretly working for the land thieves.

Senator Martínez's constituents in Peñasco had recently lost their Santa Barbara Land Grant, which fell into the hands of a land speculator. Soon, nearly 25,000 of the forested mountains above their homes would be controlled by a New Mexico Supreme Court Justice named Napoleon Bonaparte Laughlin. When Judge Laughlin looked at the pine-blanketed mountains above Peñasco, he didn't see a living forest—he saw future railroad cross-ties.

Martínez's carriage continued on, winding through piñon hills until he reached Trampas, a venerable settlement founded before the American Revolution. The old adobe wall that once helped protect the town was now a crumbling ruin. The people here were also in an agonizing situation. A double-crossing attorney, working with a single turncoat land heir, had stolen away their entire ejido. Those lands were now controlled by a millionaire named Frank Bond, who gleefully described his new acquisition as "undoubtedly the best timbered grant in this section of the country."[1]

Farther south, as the road began twisting down from the mountains toward the desert, Senator Martínez reached the village of Cundiyó. This settlement lay along a fertile green strip nestled between sagebrush-studded hills. Established in the early 1700s with a Spanish land grant, Cundiyó had lost nearly twenty thousand acres of its common lands. Those now belonged to Thomas Catron, a hefty lawyer originally from Missouri. Senator Malaquias Martínez knew Catron very well. A fellow Republican, Catron was New Mexico's longtime political boss and leader of the notorious Santa Fe Ring. Catron and his allies—judges and politicians, bankers, and attorneys—had amassed vast personal fortunes through widespread corruption, targeting lands belonging to Hispanos and Indigenous people. Catron had gained ownership of some three million acres in New Mexico, making him the largest individual landowner in the entire United States.

Malaquias Martínez was an ally of Catron's, and he understood that political graft was a fact of life in New Mexico. It pained him to see so many of his constituents, fellow Hispanos, suffering and losing their lands. But he was enough of a realist to understand that no one person could stop this wave of dispossession. Private ownership was the driving engine of the expanding Anglo nation. Even his charismatic grandfather, the famous Padre Martínez, would have been powerless to stop these changes, just as he was unable to prevent the slaughter of the buffalo. The best a man could do in these modern times, Senator Martínez knew, was to look out for himself.

In Santa Fe, Martínez's political allies were increasingly alarmed by their fellow Republican, Theodore Roosevelt. The president's progressive rhetoric denouncing corrupt political machines was bad enough, but even worse was his holy crusade to conserve natural resources. Just three months into his second term, Roosevelt had already created ten new forest reserves in Western states, taking millions of acres out of the public domain.

Roosevelt argued that the newly protected lands would ensure "the good of the whole people [over] the profits of the privileged few . . . none will quarrel except the men who are losing the chance of personal profit at the public expense."[2]

As 1906 dawned, the president kept expanding his conservationist domain. He added several new wildlife refuges, and he enlarged Yosemite National Park by 27,000 acres. He signed legislation establishing Mesa Verde as a new national park and he created three new national monuments, including one in New Mexico. Meanwhile, new forest reserves kept piling up, twenty in all. On November 7, 1906, he added his twenty-first:

> Whereas, the public lands in the Territory of New Mexico, which are hereinafter indicated, are in part covered with timber, and it appears that the public good would be promoted by setting apart said lands as a public reservation... Now, therefore, I, Theodore Roosevelt, President of the United States of America, by virtue of the power in me . . . do proclaim that there are hereby reserved from entry or settlement and set apart as a Public Reservation, for the use and benefit of the people, all the tracts of land, in the Territory of New Mexico, shown as the Taos Forest Reserve. . . .
>
> Warning is hereby given to all persons not to make settlement upon the lands reserved by this proclamation.

Roosevelt's newest reserve covered more than 233,000 acres, including some 50,000 acres of pristine forests in the Blue Lake watershed above Taos Pueblo. The president's proclamation made no reference to the Taos People's long-standing occupancy of the region—nor any mention of their continued rights to the Blue Lake area.

The artist Bert Phillips now had far more pressing concerns than worrying about Taos Pueblo's sacred homeland. After years spent painting canvases in his dimly lit studio, illuminated only by oil lamps and a corner fireplace, his eyes began to fail. This was an occupational hazard of artists, he knew.

Figure 10. Bert Phillips, 1932. Photograph by Will Connell. Courtesy of the Palace of the Governors Photo Archives (NMHM/DCA), Negative Number: 059761.

His doctor told him that he risked permanent blindness unless he took a long break from painting.

At age thirty-eight, with a wife and two children to support, Phillips had not prospered as an artist. Yet the Taos Valley was booming and fresh arrivals continued pouring in. Men younger than him were getting ahead and leaving him in the dust. He'd tried his hand at business, but his Taos Indian Curio Shop never became profitable and he finally shuttered it. His wife, Rose, was patient and loving; she believed in him and his art. But what kind of future would his family have if he became blind?

His government friend, the naturalist Vernon Bailey, had a suggestion: The new Taos Forest Reserve would need its own forest ranger and Phillips was an ideal candidate. Thanks to his friendship with Sun Elk, the painter had become an experienced backcountry traveler. He knew how to kindle a campfire without a match, and he could chop into an ice-covered stream with an axe to water his horse. Phillips had come to know the mountains above Taos as well as any white man. The pay for forest rangers was an insult—only sixty dollars a month—and men were expected to supply their own horses. Yet he had few other options.

In Santa Fe, Phillips took the Forest Service examination under the watchful eye of the area supervisor. After three days of firing guns, packing and riding horses, and answering questions about surveying, timber, sawmills, and how to fight fires, Phillips passed with flying colors.

In early 1907, he reported for duty. Joining him was another new forest ranger, a man Phillips knew quite well. Lester Myers had been his accomplice in sparking the "Taos Riot" back in 1898, when Malaquias Martínez freed them both from jail and then stopped the mob from attacking the general store. Like Phillips, Myers had gotten married and started a family. He'd aggressively pursued new business schemes, but each had failed. In one instance, Myers was attacked by a partner who accused him of fraud. His financial situation had become even more precarious than Phillips's. The local paper recently published a notice that Myers was delinquent on his taxes.

Myers was eager to get his hands on a government post—which in New Mexico was often a stepping stone toward making *real* money. Everyone knew the story of Edward Hobart, a government surveyor who gained thousands of acres of prime land that once belonged to Santa Clara Pueblo. In Taos, an English speculator named Arthur Manby had bribed government officials while acquiring fifty thousand acres from an old Spanish land grant. Such extravagant thievery was beyond Lester Myers's pay grade, but he knew of low-level government employees who had doubled their annual income by simply looking the other way. He had every expectation that serving as a US Forest Ranger would ultimately reward him with far more than a measly sixty dollars a month.

Myers was assigned to Questa, a mining town about twenty miles north of Taos. Phillips, meanwhile, was given the Taos District, which included the mountains above the Pueblo. The Taos People had been worried about Roosevelt's proclamation but were reassured to see their old friend become a forest ranger. Knowing that Phillips was assigned to protect their Blue Lake watershed gave them more confidence in the new arrangement with the US government.

In the lands soon to be renamed Kit Carson National Forest, Ranger Phillips rode through snowstorms and battled forest fires. He strung miles of telephone wire across remote cañons, and he marked timber for cutting while planting hundreds of new trees. He was resolute in expelling trespassers from Taos Pueblo's Blue Lake watershed, refusing to grant any outsider permits for grazing or logging.

Phillips also helped Taos Pueblo gain a welcome pledge of support from Ross McMillan, the supervisor of Carson National Forest. At Phillips's urging, McMillan wrote to Taos Governor Cruz Suazo: "The Forest Service is protecting and will protect the interests of the National Forests in this watershed, and also of the Taos Pueblo Indians. I beg to inform you that there need be no uneasiness upon your part or upon the part of the Taos Indians that you will not receive full protection."[3]

As the lame duck Roosevelt's second term wound down, resentment mounted in the West that so many prized lands had been set aside for conservation. In 1907 Congress passed a bill preventing the president from unilaterally declaring any more national forests. Roosevelt, backed into a political corner, was forced to sign the measure. Yet he was determined to go out in a final blaze of glory. On the eve before the new law went into effect, Roosevelt, working with his Chief Forester Gifford Pinchot, announced twenty-one new national forests and enlarged eleven existing ones. The president delighted at creating these "Midnight Forests," gleefully imagining that "opponents of the Forest Service turned handsprings in their wrath."[4]

Roosevelt's opponents lost that round, but they kept chipping away at his conservation empire. Another new law extended the old 1860 Homestead Act by opening up national forests to settlers. The Forest Reserve Homestead Act allowed individuals to file for land claims up to 160 acres in national forests, provided the lands were chiefly suitable for agriculture rather than timber. In Taos, one man paid very close attention to this new homestead law.

Senator Malaquias Martínez had his eyes on a tempting piece of land just north of Taos Mountain, where the Río Lucero spilled out of a cañon and on to the sagebrush plain. Taos Puebloans had long used this area as a seasonal pasture for their livestock. The new national forest now extended to the very edge of this domain, though Martínez realized that many locals were still uncertain about the actual boundaries.

The senator, mindful of the recent Forest Reserve Homestead Act, saw an opportunity. He knew that enlisting Lester Myers could help him carry out his plan. With a little bluffing from Taos's most powerful man, backed by a uniformed US Forest Ranger, it should be easy enough to convince everyone this acreage could be homesteaded.

The land by itself wasn't worth a great deal, for it wasn't irrigated. But if the occupants could also wrest the Río Lucero's water rights away from Taos Pueblo, the real estate would suddenly become very valuable indeed. Senator Martínez, as it happened, sat on the legislative committee that decided such matters.

Martínez's plan was to create a partnership with four others. Each man would claim the maximum 160 acres as a homestead for a total of 800 acres in all. Martínez's banker in Taos would front all the expenses for the homesteaders' cabins, fencing, and livestock. Once the land was patented, Martínez's accomplices could keep a slice for themselves and sell the rest back to the Senator for a healthy profit.

Lester Myers readily agreed to the proposal, seeing it as a welcome chance to improve his fortunes. Three others also signed on as partners: a local engineer named Parker Black, Myers's father-in-law Thomas Bryan, and another US Forest Ranger. The financially struggling Bert Phillips, in a decision that would haunt him the rest of his life, agreed to join the scheme.

On an early morning in April 1908, a group of Taos Pueblo men left their homes to work some land in one of their northern pastures. The winter snows had finally melted, and the earth was reawakening. The men intended to plant a bit of corn and check on the condition of their grazing lands. They rode their horses along the well-worn path that curved around the western flank of their sacred Taos Mountain. They followed the small stream, the Río Lucero, a thin ribbon of light winding between the silvery cottonwoods.

They approached Lucero Cañon, where the clear water flowed out of the mountains. There they encountered something very odd. A work crew was raising a wooden cabin on this land—on *their* land. They rode up to find out what was happening. They were told that this new home belonged to Mr. Lester Myers, and that he was laying claim to this land in accordance with the Forest Reserve Homestead Law of 1906.

Clinton J. Crandall, the blunt-spoken, battle-hardened superintendent in charge of New Mexico's Pueblos, had seen a lot of bad dealings at the expense of his charges. "The people of New Mexico are not in sympathy with the Indian and think that even now the Indian has too much land," Crandall observed. "They would often be glad to see the Indian become extinct and do not hesitate to say so."[5]

Crandall, who'd taken over as Pueblo superintendent in 1900, had come under increasing fire in New Mexico for his tolerant management of the Santa Fe Indian School. He was supposed to break the family and tribal bonds of his pupils, who were often forced conscripts from New Mexico's nineteen Pueblo communities. Yet Pueblo leaders had talked Crandall into allowing the students to return to their homes for two months each summer. The superintendent also made allowances for parents to come see their children during the school year, even requesting a budget increase to furnish hay for the visitors' horses. Worst of all, as detractors saw things, Crandall was accused of allowing his students to converse with one another in their native languages, rather than enforcing an all-English campus.

Crandall didn't consider himself pro-Native by any stretch. He was simply a pragmatist who realized that he could gain greater cooperation from the Pueblos by making these allowances. He also believed in fair dealing. He rose to battle whenever any of his Native wards were threatened. When Crandall learned of the land theft at Taos, he fired off a demand letter to Lester Myers on official letterhead:

> You are hereby notified that the land upon which you have constructed a small house . . . is claimed, held and owned by the Indians of the Pueblo of Taos and that the construction of your house thereon, is regarded by such Indians as a trespass on their property. If such house is not removed by you within 60 days after the service of this notice, said Indians will claim and exercise the right to remove the same themselves.[6]

Malaquias Martínez scoffed that the Pueblo superintendent was bluffing and had no power to back up his threats. Soon, another cabin went up. Then another. And another. Before long, five homesteader residences were established in the shadow of Taos Mountain. Taken together, they served notice that these men, led by the territorial senator and two US Forest Rangers, now occupied these eight hundred acres.

Bert Phillips lost many of his friends at Taos Pueblo, including Sun Elk. When Florence Merriam Bailey wrote to Sun Elk inquiring how he was doing, she asked if Phillips was still continuing to help the Taos People. Sun Elk responded with a single word: "No."[7]

Phillips rationalized his actions, insisting that the parcel he'd claimed really was public land and there had only been a misunderstanding. He continued protecting the Blue Lake watershed for the Pueblo as part of his official duties, viewing himself as a notable defender of the Taos People in that regard. Yet when Phillips entered the Pueblo in his Forest Service uniform, people now turned away at his approach. In the shadows that followed him, voices could be heard murmuring, *Americano está muy diablo.*[8]

As Phillips patrolled his territory, often riding through dark forests or entering a lone cañon, it was easy enough to imagine a deadly ambush. He startled at unexpected noises and kept alert for danger. One day he rode up to Blue Lake as part of his regular survey of the area. Near the water, he dismounted and left his horse to graze. Approaching on foot, he startled at a sudden movement. An enormous grizzly lumbered out of the woods just a few yards away.

The bear, startled, swung around to regard the interloper. Phillips's own eyes rose to meet the bear's. He saw no mercy in those depths. Even on all fours the animal towered over him. For a long moment the bear sniffed at Phillips, as if deliberating his fate. The artist's mind emptied into an accepting calm, just as when the Taos Sheriff had stuck a gun in his face ten years before. Finally, the grizzly turned and loped away, its massive shoulder muscles rippling. When it reached the woods at the far end of the lake, it stopped and turned to study Phillips again. Then it disappeared into the darkness.

Pueblo Superintendent Crandall's sixty-day deadline had long since passed, and all five of the homesteaders' cabins remained standing. Malaquias Martínez was right. Crandall had been bluffing, and no one in Washington supported his position. Crandall's boss, Roosevelt's Commissioner of Indian Affairs, Francis Leupp, had little sympathy for Native land claims. "All primitive peoples are, from our economic point of view, grossly wasteful of their natural resources," Leupp maintained.[9]

At the same time, Crandall knew that Commissioner Leupp considered himself a progressive reformer in the Roosevelt mold. "I have no sympathy with grafters," Leupp had declared upon taking office. "They will not find any rest as long as I am Commissioner of Indian Affairs."[10]

Trying to persuade the commissioner to act, Crandall appealed to Leupp's sense of law and order and government ethics: "These claim shanties are not on the public domain, as stated by Mr. Bert Phillips,"[11] Crandall argued. He pointed out that the Taos People had purchased the property nearly a hundred years earlier and possessed the original deed, proving their ownership.

He closed his letter by demanding action against Phillips and Myers for abusing their government positions:

> I further believe that the Indian Office should notify the Forest Department at Washington that Bert Phillips, ranger, and L. S. Meyer, ranger, have taken advantage of their positions as rangers to attempt to

> secure land which properly belongs to the Indians; that they as Government officials should be warned against this practice, and required to withdraw their illegal claim to Indian land. I assume that the Forest Service will not tolerate such actions and conduct.[12]

Instead, the Forest Service supported Phillips and Myers. The agency notified its two rangers: "the Forest Service will not make any objection to your entering and occupying the land." The approving official added a handwritten postscript: "How goes it?" Ross McMillan, supervisor of Carson National Forest and the son of a powerful New Mexico judge, gave his men glowing evaluations. He also told Lester Myers he "anticipated being able to do more for you and Mr. Phillips in the future."[13]

Pueblo Superintendent Crandall pressed the Special Attorney for the Pueblo Indians, appointed by the US government to look after their legal interests. But that attorney, A. J. Abbott, showed little inclination to act. Abbott had previously let trespassing cases at other Pueblos go unchallenged. When Taos Pueblo leaders gave Abbott the original land deed, which proved that they owned the land in question, the Special Attorney conveniently "lost" the document.

Then came more bad news. Senator Martínez and his accomplices had engaged the high-powered attorney Napoleon Bonaparte Laughlin, who sat on New Mexico's Supreme Court, to defend their claim. Judge Laughlin was a law partner of Thomas Catron, leader of the Santa Fe Ring. Laughlin soon assembled a formidable legal team that, as Superintendent Crandall glumly noted, "includes about all of the prominent attorneys of Santa Fe."[14]

This was not quite the equivalent of the US Army wheeling its mountain howitzers into Taos Pueblo in 1847 and blasting twelve-pound shells at their church, but the overwhelming show of force was designed with the same goal in mind: to force the Puebloans to surrender.

CHAPTER 5

AN OLD-FASHIONED SCALPING EXPEDITION

1909–1910

More than a year had passed since the squatters' cabins had gone up along the Río Lucero. Lester Myers and his family occupied one of the homes while his wife's father lived in another. The other cabins—"claim shanties" as Pueblo Superintendent Crandall described them—were merely for show. Bert Phillips and Malaquias Martínez continued to maintain their homes in Taos. The real homesteading work was left to Myers. Fronted by Martínez's bank, Myers fenced in his 160 acres and ran several cattle where Taos Pueblo's own stock used to graze.

Crandall had seen a lot of land theft during his short time in New Mexico. Now he was certain the squatters would try to secure water rights from the Río Lucero. While Taos Pueblo held an existing claim on the Lucero, they had never used their full allotment, allowing excess water to remain in the river. While this made good sense from a conservation standpoint, New Mexico law saw things very differently. By neglecting to drain the river dry, the Pueblo was vulnerable to charges that it had been negligent.

Crandall sent a plea to Indian Commissioner Leupp: "In order to protect the rights and provide for the coming needs of these Indians, it behooves us to see that all prior [water] appropriations in their favor are protected."[1]

But Malaquias Martínez was already maneuvering. Before Washington could act, New Mexico's Superintendent of Irrigation ruled that Taos

Pueblo had failed to put the waters of the Río Lucero to "beneficial" use. As Commissioner Leupp might have put it, the Natives were "grossly wasteful of their natural resources." Just as Superintendent Crandall feared, the Pueblos' rights reverted to the Territory.[2]

A new application was immediately filed by Martínez, Phillips, Myers, Bryan, and Black "for a permit to appropriate from the Public Waters of the Territory of New Mexico. Such appropriation is to be made from Río Lucero. . . . By means of ditches and there used for irrigation of 800 acres."[3]

The man who would decide the case was Vernon L. Sullivan, the territorial engineer. Sullivan's work was overseen by the Senate Committee on Irrigation in New Mexico's territorial assembly. Malaquias Martínez, as it turned out, sat on that very committee. To no one's surprise, the territorial engineer quickly ruled in favor of Martínez and his partners, awarding them the coveted water.

As the legal noose tightened around Taos Pueblo, the possibility that the Natives might be stirred to revolt buzzed at the back of the schemers' minds. The Pueblo's history was punctuated with rebellions against the Spanish, Mexican, and American governments.

Across New Mexico and the Southwest, as native peoples were pushed out of their ancestral homelands, the slightest sign of discontent stoked white paranoia about "Indian Uprisings." Newspapers inflated the smallest incidents into modern-day "depredations," arousing bitter memories of the bloody nineteenth-century wars. In western New Mexico, a report that two Navajo men had illegally butchered a rancher's cow led to published warnings about an imminent Navajo uprising. When two teenagers at the Santa Fe Indian school got hold of a bottle of whiskey and confronted a white neighbor, the papers reported the youths were "on the warpath." When guests at a Santa Fe hotel were awakened in the middle of the night by drunken tourists shouting on the plaza, the papers reported that some "were under the impression that an Indian uprising had occurred." Out in Hopi country, a group of travelers described the local Natives as "restless" around the cattle-ranching homesteaders who'd invaded their territory. The next day's headline read: UPRISING OF HOPI INDIANS THREATENED.

Superintendent C. J. Crandall was determined to keep fighting for Taos Pueblo. He made a surprise visit to the Taos County Courthouse and looked through old land records. There, he located a copy of the original deed proving that Taos Pueblo legally owned the land now claimed by the homesteaders. It remained questionable whether any New Mexico judge would admit a copy as evidence, especially for Native plaintiffs. But the document certainly bolstered the Pueblo's case.

Yet the Pueblo's Special Attorney, A. J. Abbott, still declined to press the matter. In November 1909, Crandall vented his frustration at Indian Commissioner Leupp. His fiery letter bordered on insubordination: "I feel that delayed action at Taos is working against the rights and interests of these Indians, and still I fail to see what more I can do to put this matter properly before you."

The superintendent's frustration boiled over as he closed his letter: "These poor Indians are trusting me implicitly to protect them, while I feel that I am doing nothing."[4]

On a warm spring morning in April 1910, a group of Taos men set out from the Pueblo. They planned to move some of their cattle from winter pasturage in the desert and drive the animals up into the mountains, where fresh grass awaited. The route they followed curved alongside the Río Lucero, just below sacred Taos Mountain. Their ancestors had used this same road for hundreds of years.

Two years had passed since the gang of squatters built their homestead cabins. Now the entire eight hundred acres had been fenced off. The Taos men were not happy about this, but there was little they could do. They would bypass the squatters' claim and follow their ancient trail to Lucero Cañon—where they held grazing rights in the new national forest.

But as they approached the cañon, they encountered a barrier. Lester Myers had expanded his fence, which now blocked off the road to the mountains. Along with the new fence, the local newspaper printed a public notice explaining that anyone who desired to make use of that route, "which is on the property of Martínez, Myers, Phillips, Black, and Bryan"—must "enter into satisfactory arrangements with the referred owners."[5]

Anger mounted at the Pueblo and Superintendent Crandall hurried up from Santa Fe to try and calm emotions. He was joined in his peacemaking by some of the older Taos men—those who had been children in 1847 and vividly recalled the US Army killing so many of their people. Everyone understood that any violence would potentially place the entire Pueblo at risk.

The tribal council discussed hiring an independent outside attorney, but Crandall advised against it. Not only would the lawyer be expensive, there was little chance anyone could prevail over the powerful New Mexico establishment. While the Pueblo stewed, a bolt of welcome news arrived from Washington. Indian Commissioner Leupp had at last agreed to replace the useless A. J. Abbott as Pueblo attorney.

A fresh-faced thirty-three-year-old, Francis Cushman Wilson came from an affluent Eastern family and spoke with a pronounced Boston accent. He'd attended Harvard and graduated from Columbia Law School. Inspired by his hero, Teddy Roosevelt, Wilson wanted to see the West. He also longed to fight political corruption. Coming to New Mexico gave him the opportunity to do both.

Wilson showed up in Santa Fe in 1907 as part of a government team investigating local graft. He stood out as a dandy, favoring expensively tailored suits and fine wines. Yet he also proved to be a brilliant, fearless attorney. After completing his government work, Wilson decided to stay in Santa Fe and open his own law office.

He had barely established his practice when he received the summons to become the US Special Attorney for the Pueblo Indians. The position offered only $1,500 annually plus a small expense account. This was far less

Figure 11. Francis C. Wilson, ca. 1905. Courtesy of the State Archives of New Mexico. Francis C. Wilson Papers. Box 39638, Image no. 38211.

than he could earn in private practice, but he was assured that representing the Pueblos would only be part-time.

Soon after Wilson accepted the appointment, he heard from Pueblo Superintendent Crandall: "A bad state of affairs exists at Taos and I am free to say I do not know how to correct it. Anything you can do to help out conditions will be appreciated."[6]

Wilson journeyed to Taos to meet with Pueblo leaders. At the governor's residence, he found many anxious men. He was shown the copy of the deed proving that the Pueblo was the rightful owner of the land. A group escorted him out to see where the squatters' cabins were built. Wilson observed Lester Myers's cattle grazing, and he saw where the fence now closed off the Pueblos' old road.

Wilson knew very little about Pueblo People. Like many highly educated Easterners, he was convinced of his own cultural superiority. Others considered him to be haughty in manner. Yet he was also a resolute progressive in the Roosevelt mold. Dirty-dealing deeply offended him. He informed the Taos leaders that they could count on him. He would file a lawsuit to evict the trespassers.

Before returning to Santa Fe, Wilson also addressed the matter of that fence strung across the Pueblo's road. The homesteaders had no legal right to block off an existing roadway, he said. Then Wilson explained very carefully what action the Taos People could take in response.

MAY 13, 1910

Anyone venturing outside early on this day could see a small slash of light in the eastern sky. Halley's Comet was nearing its closest pass to Earth, sparking fear and superstition around the globe. But on this morning in Taos, War Chief Donaciano Cordova had no time for comet viewing. He led a group of about a dozen men on horseback out of the Pueblo. Several in the party carried shovels. They rode north along their traditional route toward the Río Lucero Cañon. When they reached Lester Myers's new fence, the men grabbed their shovels and began digging, pulling out several of the posts. Once the wire had enough slack, they simply laid the fence across the road. They were careful not to cut any of the wire, just as Francis Wilson had advised. After the fence was down, they had free passage—without damaging any man's property.

They proceeded along the road, which had become overgrown with sagebrush. The Taos men were prepared for this. They spread out and began lighting small fires to burn off the plants. The aroma of burning sage filled the desert air.

From inside her cabin, Lester Myers's wife, Maude, looked out the window and noticed smoke rising from the road. She was alone with their two children, including a baby daughter just five months old. Her husband was in town on business. She moved to get a better look. Then she saw what was happening. Natives had set fires, and now they were riding toward her house.

Mrs. Myers had heard both her father and husband express concern that the Taos Puebloans might turn violent. Like many Americans, she had been raised on lurid tales of Native depredations, sensational accounts of fearsome savages who massacred innocent settlers, raping women and smashing babies against boulders.

The Taos men arrived at the Myers's cabin. Dismounting, War Chief Cordova came up on to the porch. His intention was to tell the squatters that the Taos People had now reopened the road, as was their legal right. He was alerting the Myers family so that they could prevent their stock from escaping through the gap in the fence. In this manner, he was precisely following the instructions Wilson had given.

Mrs. Myers saw the Pueblo man speaking, but she didn't register his words. She scooped up her children and ran from the home, terrified. The Taos men did not follow. They returned to the Pueblo, their work complete. Mrs. Myers took refuge a short distance away at her father's cabin. Her husband, Lester Myers, soon arrived. When he heard what happened, he immediately spurred his horse and raced back to Taos. Stopping at Bert Phillips's house, he roused his friend with the news, sounding like a frontier Paul Revere: *The Redskins are Coming! The Redskins are Coming!*

Together, the two men made a mad dash for the plaza, shouting that the Taos Puebloans were on the warpath. They burst into the courtroom, where a federal district judge, John McFie, was presiding. Panicked accounts of Native depredations tumbled out. Judge McFie knew there was no time to lose. He rushed to the telegraph office and sent an emergency wire to the governor in Santa Fe:

> Taos Pueblo Indians fifty strong under War Captain raided settlers, tearing down fences, drove off stock, threatened women and children and intimated worse violence. . . . Conditions serious and aid of troops or militia imperative immediately . . . military action to prevent more serious conditions involving life of citizens.[7]

Taos County Sheriff Elizardo Quintana shot off his own telegram: "Immediate aid of troops to suppress disorder of Pueblo Indians here."[8]

In Santa Fe, Territorial Governor William J. Mills promptly activated the National Guard. Fifty armed troops boarded a specially commissioned train, bound for the closest railroad stop to Taos. There, fifty freshly saddled horses would be waiting for the soldiers to ride the remaining distance to Taos and engage the marauding Puebloans.

In Washington, President Taft was alerted to the escalating crisis. He conferred with his Secretary of War and ordered the Fifth Cavalry from Fort Wingate, Arizona, into action. These battle-hardened troops had earlier been fighting rebels in the Philippines. They were supplied with two hundred bullets each as their train steamed toward New Mexico. The Thirty-Eighth Company, Coast Artillery was also ordered to prepare for battle in Taos.

The Santa Fe newspaper published a special report: PUEBLO INDIANS ON THE RAMPAGE. The story began: "A lot of intoxicated Indians from the Pueblo of Taos raided the ranches of homesteaders north of town and after cutting fences drove off all the stock. They assaulted Mrs. L. S. Myers and babies."[9]

The news instantly ricocheted around the nation, gaining fresh details as the story spread. Newspapers reported "a possible massacre of white ranchers." Readers were told that the attacking Taos Puebloans "raided the valley, driving off horses and cattle and setting fire to many buildings. Mrs. L. S. Myers, wife of a settler, and her babies, were assaulted and left for dead. Settlers who attempted to resist the Indians were driven away." The Natives were said to have "cut all telephone and telegraph wires from Taos." Rumors spread that Apaches were headed to Taos to join their Pueblo brethren in "an old fashioned scalping expedition."[10]

The *Los Angeles Times* described the situation as "the most serious Indian uprising in the Southwest since Geronimo and his bloodthirsty band of Apaches terrorized the southern part of the Territory." The *Washington Post* worried of "Artists in Danger," noting that "Several Eastern artists are believed to be in or near Taos."[11]

The *New York Times* solicited commentary from that noted authority on Indigenous people, Buffalo Bill, who'd performed the previous evening at Madison Square Garden. The entertainer opined, "I have never thought much of the Indians there [in Taos.] They are poor fighters." He added, "I think these Indians must have gotten into a squabble among themselves over their lands."[12]

The fifty National Guard troops from Santa Fe finally arrived at the Barranca train stop at 4 a.m. No one was there to greet them. Nor were there any saddled horses. Taos remained thirty miles away. Undaunted, the commander, General A. S. Brookes, ordered his men to begin marching in the dark.

By the time the general and his troops arrived, the sun was blazing and it was clear there had been no uprising. Instead, a fence had simply been laid flat so that it no longer blocked a legal road. And, incredibly, the same two men who'd sparked the Taos Riot in 1898 had once again caused a mass panic.

President Taft fumed. Newspapers gamely reported that a "truce" was achieved, but it was clear that hysterical Anglos had panicked, which could have led to a massacre of innocent people. New Mexico's leaders, who had been lobbying Taft for statehood, had acted as anxious fools in front of the entire nation.

Malaquias Martínez's land and water grab, though trivial by ordinary New Mexico standards, necessarily required a certain measure of stealth to succeed. Now his cover was blown, and a harsh spotlight exposed the entire operation. Worse, the very judge slated to hear the homesteaders' case, John McFie, had been ridiculed in the press for sending that panicked telegram. McFie would not provide a sympathetic hearing.

Revista de Taos, the Spanish-language newspaper in Taos, operated by Senator Martínez's son-in-law, summed up much of the local anger toward Bert Phillips and Lester Myers: "La fatal jornada de esos mismo individuos que causaron este excitamiento—Phillips y Myers—y que causó la muerte del Alguacil Mayor en años pasados por necedades estúpidas . . . que muy bién pudiéra haberse repetido la historia á causa de los mismos indivíduos."[13] (The fatal journey of those same individuals who caused this excitement—Phillips and Myers—and who caused the death of the Sheriff in past years due to stupid nonsense . . . history could have very well been repeated because of these same individuals.)

Even as he worked to control the spreading backlash after the "Indian Uprising," more unwelcome news reached Senator Martínez. On a ranch he owned outside Taos, one of his cows was found killed. Soon he heard that a second cow perished—also a victim of a bloody depredation. His men at the ranch rode in pursuit, but the culprit had disappeared. Then a third cow got picked off, its torn carcass scattered across the pasture.

Clearly, Martínez was being targeted. When a fourth cow was mauled, Martínez summoned C. B. Ruggles, the best bear hunter around.

Ruggles quickly located the fresh bear tracks. Led by his dogs, he pursued an enormous grizzly, one of the last known to exist in the region. Ruggles caught a fleeting glimpse of the retreating animal, which he described as "round and fat, large as a young steer, with hips as broad as a horse, but he was not too big and heavy to get over the hills at a rapid pace when the dogs got after him."[14]

The bear headed in the direction of Taos Pueblo. Ruggles and his dogs tracked their quarry to Taos Mountain, which sat brooding under dark clouds. The grizzly entered the dense forest, clambering up steep slopes. Though it was no longer in sight, Ruggles's hounds continued baying as they followed its scent. Higher and higher the chase continued, through the pines and into the spruce and fir, the bear still somehow managing to keep ahead of the hunter and his pack. When Ruggles reached the timberline, he saw Blue Lake ahead, its waters leaden under the cloudy sky. The hunter was near the very same spot Bert Phillips had encountered an immense grizzly two years earlier. The dogs' barking suddenly changed pitch—and Ruggles knew they'd spotted their quarry. He spurred his horse ahead as the frantic howls gained volume, knowing the bear would be trapped at Blue Lake. But as Ruggles reached the water, the hounds' bays had turned to wails of disappointment. The hunter peered ahead. His dogs were pacing the rocky shore, sniffing at the empty air. The grizzly had somehow disappeared, never to be seen again.

CHAPTER 6

BAD VARMINTS

1911–1913

MAY 12, 1911

At Santa Fe's Union Station, Aldo Leopold, a sandy-haired young man with a sunlit smile, was feeling on top of the world. He'd been courting a gracious beauty from one of New Mexico's wealthiest families, fending off numerous rivals to win her affection. Leopold had also just landed an impressive new job—Assistant Supervisor at Carson National Forest. It was a heady position for a twenty-four-year-old.

The Forest Service had ousted the previous Carson supervisor, Ross McMillan, after an internal investigation revealed widespread bribery and collusion. McMillan's forest rangers, Bert Phillips and Lester Myers, were evicted from their homestead claims and each resigned from the Forest Service. The agency, stung by these embarrassing developments, brought in a new management team.

Leopold had less than two years' service, but he had risen rapidly through the ranks. Bright and ambitious, he graduated from Yale University's Forestry School, the preferred breeding ground for agency leaders. Students at Yale learned that national forests could not only be conserved but also made to turn a profit for the agency.

Leopold was well drilled in Forest Service policy, including the matter of predators, which he called "bad varmints." His sweetheart's family, the powerful Luna clan, controlled New Mexico's largest sheep empire, and

Figure 12. Aldo Leopold and Estella Bergere Leopold, ca. 1912. US Forest Service, Pacific Southwest Region 5 © Wikimedia/Creative Commons.

Leopold was well aware of their animosity toward wolves. The Lunas and other prominent stock raisers in New Mexico were besieging his agency with complaints about wolf depredations. In response, the Forest Service had begun hiring trappers. It also distributed a manual on wolf-killing to Leopold and other employees. That guide, *Wolves in Relation to Stock, Game, and the National Forest Reserves*, was authored by none other than Vernon "Wolf" Bailey, Chief Naturalist for the US Biological Survey and would-be benefactor of Taos Pueblo.

In his guide, Bailey suggested strychnine as "the only practical poison that can be recommended." But his favored method of reducing wolf populations involved locating dens. In that way, he could ambush the parents and then clear out the pups. "The dens are generally large enough for a man to crawl into," Bailey noted. He described finding a litter of eight wolf pups: "they were about 6 weeks old [and] fought as fiercely as their strength and puppy teeth would admit, but they could not cut through my buckskin glove."[1]

"Wolf" Bailey would have been proud of young Aldo Leopold. On Leopold's very first assignment, in Apache National Forest along the Arizona-New Mexico border, he'd been lunching on a ridge when he spotted a shaggy creature splashing across a mountain stream. It was a mother wolf, returning to her den. A pack of pups scampered out, tumbling over one another and wagging their tails furiously as they raced to greet her. Leopold sprang into action. He reached for his Winchester and began blasting away. Then he clambered down to inspect the damage. One crippled pup that survived the initial shooting desperately heaved itself away from him. The mother was down on her side, her breaths shortening. Leopold approached cautiously and stared in fascination. He saw "a fierce green fire dying in her eyes."[2] He'd done right by the Forest Service. Exterminating an entire wolf pack was citation-worthy.

Beyond controlling wolves and other predators, Leopold's marching orders for Carson National Forest were clear. He would need to maximize timber yields, which had so far been disappointing. The range also remained vastly overstocked with sheep. More than 225,000 were known to be on Carson lands, and Leopold's job was to reduce those numbers to 200,000. He would have to confront local stockmen and enforce grazing limits for the first time. He'd been given a six-shooter to wear for protection while doing so.

The most nettlesome challenge awaiting Leopold would be the Taos People. The disgraced Forest Ranger, Bert Phillips, had foolishly allowed the Pueblo exclusive use of the heavily timbered Blue Lake watershed. Former Carson Supervisor Ross McMillan had even sent the Pueblo assurances on Forest Service letterhead, pledging to protect their long-standing rights to the Blue Lake region. Now it would be Aldo Leopold's job to change things. He would be tasked with squeezing the Natives out of the national forest.

In Santa Fe, Leopold boarded the narrow-gauge Chili Line for the eight-hour journey to Carson headquarters. The steam-powered locomotive chugged northwest across the sandy, sagebrush-covered hills. Just south of San Ildefonso Pueblo, it crossed a wooden trestle over the Río Grande. Leopold looked out to the water and saw an extraordinary sight: the river was filled with thousands of logs, all bobbing and floating downstream.

The lumber, cut and squared into eight- and sixteen-foot segments, came from the mountains just south of Taos. Known as the Santa Barbara Land Grant, the land had once belonged in common to Hispano villagers in Peñasco. Then the New Mexican Supreme Court Judge, Napoleon Bonaparte Laughlin, managed to legally steal the entire grant, some 25,000 acres in all. Judge Laughlin soon partnered with the Atchison, Topeka, and Santa Fe Railway. The railway was expanding, and it needed millions of new cross-ties to lay down more tracks.

The Santa Barbara Tie and Pole Company, named in honor of the pillaged land grant, supplied the raw material. Nearly the entire area, some forty square miles of forest, was in the process of being clearcut. Sawmills buzzed all the way to the timberline at eleven thousand feet. Many of the laborers were displaced Hispanos, who earned sustenance wages and were supervised by armed guards. To get the timber down to the Río Grande, workers dynamited the small feeder streams, straightening their courses and turning the waterways into giant sluices. Once the finished logs reached the river, workers tossed them into the water for their journey downstream to Albuquerque's creosoting and fitting plant.

Leopold's employer, the US Forest Service, was quite aware of this massive clearcut. In fact, the agency helped engineer it. This land was slated to be added to Carson National Forest in what would become another lucrative deal for Judge Laughlin. But first, teams of forest rangers were sent to oversee the cutting and sawmill operations. In the agency's view, the old growth, mixed-species forests found on the Santa Barbara Grant were grossly inefficient. Centuries-old trees had long passed their peak lumber utility. The best policy, according to America's most highly educated foresters, was to strip the woods bare. Then, neat rows of a single species could be planted, the trees grown and harvested just like any other crop.

New Mexico had been denied statehood ever since the United States claimed it as a spoil of war in 1846. Meanwhile, other western territories had successfully petitioned for admittance: Colorado, Oregon, Washington, Montana, Idaho, Wyoming, Nevada, and Utah. New Mexico's secondary status as a territory was more than just a blow to civic pride. It also kept the political establishment on a tight federal leash, preventing its leaders from exercising the full powers of statehood.

It was no secret why New Mexico had been left behind—deeply rooted prejudice against its majority population of Spanish-speaking Hispanos. In 1903, the chairman of the US Senate Committee on Territories judged that "the people of New Mexico are not fit for statehood," blaming, "this mass of people, unlike us in race, language, and social customs." Others were less circumspect. The *Chicago Tribune* editorialized that New Mexicans were "not American, but 'Greaser,' persons ignorant of our laws, manners, customs, language, and institutions." The *Washington Post* added: "We are not anxious for a government of the 'greasers,' for the 'greasers,' and by the 'greasers.'"[3]

After many failed attempts to gain statehood, one of New Mexico's Spanish-language newspapers, *La Voz del Pueblo*, concluded that the Territory would never join the Union until "frogs grow hair, mules have children, and donkeys learn to read." The donkeys, the paper added, would also be required to "bray in English."[4]

Yet, from 1900 to 1910, a wave of some hundred thousand new Anglo-American immigrants swept into New Mexico, substantially altering the territory's demographics. Political calculations swiftly changed. At last, the nation judged New Mexico qualified to join the Union. With President Taft's endorsement, Congress passed the Enabling Act, finally setting New Mexico on the course to statehood.

A new state constitution would need to be drafted, and Malaquias Martínez of Taos was among the one hundred delegates who assembled in Santa Fe for the noble mission. He joined other prominent Republicans, including Thomas Catron, the fat-cat boss of the Santa Fe Ring, described by one newspaper editor as "the most unscrupulous man in the

Southwest."[5] Also present was Solomon Luna, the territory's largest sheep owner and considered New Mexico's richest man. Luna was also the uncle of Miss Estella Bergere, who Aldo Leopold had been courting in Santa Fe.

The most flamboyant delegate was fifty-year-old Albert B. Fall, a cigar-chomping lawyer and rancher who walked with a cowboy's swagger. Six feet tall, the sullen-eyed Fall wore a black Stetson and carried a six-shooter on his hip. Born in Kentucky during the Civil War, he came from a wealthy, slave-owning family. Fall had gravitated west as a young man, finding his fortune in New Mexico, where he became a Supreme Court justice and prominent landowner. A fearsome political force, Fall was known for his grandiloquent oratory—and for sometimes physically assaulting opponents. After his chief rival in southern New Mexico was murdered, Fall defended the accused men and won acquittals for all.

As the convention delegates were seated, Fall, Catron, Luna, Martínez, and the other Republicans enjoyed an overwhelming 71–28 majority. Albert Fall wasted no time establishing his personal dominance over the proceedings. When a Democrat named Jacob Crist began speaking, Fall rose and strode furiously toward the podium, swearing and threatening to pistol-whip the man. The shaken Crist left the capitol, never again to return to the convention.

In drafting the new constitution, Fall and the Republican majority dispensed high-minded rhetoric while fashioning a reactionary document beholden to monopolies and the privileged few. Rather than direct elections of US senators, the constitution awarded that power to the state legislature. Though several Western states had already granted women the right to vote, New Mexico barred women from voting or serving on juries. Nor were any Native Americans extended those rights. Once the final document was approved, Fall and the others lit victory cigars as three barrels of beer were wheeled into the capitol for the celebration.

In November 1911, New Mexico held its first-ever statewide elections and Malaquias Martínez became the Republican nominee for lieutenant governor. Martínez, carefully groomed for leadership, would at last get a chance to deliver on his political promise. Yet questions about his ethics lingered. Three weeks before the election, his business partner in Taos, a bank president named Arthur Clarence Probert, was arrested for fraud.

The bank closed and Probert was unmasked as a serial con man, a fugitive wanted in several states.[6] Bruised by this fresh scandal, Martínez narrowly lost the race.

Selecting the new state's first US senators involved far more intrigue than an open election. After days of backroom wrangling and exchanges of cash-stuffed envelopes, two Republicans were named: political boss Thomas Catron and the evil-tempered Albert B. Fall.

Catron, at age seventy-one, was no longer in his prime. It would be the younger, far more vigorous Albert B. Fall who claimed the starring role in this new political era. Now that New Mexico was at last "relieved of territorial shackles,"[7] Fall understood better than anyone what the stakes were. He and his cronies now stood poised to finally gain control over the most desirable lands within New Mexico's borders—those areas belonging to the Pueblo People and the US Forest Service. To accomplish this, the brand-new state would need to elbow the overprotective federal government out of the way.

In Fall's maiden speech before the US Senate, he rose to denounce federal management of New Mexico's forests. "The conservation of the natural resources in New Mexico means a restriction upon the individual," Fall complained. He argued that "little thrifty cities would grow up all over New Mexico, if we could use our forests." Appealing to his new colleagues, he pleaded, "We ask you simply to give us the administration of the forest reserves in the State of New Mexico. . . . These lands should be turned back to the people."[8] Fall's quixotic measure failed, but his campaign against the Forest Service spooked agency leaders, who were already under attack from stock raisers, timber companies, and mining conglomerates.

The New Mexico establishment also moved quickly against the Pueblos and other Indigenous people. The new State Legislature, in its first joint resolution, called upon Congress to dissolve New Mexico's federal reservations and grant the state control over those lands. In the senate, Albert Fall quickly introduced the necessary legislation. When Congress rejected his bill, the senator exploded in fury. He vowed that he would eventually abolish the entire Interior Department and its Office of Indian Affairs.

With New Mexico's drive to commandeer Pueblo lands stymied in Washington, the state's first US District Judge, William H. Pope, found an inventive solution. A member of the Santa Fe Ring, Judge Pope reviewed the conviction of Felipe Sandoval, a Hispano man who'd been arrested for selling liquor at Santa Clara Pueblo. The charges against Sandoval seemed clear—he'd been caught with the alcohol and federal law forbade the sale of intoxicants to Indigenous people. But Judge Pope rejected the premise of that statue as it applied to New Mexico. He determined that the bootlegger had committed no crime, for "the Pueblo Indians are not tribes within the meaning of the Constitution."[9] As Pope saw it, the Pueblos, independent and largely self-sufficient, did not qualify as wards of the federal government. He ruled that the Pueblo People were instead ordinary citizens of the state of New Mexico, never mind that they were barred from voting.

Judge Pope's decree struck New Mexico like a thunderclap. His ruling meant that the state, not the US government, now held legal jurisdiction over the Pueblo People—and their lands.[10] The path had been cleared. Stripped of federal protection, the Pueblos would now become subject to state property taxes. When the cash-poor tribes fell behind on their payments, the state would swoop in and seize their property. Then the lands could be auctioned off to preferred bidders.

At Carson National Forest, Aldo Leopold threw himself into his new assignment with gusto. He opened thousands of acres to timber harvests, pleasing lumbermen who kept sawmills buzzing across northern New Mexico. He also worked to reduce the long-standing problem of overgrazing. He encountered a few tense situations, but Leopold was at his diplomatic best in these moments, disarming opponents with his friendly smile and clear orders.

Within months, he was promoted to Forest Supervisor, an extraordinary rank for such a young man. In October 1912 he married the lovely Estella Bergere in a glittering wedding at Santa Fe's St. Francis Cathedral. The Forest Service built the newlyweds a supervisor's cabin overlooking the Sangre de Cristos and Taos Valley.

By now, the Forest Service had settled on its plan to rid the forest of the

Taos People: It would price the Natives out, choking them on permit fees. Supervisor Leopold went to Taos Pueblo flanked by armed rangers. There were no smiles and none of his cajoling diplomacy on this occasion. Leopold was polite but firm. The young man informed tribal elders that their people would henceforth be required to apply for federal permits—and pay usage fees—in order to gather timber, hunt game, or graze their animals within the boundaries of the national forest. The Natives were now to be charged for the same rights their ancestors had known for a thousand years.

Taos Pueblo was still represented by its skillful attorney, Francis Wilson, who immediately lodged a protest. In Washington, the Interior Department agreed to act, motivated less by sympathy for Natives than a desire to protect its bureaucratic turf from the Agriculture Department. After some wrangling in the capital, the Forest Service finally backed off. It would not charge any fees, though the Taos People would now be required to apply for use permits.

Leopold kept the pressure on, quickly moving ahead on another front. He decided the time had come to survey the Blue Lake area's thick forests—"with a view of securing a timber sale and starting a sawmill."[11] This new threat alarmed Pueblo leaders, who were well aware of the massive clearcuts that had decimated the nearby Santa Barbara Grant.

When Leopold's squadron of Forest Rangers rode toward Blue Lake, the Taos war chief and several mounted men massed to block them. The Taos People meant to protect their ancient forests, those living saints. After a tense standoff, the rangers finally retreated. In Washington, the bureaucrats again worked out a solution. Any logging around Blue Lake would be postponed—for the time being.

But Leopold refused to give up. In the mountain forests above the Pueblo existed many religious shrines, natural altars where the Taos People regularly performed holy rituals and made offerings throughout the year. These ceremonies required strict privacy to be carried out properly. Leopold knew this, yet his forest rangers soon developed a pattern of harassing the Taos People.

One morning, C. E. Hulbert, who had replaced Bert Phillips as the ranger for the Taos District, rode into a thick cottonwood grove called Glorieta. A Pueblo religious retreat was underway, but the ranger entered the camp anyway. A group of Taos men instantly swarmed him. Two subdued Hulbert while two others secured his horse. The Puebloans tied a scarf over the ranger's eyes. Then they turned his horse around and guided the blindfolded man back to the Pueblo. There, the scarf was untied. Once he was set free, the ranger was admonished: *This is Indian time in the forest.*[12]

One August, Ranger Hulbert and two other men rode into the mountains. Their job was to string telephone wire to a new fire lookout. They decided to follow a trail that led to Blue Lake, knowing full well the Taos People were on their annual religious retreat and this was the Pueblo's holiest time of year. As the rangers approached the Lake, they encountered a wondrous sight. Dozens of Native horses were staked out on a grassy meadow, their thick manes delicately threaded with wildflowers: blue columbine, yellow coneflowers, purple bellflowers, and scarlet paintbrush. Even the horses' tails were braided with fresh flowers.

The men could have turned back. Instead, they rode on toward the lake. They could see the Puebloans gathered on the shore, many with prayer feathers. Still the rangers continued to advance, deliberately steering their horses through the gathering. Some Taos People slipped into the forest while others rose to their feet and stared angrily at the intruders.

A few days later, one of the rangers was in Taos, getting supplies at the general store. He was confronted by a Taos Pueblo man, Tony Luján, who stood six feet tall and was built like a bear. Luján nodded in the direction of Blue Lake and told the ranger, "I saw you there." Then he gestured to a nearby tree stump. "Was as close as that stump to you." Then Luján gave the ranger a hard look. "Could have killed all three of you."[13]

In the Senate, Albert B. Fall kept up his attacks on the US Forest Service. He charged that the federal lands offered safe harbors for malicious predatory animals—which in turn preyed upon independent stock raisers. "Upon such forest reserves . . . the gentle bear, the mountain lion, and the timber wolf are conserved," Fall scoffed, "so that they may attack his herds, his cattle, and his sheep." The senator sourly concluded, "That is conservation in New Mexico."[14]

The Forest Service, sensitive to such criticism, responded by launching a massive, well-publicized killing campaign targeting native animals with close cultural and spiritual ties to Indigenous people. Wolves, bears, mountain lions, coyotes, bobcats, badgers, hawks, eagles, and others were poisoned, trapped, and shot by the tens of thousands. The Forest Service aimed to do more than simply reduce these populations—it hoped to placate Fall and other critics by clearcutting the "varmints" out of the forest completely.

In New Mexico, Aldo Leopold saw a fresh opportunity and moved quickly to claim leadership of this holy war. He barnstormed across New Mexico, delivering a series of fiery speeches to rally the citizenry. "It is well known that predatory animals are continuing to eat the cream off the stock grower's profits,"[15] Leopold charged. Such actions brought favor from his wife's family, including his influential father-in-law—who owned fifteen thousand sheep as part of the family's empire.

In his public talks, Leopold praised the Forest Service's efforts while also conceding that the agency hadn't done enough. "Whatever may have been the value of the work accomplished by bounty systems, poisoning, and trapping," he argued, "the fact remains that varmints continue to thrive." His call to arms was simple and direct: "The varmints must be killed not only as fast as they breed, but even faster."[16]

Leopold identified the wolf as Public Enemy #1. He created a new alliance that partnered cattlemen and hunters with the Forest Service in a focused campaign to eradicate the animal. He also successfully lobbied for taxpayer funds to be devoted to the effort. Within three years of Leopold's announced crusade, the state's wolf population fell by 90 percent. A few years later, when the last wolf was finally hunted down and destroyed, Leopold could claim victory.[17]

In representing the Pueblos, attorney Francis Wilson had been on the losing end of the notorious *Sandoval* case in Judge Pope's courtroom. While New Mexico's establishment rejoiced, even Wilson admitted a grudging respect for the dark brilliance of Pope's ruling. Still, the attorney wasn't about to give up. He appealed the decision, and the US Supreme Court agreed to hear the case.

In October 1913, the High Court issued its ruling: "The people of the pueblos, although sedentary rather than nomadic in their inclinations and disposed to peace and industry, are nevertheless Indians in race, customs, and domestic government . . . adhering to primitive modes of life, largely influenced by superstitions and fetishism, and chiefly governed according to the crude customs inherited from their ancestors, they are essentially a simple, uninformed and inferior people."[18]

This was hardly the wording that attorney Wilson and the Pueblos wished to see. Yet in a unanimous vote, the Supreme Court had overturned Judge Pope in New Mexico. The Pueblo People were confirmed as wards of the federal government. As such, they could not be subjected to taxation by the State of New Mexico. Their land was safe—for the time being.

Wilson had won this battle, but he felt little cause for celebration as he knew a long war lay ahead: "With a state legislature alive to the value of the development and settlement of the broad acres owned by these Indians, it will be but a short time before legislation will be adopted by which title [for whites] can be safely acquired. When the time arrives only a short period will elapse before the Pueblo Indians will be stripped of his only resource—his land."[19]

CHAPTER 7

CULTURE WARS

1913–1917

By the time Bert Phillips resigned from the Forest Service, his ailing eyes had healed and he was able to return to painting. He'd lost many of his established models, including Sun Elk, but he was able to hire others. He drifted away from formal studio portraits and increasingly embraced the outdoor splendor of the Taos Mountains. His Pueblo subjects became part of the landscape, often shown lost in reverie.

Phillips was prospering as never before, and for that he could thank the Atchison, Topeka, and Santa Fe Railway. The company, seeking to increase ridership along its tracks, had launched an ambitious plan to transform New Mexico into a tourist destination. The Taos painters, with their soothing depictions of peaceful Natives, were the ideal image-makers for the railroad's marketing campaign.

The Santa Fe Railway had become a major arts patron, buying up paintings and paying premium prices to secure advertising rights. The artwork was displayed at train stations back east and featured in brochures and postcards. The publicity boost helped Phillips sell more work and now, at age forty-five, his art finally began to sustain him financially. He and his family moved into a larger, freshly remodeled adobe home just off the main plaza. The residence included a spacious studio with a panel of north-facing windows offering a framed view of Taos Mountain.

The little art colony in Taos was flourishing. Joseph Henry Sharp, who'd earlier sold Phoebe Hearst enough paintings to fill her fifty-room mansion, joined Phillips as a year-round resident. Now in his mid-fifties, Sharp had come to favor the slow and easy tempo of Taos. His California agent complained that he could sell a lot more paintings if he moved to the West Coast, but Sharp told the man, "I'd rather have boiled dog in Taos than lamb and asparagus in Pasadena."[1]

Next door to Sharp was the summer home of E. Irving Couse—the portly "Green Mountain." Couse had mastered the technique of soft firelight scenes with breechcloth-clad Natives, in the process establishing himself as the Santa Fe Railway's favored artist. In 1914, the company selected his painting—*Wal-si-el—Good Medicine*—to be its chief promotional image. Couse's picture portrayed a gentle Taos man crouched before a fire with a clay pot. The painting appeared on 300,000 copies of the Railroad's calendar and was seen by millions, displayed in homes, offices, and schools around the country. The Santa Fe's patronage was lifting the already popular Couse to entirely new realm, making him a wealthy man.

More artists began appearing in Taos, among them Ernest Blumenschein, who had first arrived back in 1898 with Bert Phillips. For years, Blumenschein had lived a glittering life in Paris as a top commercial illustrator. He'd married the painter Mary Shepard Greene, who came from a prominent New York family and won major French art prizes for her work. The couple returned to the United States in 1909, taking an apartment in Greenwich Village.

For Blumenschein, working as an illustrator paid the bills, but the commissions hardly stirred his soul. Now nearing forty, he burned with ambition to make great paintings—and he saw Taos as his muse. He began spending his summers in New Mexico, taking advantage of the free train passage provided by the Santa Fe Railway to notable artists. Yet once in Taos, his intention to make "art" faltered before the railroad's tempting financial offers. He sold several market-ready works to the company, including "Taos Indian Holding a Water Jug"—which depicted a man in a stereotypical Plains headdress standing in front of the Pueblo, clutching a clay pot as though offering it for sale.

While the middle-aged artists in Taos created romantic images of an Edenic past, the modern world continued hurtling forward. Traffic lights went up in cities and wind-up Victrolas brought opera into peoples' homes. In Detroit, Henry Ford set up a moving assembly line for his Model-T, manufacturing a new car every three minutes.

The tumult of change reached far beyond new products. The theories of Darwin, Freud, and Einstein were undermining religious certainty. Anthropologist Franz Boas's vision of cultural relativity challenged notions of innate European superiority. These new ideas inspired artists, leading to radical experimentation. In Paris, where Bert Phillips and other Taos painters had been trained in the genteel Beaux-Arts style, an upheaval was shaking the foundations of Western art. Pablo Picasso, influenced by African tribal art and other "primitive" styles, painted with an intentionally decentralized perspective. Picasso and other artists began thinking of themselves as revolutionaries. "Painting is not done to decorate apartments," Picasso snarled. "It is an instrument of war for attack and defense against the enemy."[2]

In the United States, this confrontational "modern" art arrived in February 1913 at New York City's 69th Regiment Armory. Dubbed "The Armory Show," the exhibition featured the latest avant-garde works from Europe, introducing Americans to the complexities, and perplexities, of nonrepresentational painting. Pablo Picasso's cubism and Henri Matisse's intensely colored "Blue Nude" were condemned as "perverse" and "grotesque." The most notorious work became twenty-five-year-old Marcel Duchamp's futuristic "Nude Descending a Staircase," which a critic panned as resembling "an explosion in a shingle factory."[3]

In faraway New Mexico, none of the Taos artists were breaking new ground. Their paintings, crafted in a realistic, sentimental style, were familiar and comfortable to many Americans. The Santa Fe Railway's marketing campaign was proving to be a phenomenal success, steadily transforming New Mexico into the "Land of Enchantment." A sprawling new business empire grew along the tracks, with full-service restaurants and hotels managed by the Fred Harvey Company. The ancient capital of Santa Fe, blessed with railway access, became a popular destination and began developing its own artist colony that would soon rival Taos.

The Taos artists had begun with a very simple idea—they wanted to paint "the vanishing race" before it disappeared. Now their work, fueled by an expansionist railroad's marketing zeal, was becoming national iconography. None of the artists thought of themselves as revolutionaries, but their paintings were becoming quietly radical propaganda. The popular images helped redefine Native Americans in the national consciousness. By celebrating the peaceful Pueblo People and their beautiful homeland, the works were helping undermine the US government's long-standing policy of forced assimilation and dispossession of Native peoples.

Matilda Coxe Stevenson, the venerable Smithsonian anthropologist, was keenly aware of the Pueblos' devotion to privacy in safeguarding their religion and culture from outsiders. Such conditions were a challenge she relished. The imperious Stevenson had made her reputation extracting precious secrets from the Zuñi People in western New Mexico. Later, she descended on Taos Pueblo, brazenly outlining her objectives to a reporter: "At Taos I want to learn all about the practice of the priests, the religious ceremonials, the secret societies of which there are many." The anthropologist clarified, "I am not an Indian myself—don't even eat Indian food, but . . . to get among the people I am studying I first have to win their confidence. This I do by kindness, combined with firmness."[4]

What Stevenson didn't mention to the press is that she ordered whiskey by the case and charged it to her government expense account. The alcohol was necessary, she claimed, "since nothing else would induce the Indians to give out their more secret information."[5]

After her newspaper interview, Taos leaders swiftly banned her from the Pueblo. Undaunted, the anthropologist took up residence in a log cabin outside Taos, naming it Camp Defiance. There, Stevenson spent six months prodding informants drawn to her supply of liquor. Then she moved on to investigate other Pueblos. At Santa Clara, she questioned a man about an old legend that the Puebloans had once practiced human sacrifice to appease a snake god. Tumblers of whiskey were filled and refilled until finally, the man rewarded Stevenson with the biggest discovery of her career. In January 1915 the Smithsonian Institution made her report available to the press.

PUEBLO HUMAN SACRIFICES, shrieked the newspaper headlines. Stevenson, credited as "an expert on Indian affairs for thirty years," affirmed that she'd cracked open the greatest secret of all: Puebloans had not only sacrificed humans in ancient times, but they continued to do so in the modern world. She described in lurid detail how babies and unmarried women were stripped naked and given narcotics in underground kivas. The victims, she reported, were "placed upon a sand painting before the altar, and the ceremonies proceed amid incantations and strange performances."[6]

Then things got even weirder. Religious leaders brought several clay vessels into the kiva, each bearing an enormous rattlesnake. Stevenson described how "the rattlesnakes, which have been starved, are turned loose from the pottery vases and allowed to feast upon the body until not an atom of flesh remains."[7]

This shocking report of present-day human sacrifice scandalized people across the nation. No one had imagined those gentle, pot-decorating men in the Santa Fe Railway's paintings were in reality murdering women and babies by feeding them to flesh-eating snakes.

Detractors in New Mexico immediately lambasted Stevenson's account as ridiculous, pointing out that such tall tales had duped gullible outsiders for years. The Smithsonian Institution's own naturalists conceded that rattlesnakes were not physically capable of tearing flesh off a human body and ingesting it.

Though mocked by experts, Stevenson's report served the forces of conquest as capably as any battlefield general. Her story galvanized pro-assimilationist forces bent on eradicating Indigenous cultures. Newspaper editorials warned that if "women and babies still are sacrificed to propitiate the Indian gods," the Pueblos "are far from being civilized within the Anglo-Saxon acceptance of the term." Frederic J. Haskin, president of the National Press Club, complained of the Pueblos' "despotic" religion and called for stricter government controls: "It is a well-known fact that upon returning to the pueblo from an Indian school, the Pueblo Indian immediately relapses into barbarism. He discards his civilized garb, forgets all he has learned, and proceeds to live the rest of his life pretty much as though Columbus had not discovered America."[8]

While the Taos artists portrayed the Taos People as static relics of the past, in truth profound changes were occurring within the Pueblo. Perhaps no person embodied these developments more than a young man known as Star Road. In his late twenties, the rebellious Star Road had begun adopting American-style clothing. He favored boots over moccasins, and he was most comfortable in a pair of denim jeans. Instead of using a blanket for protection from the sun, he preferred a cowboy hat. Tribal elders did not approve.

Star Road was a familiar figure to the Anglo artists in town, who knew him as Gerónimo Gómez. The lean, sinewy Puebloan was one of Eanger Irving Couse's favorite models. He'd posed for dozens of paintings, and he'd been photographed hundreds of times. He spent many hours wearing nothing more than a breechcloth, directed to squat, kneel, or sit cross-legged before a fire as he pretended to decorate pottery or weave a blanket. His real life was nothing like this. No Pueblo man he knew walked around in a breechcloth. Nor did Star Road make any crafts. Instead, he was a farmer, and he grew corn while tending an apple orchard behind his home. He was also a founding father of the peyote cult at Taos.

He had learned about peyote in 1907, when he joined other young Taos men who traveled to Oklahoma to visit Arapaho and Cheyenne friends who'd been classmates at Carlisle Indian School. There, Star Road took part in a peyote ceremony. He emerged feeling renewed, closer to God. He and others soon formed a peyote group in Taos. They viewed the new practice as a supplement, not a replacement, for their traditional religion. But tribal elders disagreed. They considered peyote use heresy. They raided the ceremonies, confiscating belongings and levying fines.[9]

Star Road not only challenged tribal elders, but he also took sharp notice of how the Anglo painters were exploiting Native models. As the Taos art colony gained increasing fame, Star Road had seen himself on those famous Santa Fe Railway calendars. He knew that Green Mountain

Figure 13. "The Quiver Maker." Painting by Eanger Irving Couse, 1918. Collection of the Panhandle-Plains Historical Museum. © Wikimedia/Creative Commons.

was getting rich—and was doing so off his image. And yet Star Road and other Pueblo models were still only receiving twenty-five cents an hour to pose.

The artist Couse often proclaimed his love for Native people. His paintings, he said, were created "to remove the misconception and contempt in which the Indian has been held, and to show that they are human beings worthy of consideration and a place in the sun."[10] Couse might have really believed that, but it was also true that Taos appealed to him for its cheap labor.

Star Road and the other models were painfully aware of Couse's cost-saving tricks. Rather than paying them to pose for long periods of time, the painter developed a shortcut. He took hundreds of photographs of his models in various positions. When he returned to his brightly lit New York studio in the winter, he worked from the photographs to crank out dozens of new market-ready paintings.

Growing dissent among Taos Pueblo models erupted when a notice appeared in local newspapers announcing that E. Irving Couse's recent painting, "A Vision of the Past," won a major art prize carrying a cash award of $500. The men who posed for the picture had received only a dollar or two. When Star Road heard the news, he led the other Pueblo models on a strike. Their demand was simple: half the money for each painting.

Star Road's boycott brought a long overdue reckoning. Several of the Taos models also worked for the artists as handymen, cutting firewood, tending to gardens, and repairing leaky roofs.[11] Women were often hired to cook and clean. As models and domestic servants, the Puebloans provided low-cost labor for the Anglos. Yet the painful truth was that the wages, insulting as they were, provided more cash than most other work around Taos.

Eventually, the strike's momentum waned and an uneasy peace prevailed. Seeking to head off future labor disputes, Couse contacted the Taos and Santa Fe newspapers and asked them to quit publishing the dollar amounts earned by the artists—"because such information was creating problems." In a letter to the *Santa Fe New Mexican*, Couse added a threat: "Unless these impressions are nipped in the bud the whole future of the Santa Fe Taos Art movement will be seriously handicapped [and] the artists will be compelled to go elsewhere for models."[12]

Ernest Blumenschein, far more than the other painters in Taos, felt driven to achieve artistic greatness. Yet he was continually frustrated by the need to make a living. When his wife received a substantial inheritance, he at last escaped the commercial treadmill. The family moved to Taos so he could pursue his artistic vision. Blumenschein would prove far more open

Figure 14. "Star Road and White Sun." Painting by Ernest Blumenschein, 1920. Collection of the Albuquerque Museum. © Wikimedia/Creative Commons.

to experimentation than his colleagues in the art colony. He had attended the controversial Armory exhibition in New York and was intrigued, considering the new modernism "a very healthy affair."[13] In Taos, his brush strokes began loosening from the cautious Académie Julian training.

Meanwhile, Star Road drifted away from Couse and began posing for Blumenschein instead. He also worked as the Blumenschein family's handyman. He and the artist developed a warm rapport, and the two often went fishing along the Río Grande or camping in the mountains. The Pueblo man never revealed any tribal secrets, but as their relationship strengthened he opened Blumenschein's eyes in many ways. Blumenschein learned of the renegade peyote movement at Taos and he gained a deeper understanding of the bracing challenges the Taos People faced in maintaining their homeland and culture.

The newly inspired Blumenschein soon began creating a series of masterworks that eschewed his past romanticism. His best was a life-size canvas titled "Star Road and White Sun." This new painting depicted Star Road, at long last, as he really was: He posed wearing his cowboy hat and a modern work jacket, along with the red-and-blue neckerchief associated with the peyote movement. Pictured with him is White Sun, a tribal elder wrapped in a traditional blanket. The defiant Star Road is standing in front, eclipsing the older man and staring directly at the viewer.[14] The message in Blumenschein's painting was unmistakable—a new generation was becoming ascendent, but the resilient Taos People would endure.

Along with the evolution in his painting, the eloquent Blumenschein began writing articles defending the Taos People from the likes of Matilda Coxe Stevenson and others who condemned the Natives as "savages." In an essay for the *Magazine of American Art*, Blumenschein wrote: "The Indians of Taos have resisted all enemies for these many centuries during which they gradually developed the grand little democracy of the Pueblos, self-governing, self-supporting, and self-respecting.[15]

Blumenschein also gave a press interview criticizing the Indian Bureau for its unsparing drive to assimilate the Pueblos and other Indigenous people: "If in the adoption of a 'higher' civilization the Indian gives up his own remarkable gifts to the world, the loss will be irreparable."[16]

Blumenschein's outspokenness soon inspired an old friend. Bert Phillips's earlier betrayal of Taos Pueblo had been spurred by economic need, but now his finances were steady and he sought to make amends. Emboldened by Blumenschein, Phillips re-emerged as a Pueblo advocate. He began promoting the Taos People's virtues to white audiences, arguing that the Puebloans defied "primitive" stereotypes and were instead quite sophisticated in their thinking. "I cannot doubt that there is a culture behind the Pueblos we cannot understand," Phillips said. "Thousands of years in close communion with nature, a religion and knowledge based on this, has given them a power we do not possess. They see thousands of things that we do not; they hear things that we do not hear, and they believe things that only some of our advanced thinkers are preaching."[17]

Phillips also lavished praise on Pueblo aesthetics, telling the *Albuquerque Herald*, "Their contribution to art has been invaluable. We come out here to learn from them and find an apparently inexhaustible store of beauty and originality. . . . There is a great future in Indian art; of this we artists are confident."[18]

Like Blumenschein, Phillips bemoaned the US government's continuing policy of forced assimilation: "Their very methods of 'civilizing,'" he said, "are largely responsible for the destruction of the Indians' gifts to the world."[19]

Phillips and Blumenschein could take pride in speaking out, but their voices gained little traction. The *Magazine of American Art* and the *Albuquerque Herald* were hardly required reading on Capitol Hill. Nor did the US Indian Bureau seem concerned by the artists' objections to its policies. Native American advocacy organizations such as the Indian Rights Association did exist, but these were missionary-dominated groups focused on issues of health and welfare. Their goal was to ensure that the grinding dispossession and cultural extinction of Native peoples mandated by the 1887 Dawes Act were carried out as humanely as possible. There was no unified national movement to defend Native cultures or protect Indigenous lands—only a few scattered voices of protest, including the artists in Taos.

But seeds of resistance were being planted. Change was coming.

PART II

RESISTANCE

CHAPTER 8

A STRANGE RELATIONSHIP

1917–1918

NOVEMBER 1917

The New York heiress was just a few weeks into her third marriage when she caught her husband, a noted artist, eying another woman. Though she had often extolled the merits of free love in principle, in her own relations she was always passionately jealous. She quickly settled on the proper punishment. She'd been hearing that other New York painters were traveling to far-off New Mexico for inspiration. Imagining her new husband in such remote surroundings appealed to her. As she put the reluctant man on a train, she told him the change in scenery would be good for his art.

Mabel Ganson Evans Dodge Sterne was the iron-willed daughter of a banking titan, and she was used to calling the shots. She was not regarded as conventionally beautiful. Her artist husband described her square features as "robust . . . without the fine bone structure in which I had always taken such pleasure."[1] But Mabel had a powerful magnetism that drew others to her.

At age thirty-eight, Mabel was the darling of the American avant-garde. Fascinated by modern art, radical politics, feminism, mysticism, and psychoanalysis, she championed rebels and promoted their causes. Muckraking journalist Lincoln Steffens considered her "one of the most wonderful things in the world . . . a woman that has done whatever it has struck

Figure 15. Mabel Dodge Luhan. Photograph by Carl Van Vechten, 1934. Mabel Dodge Luhan Papers. Yale Collection of American Literature, Beinecke Rare Book and Manuscript Library. © Van Vechten Trust.

her fancy to do." Modernist painter Marsden Hartley praised her as "the most remarkable woman . . . a real creator of creators." One wag, less reverent, labeled her "an aeroplane laden with explosives."[2]

In New York, Mabel had helped stage the audacious Armory Show that introduced Pablo Picasso and other revolutionary artists to America. At her luxury apartment in Greenwich Village, she presided over weekly salon discussions that became renowned among the cultural elite. Birth control crusader Margaret Sanger and anarchist Emma Goldman attended, along with a fledgling painter named Georgia O'Keeffe. Among the writers Mabel cultivated were two young men who would go on to win Nobel Prizes for literature: Sinclair Lewis and Eugene O'Neill.

In 1915 Mabel met Maurice Sterne, a handsome painter who'd won acclaim for his colorful portraits of Bali. They carried on an affair at the famous Provincetown art colony, where Mabel kept a house. In August 1917 they impulsively married. Sterne admitted to Mabel that her money was part of the attraction. The couple bickered constantly while living under the same roof, but after Mabel dispatched Maurice to New Mexico and he was living two thousand miles away their relationship improved. They exchanged regular letters that grew increasingly tender. Sterne shared gossip about other New York artists who were in New Mexico, and he told Mabel that everyone was busy painting the Natives.

Mabel had been thinking a lot about Native Americans. While the Great War raged in Europe, killing millions, several in Mabel's circle had begun touting New Mexico's Pueblo People and their peaceful lifeways. The art critic Leo Stein, an early champion of Picasso and Matisse, told Mabel that the Pueblos lived in communal villages that functioned as model egalitarian societies. Others considered the Puebloans religious mystics who possessed telepathic powers. When Mabel sat by the poet Ridgely Torrence at a dinner party, he assured her that the Pueblos had the power of levitation, telling her, "People went on journeys in the air."[3]

At one of her weekly salons, an anthropologist named Raymond Harrington spoke of a magic cactus sometimes ingested by southwestern Natives. He reported that it gave them the power "to pass beyond ordinary consciousness and see things as they are in Reality."[4] The more he talked, the more animated Mabel became. She pressed Dr. Harrington until he admitted that he had brought a sample of this cactus with him to New York. He warned that the substance was not to be trifled with, but he was no match for the determined Mabel. And so that very same evening, Mabel and her guests began chewing on peyote buttons.

The experience began pleasantly enough. Some people enjoyed idyllic visions. One man "saw the walls of this house fall away and . . . was following a lovely river for miles through the most wonderful virginal forest."[5] Mabel, maintaining her ego, thought everything seemed ridiculous and fought back wild urges to laugh. Then, as the drug took stronger hold, one panicked guest fled the apartment and disappeared into the New York night. Fear and paranoia took over, leaving Mabel and the others jittery. When everyone finally came down, Mabel felt that they had tapped into some powerful, elemental force, something beyond her control.

In November 1917, with her husband still in New Mexico, Mabel learned of a new exhibition. The founding Taos artists had been granted their first-ever group show in New York, their work displayed at the opulent Majestic Hotel on Central Park. The *New York Times*, in its review, judged the painting styles to be a bit dated but praised the artists for having "the right spirit, when it is an affair of making records of a race certain to vanish."[6]

Mabel went to see the show, even though she was already familiar with the art from the Santa Fe Railway's advertising campaign. While there was nothing avant-garde about the paintings, she studied the subjects with interest.[7] She saw one of Eanger Irving Couses's nearly nude, breechcloth-clad men kneeling before a fireplace, fashioning a small katsina figure. Bert Phillips contributed a heart-rending portrait of a young Taos boy contemplating an old buffalo skull, along with a picture of four vibrant Taos maidens balancing baskets of freshly shucked corn on their heads. Ernest Blumenschein, whose featured work was called "Wise Man," supplied the exhibition text:

The Pueblo People, Blumenschein pointedly noted, "have always maintained their own customs and their religion even until now, when they are struggling against the mighty white race that threatens to swallow them up and spit them out again, servants with short hair and clad in overalls!"[8]

Mabel was enchanted by these gentle Pueblo people and their homeland's luminous beauty. Why were her fellow countrymen so intent on destroying them? What threat did they pose to the nation?

She returned home from the exhibition and lay down for her customary afternoon nap. Drifting toward sleep, her husband's face suddenly appeared overhead, as if in a vision. She observed him for a long moment, curious about this strange phenomenon. Then his image began to dim, and another man came into view. This new person was clearly a Native, with high cheekbones and golden-brown skin. She studied his handsome face with curiosity. Strong and noble-looking, his brown eyes smoldered with compassion—and hinted at deep knowledge. Mabel awoke with a start. What could this vision mean?

The next day a letter arrived from her husband. Maurice Sterne missed his wife dearly and hoped to persuade her to join him in New Mexico. "Dearest Girl," he wrote. "Do you want an object in life? Save the Indians, their art—culture—reveal it to the world! . . . You could if you wanted to, for you have the energy and are the most sensitive little girl in the world—and above all, there is somehow a strange relationship between yourself and the Indians."[9]

Mabel had only been in Santa Fe two days but was already anxious to leave. Maurice had introduced her to painters and writers in town, but she had no interest in them. That wasn't why she came to New Mexico. When a poet invited her to tea, Mabel blurted out the first excuse she could think of: "Well, I think we'll motor up to a place called Taos."[10]

By the next morning, she had hired a man to drive them the seventy-five-mile distance. As they climbed into the open-air Model-T, Maurice sighed. He'd once hobnobbed with Picasso in Paris, but now he was bound for a remote village inhabited by those he considered "ghastly" painters. Trying to look on the bright side, he told Mabel, "almost all the artists are away"[11] for the winter.

The primitive road, a former burro path, was deeply rutted and the driver stopped frequently to attend to his boiling radiator. Yet Mabel was enthralled by the ever-changing play of light and shadow upon the desert and mountains. By afternoon they reached the mouth of the Río Grande Gorge, about halfway to Taos. Here green water poured over polished black rock as it emerged from the cañon. They stopped for lunch, and Mabel sat away from the two men, alone with her thoughts beside the flowing river and the chattering birds. She looked up to the yellow sandstone spires that cut against the blue sky. Everything here has a *Being*, Mabel suddenly thought. An energy.

Their driver cranked the car back to life, and they chugged into the cañon. They followed the river upstream past fruit orchards and small Hispano settlements. The sun was setting by the time they could see Taos ahead, cradled by dark purple mountains. As the car rode over clumps of desert brush, the sweet smell of sage came wafting up. It was dark when they reached the village. The small plaza was deserted.

Maurice looked around, unimpressed. "This seems to be just about the end of the world," he murmured.

But Mabel breathed in the fragrant aroma of piñon curling from chimneys. "I couldn't see Taos," she thought, "but I loved it already."[12]

The next morning, over Maurice's protests, she began looking for a place to rent. They visited an Englishman named Arthur Manby, who lived alone in a rambling, nineteen-room adobe compound. Mabel hoped to talk him into leasing part of his home to her. Manby, like many white men, had been lured to Taos by the prospect of riches. He'd earlier managed to steal thousands of acres from Hispano land grants. But his would-be empire, built by fraud, eventually collapsed. Now he was a bitter old man.

Manby had tousled hair and wild, bloodshot eyes, yet he spoke in a cultivated British accent that charmed Mabel. He was on his best behavior as he proudly showed off his flower beds and vegetable gardens. He pointed to the cottonwoods he had planted along the curving dirt road that ran alongside his home. But Mabel was looking past the trees, out to where Taos Mountain dominated the skyline. Manby followed her gaze. "You see that mountain up there? The Indians call that the *sacred* mountain. I could tell you some things about it if I wanted to. It is full of *gold* and *silver*, but those devils won't let anyone prospect up there."[13]

Manby wasn't sure about renting out his home. His British countrymen were at war, and he was suspicious of Maurice Sterne's German last name. But Mabel was persuasive and Manby needed the money. Finally, they agreed on a six-month lease. Maurice sighed in disapproval. "I was all nicely settled in Santa Fe,"[14] he complained.

Their driver was anxious to begin the journey back. but Mabel made him drive around the area. They took a road leading toward the giant mountain she had seen earlier. Drawing closer, she exclaimed to Maurice, "Look at those veils of blue and violet and plum color upon the mountain! I never saw anything so lovely! And don't you feel something different in the air here, Maurice?"

The driver cut in, "That's altitude."

But Mabel knew there was more to it. She looked upon the massive mountain and sensed a life force: "It seemed to me the mountain was alive, awake, and breathing. That it had its own consciousness. That it knew things."[15]

By New Year's Day, 1918, nearly a million US soldiers were fighting in the Great War. Many filled the trenches along the Western Front, where some two million men had already died. The days of heroic cavalry charges up San Juan Hill were long gone, supplanted by mass killing on an industrial scale: machine guns, tanks, submarines, airplanes, and clouds of poison gas.

In New Mexico, far from the war and from the powers that declared it, Mabel Dodge Sterne reveled in the crisp, clean air as she and Maurice returned to Taos in a brand-new car. The couple took up residence in a wing of Manby's compound, complete with a separate entrance and their own patio and garden. Mabel had been warned about the meager provisions in the remote village, so she ordered enough groceries in Santa Fe to fill dozens of crates. She hired an eighteen-year-old local named Anita to cook for them. She also employed an army of others to scrub away decades of Manby's accumulated filth. She paid good wages. Before long, everyone in the Taos Valley knew that a rich Eastern lady and her artist husband had moved to town.

Living across the road from Manby was one of those "ghastly" Taos painters. Bert Phillips came over to introduce himself. Approaching fifty years, Phillips struck them as a relic of the past. He proudly called himself "The Pioneer" of the Taos art colony. He gave them a tour of his studio, filled with Native curios, while relating the well-rehearsed story of his arrival twenty years earlier. Mabel had no regard for him as a painter, viewing his work as "beneath criticism"[16]—but she was fascinated by his museum-worthy collection of Indigenous artifacts.

A couple of days later, Mabel and Maurice motored out to Taos Pueblo. Mabel brought a bag of oranges, as she'd been told that it was customary for visitors to bring gifts. The morning was chilly, and the small river was crusted with ice. Thin columns of blue smoke rose from the chimneys. Nearly everyone was inside their homes. This was the "quiet time" at Taos Pueblo, when the earth rested, gathering its strength to emerge again in the spring.

Mabel's car, its engine sputtering, entered the pueblo. Slowly, they drove past the adobe dwellings. A door opened, and a woman in a black dress with a woven red belt stepped outside. Mabel stared and the woman smiled. That was all Mabel needed. She climbed out of the car and hurried forward, carrying the sack of oranges.

The woman beckoned. "Entre."

They walked into a warm room with clean, whitewashed walls. A corner fireplace crackled, and sunlight streamed through a small, high window. A man wrapped in a white blanket sat on a low stool beside the fire, singing softly and beating a drum. He looked like an E. Irving Couse painting come to life.

The man was so intent on his song that he didn't appear to notice the visitors. His wife, very attentive, gestured for them to sit. It was a show staged for the tourists, but Mabel had no idea. He seemed lost in his song and soon Mabel was lost with him. She heard the music as "the glad, solemn voice of the tribe,"[17] a sound rising and falling like the wind.

When he finished, the man looked up at Mabel. She stifled a gasp. This was the very same man she'd seen in her dream back in New York, the same face that had blotted out Maurice's. She and the Taos man stared at each other for a moment, seemingly in instantaneous recognition. Yes, she saw "the same face, the same eyes, involuntarily intense, with the living fire in their depths."[18]

The man stood up. He was six feet tall and powerfully built with a barrel chest. He wore white moccasins and white leggings. His two long braids were delicately interwoven with white ribbons. He bowed gently toward them.

"I sang you a little song," he said.

"Thank you ever so much," Mabel answered as her heart raced. Not knowing what else to say, she offered him an orange. He bowed again before accepting it.

Before they left, Mabel held her hand out. "I wish you'd come and see us down in Taos."

"I seen you before, already," he said.[19]

CHAPTER 9

THE LOVE TOKEN

1918

The man Mabel had met was Antonio Luján, Deer Yellow Willows. He was fluent in Tiwa and Spanish and spoke passable English. He'd only had a dash of schooling and never learned to read or write, but he was a natural leader. At age thirty-nine, he carried himself with great authority, radiating calm assurance. He belonged to the Knife People kiva in Taos Pueblo and came from a respected family. Under normal circumstances, he would be in line to be elected Taos governor. But Luján was something of a dissident within the Pueblo. Along with Star Road, he was a member of the peyote cult.

A few days after Mabel handed him that orange, Tony Luján and a group of Taos men rode their horses to her home. She was overjoyed by their appearance, though Maurice complained that the men had shown up right at lunchtime. Mabel instructed Anita to set out extra plates for their visitors. Beefsteak and fried potatoes were served—which Mabel was beginning to realize represented the entire extent of her young cook's culinary repertoire.

Everyone ate quietly, concentrating on the food. Maurice decided to be magnanimous, observing, "Since the white man had taken their land away, it was only proper that we should feed them."[1] After the meal, the Pueblo men stood, preparing to leave. Mabel, speaking in honeyed tones, asked Tony if he could bring his drum the next time he visited. He readily agreed.

A few days later, he and the others returned and another platter of

Figure 16. Tony Luján, ca. 1918. Mabel Dodge Luhan Papers. Yale Collection of American Literature, Beinecke Rare Book and Manuscript Library.

beefsteak was shared. After lunch was over the music began, led by Tony's quietly hypnotic voice and the comforting heartbeat of his drum. Mabel listened in wonder, but Maurice had no use for this "tom-tom music." He left the room.

Mabel had every imaginable advantage, yet she was battered by neuroses. She had tried to commit suicide multiple times, and she had spent thousands of dollars on psychoanalysis. She had the money to buy anything she wanted, yet a gaping hole remained at the center of her life. When she attended her first Pueblo ceremonial dance, she was struck by the communal spirit. "For the first time in my life," she realized, "I heard the voice of the One coming from the Many." Previously, Mabel had believed, like many Americans, in a "singular raging lust for individuality and separateness." Now she understood "a different power from any I had known, and where virtue lay in wholeness instead of in dismemberment."[2]

Mabel couldn't get enough, and soon she began walking out to the

Pueblo every morning after breakfast. She took balls of yarn to share with Tony's wife and other women, sitting among them knitting long scarves and shawls. They tolerated her presence, and she kept quiet, absorbing their tender, musical language. She observed the varied human relations at the Pueblo, noting that harmony and kindness seemed to prevail. These people were materially poor, living in mud huts with dirt floors, but despite the apparent simplicity of their lives, they seemed to possess spiritual riches she lacked.

Once, on a visit to the Lujáns' home, Mabel praised its absence of cluttered possessions. Tony had a ready response: "God said Indian cannot have *things*. White people have *things*, but God give the Indians just what grows on the mountain."[3]

Later, he elaborated, explaining to Mabel the problem with white people: "Their religion is in machinery to change things." Then he added, ominously, "and now they come to want to change the Indians."[4]

One morning Mabel found Tony at his sister's house with the entire family. Tony's pretty seventeen-year-old niece, Paulita Archuleta, had come down with a common cold a few days earlier and now she'd developed a raging fever and a choking cough. Mabel quickly called the government physician assigned to Taos Pueblo. Eventually the doctor arrived—taking far too long in Mabel's estimation. To her critical eye, the man seemed unconcerned for his patient's well-being. He diagnosed Paulita with pneumonia and gave her some aspirin. He also handed the girl's mother some cathartic pills to purge the gastrointestinal tract, as was standard practice. Mabel stayed with the suffering Paulita and her family until late evening, then finally returned to her own home. The next morning she received the devastating news that the girl had died during the night.

Outraged, Mabel filed a formal complaint, charging the attending physician with neglect and malpractice. The resulting investigation exonerated the doctor but did nothing to quell Mabel's anger at such a senseless death—nor did it ease her growing suspicion that the US government had little interest in the Pueblos' welfare.

~

Maurice Sterne was a noted painter, but in Mabel's judgment he was better suited to be a sculptor. With her encouragement, he recruited a model from Taos Pueblo, a friend of Tony's named Pedro Mirabal. Maurice rented a studio space in Taos and began working long hours. Progress was slow yet he could see how well the work was coming along. He realized that his wife had been right to push him in this new direction.

Mabel soon invited friends in New York to come visit them in Taos. Chief among them was Andrew Dasburg, a stylish young modernist. Dasburg had exhibited at the groundbreaking Armory Show and made his reputation with an early cubist portrait, "The Absence of Mabel Dodge"—which became famous in part because no one could tell which was the right side up. Mabel summoned Dasburg with a command: "Bring a cook with you."[5]

Dasburg arrived with a German-speaking chef he'd found at a New York employment bureau. The language was no barrier for Dasburg and Maurice, who were both fluent in German. Mabel's ever-growing household also came to include her teenaged son and a Broadway set designer. At least once a week, more wooden crates packed with Mabel's belongings arrived from back east. In the evenings, as the group gathered in the drawing room, they had no idea that their landlord, Arthur Manby, was spying on them. The aged British man would quietly creep onto the rooftop and peer down through a peephole, his eyes widening in alarm as he heard the men sometimes conversing in German.

Dasburg had no interest in painting Taos Puebloans. Instead, he favored geometric landscapes like his idol, Cézanne. But Dasburg and Mabel both became increasingly enamored of old artifacts, particularly hand-woven blankets. As they got caught up in the thrill of the chase, Tony Luján became their willing agent, taking them to prospects' houses and conducting the negotiations in Spanish. Word quickly spread that the rich outsiders from New York were buying old things. Soon people began showing up at Mabel's house, offering items for sale.

One evening, two young men arrived struggling under the weight of a large bundle. In the parlor, they carefully unrolled an enormous Native blanket to approving murmurs. It was the most impressive specimen Mabel and Dasburg had ever seen. Blue and black stripes ran along its length, framing a red-and-white diamond-shaped design in the center. Mabel instantly agreed to purchase the treasure, paying fifteen dollars.

The next morning, she called her neighbor Bert Phillips over to show off her new acquisition. "Oh, it's a beauty!" Phillips exclaimed. "It's a real old Chief's blanket!" He bent to inspect it more closely. "These are very valuable, you know."[6] He kept fingering the blanket, studying it carefully. Then he excused himself and left. A short time later the sheriff showed up. It turned out that someone had broken into E. Irving Couse's studio, stolen his prize blanket, and sold it to Mabel.

Meanwhile, Mabel's landlord, Arthur Manby, decided the time had come to act. He'd heard this odd collective of people speaking in German even as those mysterious wooden crates kept piling up. Who knew what was inside those containers? The Germans had already tried to form an alliance with Mexico, promising the return of Texas and New Mexico. German saboteurs were known to be active in the United States and had blown up a munitions depot in New York. Who knew how far the plot extended?

The landlord alerted authorities and a federal investigator arrived in Taos. Mabel was called in for questioning. The official blew cigar smoke at her and announced: "You are suspected of pro-German activities. It is said you are receiving arms and ammunition almost weekly in large boxes and storing them in your house; that one member of your family is going among the Mexican population and enrolling them; that you, lady, are inciting the Indians to rise."[7]

Mabel's initial shock swiftly gave way to withering scorn. She pointed out that one of her relatives was a Rear Admiral and several other family members were serving as US Army officers. She told the agent, "I demand an immediate apology from your office for this ridiculous accusation!"[8]

The investigator beat a hasty retreat. By then, Mabel had become positively gleeful at the notion she and her fellow aesthetes had been mistaken for a band of revolutionaries. She wrote to a friend in New York: "We are in the maddest, most amusing country in the world—in the freakiest—most insane village you ever dreamed of and *I* would like to stay forever."[9]

Tony Luján was becoming a regular visitor, riding his pony to Mabel's house nearly every day. Mabel, in turn, felt her life's energies flowing toward this man. Beyond his handsome dignity and impressive bearing, his essential quality seemed to be a deep, unruffled kindness. After Tony admired a purple ribbon in her hair, she made a point to buy a purple shawl. Tony promised her that, when warmer weather arrived and the snow melted, he would take her into the mountains on horseback.

One bright morning, Tony and his friend, Pedro Mirabal—Maurice's model, showed up at Mabel's home in a horse-drawn buggy. They had arranged to take Mabel and Maurice to a local hot spring. Mabel climbed aboard, wearing her purple shawl pulled over her head in the manner of Pueblo women. The two Taos men sat together up front, with Mabel and Maurice on the rear bench. Tony drove them across the sagebrush desert until they came the edge of the gorge, the Río Grande rushing far below.

They descended carefully down a twisting road, squeezing past black lava boulders and scraping against juniper trees. At the bottom, alongside the river, the thermal waters steamed in the cool air. Tony told them that the spring's name meant "you always live, always be young."[10]

A stone bathhouse had been constructed for privacy. Mabel went in first and then the men took their turn. Afterward, they cooked steaks over an open fire and Tony showed them petroglyphs carved into the black rocks. Later, as they sat alongside the flowing river, Tony walked casually by Mabel and dropped a small red bag to her.

Back at home, out of sight of Maurice, she was finally able to inspect the package. It was a perfumed sachet, stuffed with local plants and wrapped in silk. She slept with it under her pillow. When Maurice learned of it, he sneered at her, "Is that a love token that Indian was giving you?"[11]

With spring's arrival, Maurice finished his sculpture and began working on a new one, this of Pedro Mirabal's sister, a poised young woman named Albidia. Tony in turn saddled up a pair of horses for him and Mabel and led her into the mountains. He pointed out the blooming wildflowers and helped her hear the joyous song of young birds taking their first flight. The land now officially belonged to the US Forest Service, but he told her that it was really Taos Pueblo's, and that it was "the beating heart of the world."[12]

On one trip, he took her to Taos Pueblo's most sacred place. Riding through a driving rainstorm, they arrived at Blue Lake just as the clouds lifted. Sunlight poured down as they sat beside the water. "Bottomless, peacock blue, smooth as glass," Mabel observed. "Blue Lake is the most mysterious thing I have ever seen . . . an unknowable, impenetrable life of its own, and a definite emanation that rises from it."[13]

For once, she was not in a rush to be anywhere else. "I can see life whole," Mabel told Tony.

"Yes," he answered.[14]

One warm day, they left the horses behind and walked instead. Tony led her east of the main plaza, past an alfalfa field and up to a rising piece of land bordering Taos Pueblo's territory. A small creek flowed nearby and Tony's personal allotment of Pueblo land lay on the other side.[15] When they reached a giant cottonwood, Tony stopped underneath.

"This the nicest place I know 'cept the Pueblo," he told Mabel. "Little bit high up, good air, and you see all over."[16] He waved his hand to indicate what he meant. Mabel knew he was right. The entire valley stretched out before them, with Taos Mountain's majestic presence dominating the horizon. Tony pointed to the stream and assured her that its water was very good. An apple orchard was on the property along with a modest, three-room adobe house. Tony knew the person who owned the place, and he'd already worked out a deal. He told Mabel the man would be willing to sell it to her.

As summer arrived, the seasonal members of the Taos art colony drifted back into town. The Great War was still convulsing Europe, as thousands of men were dying in horrific battles to gain a few yards of territory. Ernest Blumenschein, sensitive about his German name, had taken a lead role in organizing artists' support for the US war effort. He captained drives for war bonds, and he painted celebratory portraits of American soldiers. He created a propaganda painting, *Long Range Gun, Paris*, showing a German shell crashing into a French cathedral packed with worshippers. The illustration was used on a poster touting "Liberty Loans."

In Taos, Blumenschein had a mission: to recruit other artists to join him in painting training targets for the US Army. These range-finders were oversized landscapes of European scenes, nearly six feet wide and made with house paint. The army used them to teach gunners how to sight and distance targets. The paintings would be shot to bits. Few of Blumenschein's colleagues were enthusiastic, but he hectored them until they complied.

While Blumenschein and his fellow Taos artists members worked on their range finders, a very different class of artists began appearing in Taos. These were the modernists, lured by Mabel Dodge Sterne to reinforce the ranks of her husband and Andrew Dasburg. Among the newcomers was Marsden Hartley, a major American painter. Hartley knew Mabel well from their days at the artist colony in Provincetown. Like his fellow bohemians, Hartley wouldn't be caught dead painting for the US Army. He also had no wish to interact with the older Taos artists, condemning them as "awful hackers" and "cheap artists."[17]

A moody, sensitive man, Hartley became enraptured by the New Mexico landscape, which he considered "the perfect place to regain one's body and soul."[18] He rented a house near the Taos plaza for ten dollars a month and began making pastel sketches of the mountains and arroyos.

Mabel was aware of the culture clash between her bohemian visitors and the Taos old-timers. In her forceful way, she decided to bring everyone together. She staged a big garden party, hiring Tony Luján and other Taos Pueblo men to sing and dance. She pointedly invited the older artists: Phillips, Blumenschein, Couse, and the others, along with their families—to join her and her modernist friends.

The evening got off to a slow start. Small clumps of people stood off on their own. The music started and the young Pueblo men began to dance, raising everyone's spirits. Still, Mabel could see that the evening was turning into a stage show: the Natives performing for a white audience. "The doom of our race," she thought, "is to watch things . . . we are only looking at life, not living it."[19]

As if reading her mind, Tony Luján lifted his drumstick high, waving it over everyone like a conductor. "Come on. Everybody got to dance. Round dance now." He started a new song. Tony's drum beat in time as the Taos dancers made a slow circle around the gathering, seeking communion and unity. The white people froze. "Come on," Tony ordered. "Everybody dance."[20] Finally, an older woman joined in. Then, one by one, the others followed. Soon, everyone was moving sideways, all part of the circle around the drum, falling together into the same rhythm on this one night, at least.

Mabel delighted in Taos's summer climate. She wanted to spend every moment outside, warming herself in the sun or finding cool relief in the shade. With Tony's help, she purchased a tipi and set it up in the yard outside her wing of Manby's home. Complaining to Maurice that the air inside their adobe was too stuffy, she began spending most evenings in the tipi. By morning, she was back in her bed, sleeping in late.

Maurice was no fool. He heard the hoofbeats of an approaching horse each evening. He knew that his wife was not alone in that tipi. He borrowed a gun from his landlord, Manby. He fondled it, darkly imagining the destruction it would cause. He slept with it under his pillow, dreaming of revenge. Yet, in the end, Maurice was an artist. He was a creator, not a destroyer. He couldn't bring himself to use the gun.

One night, as usual, Mabel went out for her "fresh air." Maurice laid in bed, listening. On this evening, there was no sound of a horse softly clip-clopping the familiar path to their home. After a couple of hours of silence, Mabel returned to bed. Maurice was waiting for her.

"Poor Mabel, poor, poor Mabel!" he jeered. "Her lover doesn't show up, and she has to go to bed without her nightcap."

Mabel shouted at him. "Tomorrow you get out—do you hear me?"[21]

Maurice left the house, but he couldn't quit New Mexico just yet, for he needed to finish his sculpture of Albidia. He retreated to the mountains, to the old mining town of Twining, near where Bert Phillips once prospected for gold. He took the piece with him to work on. For his earlier bust of Pedro Mirabal, Maurice had used plaster of paris to build the core. But by the time he started on Albidia, it'd become impossible to find more of the material in Taos. Instead, he had to use wax to shape Albidia's form. Such irritations only added to his growing dislike of Taos.

Working furiously in the mountains, Maurice finally completed the Albidia bust. His marriage might have been in tatters, but at least he had created a breathtaking piece of art sure to impress everyone back in New York. He returned to Taos and carefully packed each head into its own wooden crate. Then he rode with the containers to the nearest train station and oversaw their loading before boarding the train himself.

The four-day ride back to New York in midsummer was stiflingly hot. Even with the windows open, the train felt like a moving oven. When he finally made it back to the city, Maurice opened the crates, anxious to inspect his creations. The bust of Pedro Mirabal was perfect, just as he remembered it. Then he unwrapped the packaging around Albidia. Without a plaster of paris core, the heat of the cross-country journey had melted the wax form. His beautiful head of a lovely Pueblo maiden had become a grotesque monster. The sculpture was ruined. Enraged, Sterne stormed through the house until he found a hatchet. Then he hacked the wax head to pieces.

CHAPTER 10

THE BEATING HEART OF THE WORLD

1919–1920

Mabel's affair with a Taos Pueblo man caused an uproar in her New York social circle. Several friends notified her that they would refuse to see her unless she ended the relationship. Her expensive psychoanalyst, the renowned Freudian Abraham Brill, lashed out: "I feel that you are making a great mistake," he told his patient, adding, "Everybody thinks you are crazy and if everything that I hear is really so . . . I would agree with them."[1]

The scandal also caused distress at Taos Pueblo. Mabel no longer found a warm welcome there. Tony's wife, Candelaria, who had kindly invited her into their home, became a bitter enemy. Most onlookers predicted that the affair would soon pass, like a summer storm. Some of the men at Taos Pueblo joked that the rich white woman was simply "renting" Tony.

Mabel began to doubt her feelings. She worried about Tony's devotion to peyote—a drug that frightened her ever since she'd seen a friend lose her mind on it in New York. When she confronted him about his peyote use, he pledged to stop. "It is a big thing God put here in the world, but one doesn't have to use it,"[2] he told her. But there were other concerns. Mabel was a natural conversationalist who loved to draw people out and listen to hours of talk. Tony was not especially fluent in English, nor was he much for talking in any case. Mabel had felt a strong psychic bond between them, but how long, really, could she bear to share her life with such a man?

In April 1919, she decided to leave Taos and visit New York. She saw Maurice, but the reunion did nothing to stir her passion. While in the city, she learned of a popular new psychic, a Bryn Mawr graduate named Sarah Dudley who'd begun calling herself "Lotus" Dudley. Mabel's wealthy friends were flocking to see her, paying top dollar for spiritual revelations. Lotus Dudley spoke easily of elemental spirits, Paracelsian magic, gnomes, sylphs, and the metaphysical secrets of the universe.

When Mabel met with her, Dudley seemed to have all the answers. She told Mabel that an ancient wisdom had been kept alive by select people through the ages. The Taos Puebloans, she said, were the current possessors of this sacred knowledge, and they held "the psychic key to Nirvana on earth." Taos, she told Mabel, "is the beating heart of the world."[3]

Mabel was stunned, for Tony had earlier said the very same thing. She knew that some mystical phenomena had drawn her to Taos, but she couldn't explain why. Dudley revealed the truth: Mabel had been summoned because the Taos People were now ready to share their enlightenment with select others, in the hope of redeeming the white race. For this transmission of sacred knowledge to occur, "a bridge will be needed between the Indian and white people," the psychic said. Then she announced why Mabel and Tony Luján had come together: "You have been chosen to be that bridge."[4]

Mabel's entire life now made sense. The earlier Armory Show and her Greenwich Village Salon had merely been warm-up acts to prepare her for this enormous new responsibility. She would return to Taos and renew her relationship with Tony. There, she would seek to attract the West's "great souls" to New Mexico and connect them with the Pueblo People. This cross-cultural synergy would spark a revolutionary spiritual renaissance, heralding a grand new age in which white people no longer worshipped money and machinery, but would instead revere community, art, and nature.

Back in Taos, Mabel moved on to the twelve-acre plot of land Tony had advised her to buy. Her lover remodeled and expanded the small adobe

Figure 17. Mabel Dodge Sterne, ca. 1917. Mabel Dodge Luhan Papers. Yale Collection of American Literature, Beinecke Rare Book and Manuscript Library.

home so that Mabel could host visitors. She began writing many dozens of letters to "movers and shakers" back east, encouraging them to come visit the new utopia she had discovered.

Mabel no longer looked like a wealthy New York maven. Instead, she now wore white deerskin moccasins and favored colorful shawls. She kept her hair cut short, with bangs that mimicked the style of Taos women. Tony Luján retained his regal blanket, but he exchanged his moccasins for a stylish pair of English riding boots. He also came to prefer the comfortably tailored slacks Mabel had made for him in New York. He continued to dote on his horses, but he also fell in love with Mabel's car, quickly learning to drive and how to tinker with the engine. Soon, Mabel bought him his own Cadillac.

Thanks to Mabel's entreaties, a parade of notable outsiders began arriving: art critic Leo Stein, sculptor Grace Mott Johnson, writer Carl Van Vechten, and the anthropologist Elsie Clews Parsons. Many were veterans of Mabel's Greenwich Village salon days. Mabel and Tony worked as a team. She was an attentive though sometimes overbearing host, stage-managing everyone's experience. Tony's role was to chauffeur visitors and guide them to Taos Pueblo for an appropriately reverent introduction to the Native way of life.

Tony often made a grand impression on the outsiders, particularly the women. Sparks invariably flew between him and female guests, much to Mabel's dismay. The painter Agnes Pelton, who had exhibited at the 1913 Armory Show, was among those who adored him. He in turn was very gracious to her. He had always refused to model for male artists in Taos, but he allowed Pelton to paint his portrait. Her finished canvas showed him sitting erect before his drum, a blanket draped across his broad shoulders as he gripped a big drumstick.

Mabel's biggest early catch was Mary Austin, the famed writer and feminist based in New York City. Author of nearly a dozen books, Austin was a formidable lecturer who toured the country giving fire-breathing pro-suffrage speeches. Also known as a leading advocate for Indigenous people, Austin considered Natives "the resident genius of [their] own land." She castigated Anglos for "imposing our particular brand of civilization upon them."[5]

Upon her arrival, Austin was given a guest room at Mabel's home. Mabel dealt with her gently, for the imperious writer could be difficult. As

Figure 18. Mary Austin, ca. 1900. Photograph by Charles F. Lummis. The Autry Museum of the American West © Wikimedia/Creative Commons.

a self-proclaimed "woman of genius," Austin often expressed irritation at the shortcomings of others. Some of her friends jokingly referred to her, always carefully behind her back, as "God's Mother-in-Law."

To Mabel's immense relief, Austin immediately bonded with Tony, generously praising his "warm stability of temperament." She also found much to admire in her tour of Taos Pueblo, seeing a wholesome community guided by "psychic unity." Austin, who was divorced and had endured her share of failed relationships, was delighted to learn of the ease with which Pueblo women were said to be able to dismiss unsatisfactory husbands: "with the simple ceremony of setting the man's private possessions—his gun, his saddle, his other pair of moccasins—outside the door."[6]

The more she saw of Taos Pueblo, the more Austin came to admire what she divined to be a woman-centered society. She heard talk of matriarchal lineages, which helped her overlook the fact that the tribe's ruling council was composed entirely of men. Instead, she described the culture she saw at Taos as "Mother-rule," noting that many Taos men freely helped with domestic duties such as child care. This blending of gender roles into roughly equal halves explained for her why the Pueblo had developed such a harmonious, communal-oriented society.

Mabel's plan appeared to be working. Just as she had hoped, the eminent writer's exposure to Taos made her enthusiastic about the Pueblo's capacity for inspiring white America. Indeed, Austin was so taken by her visit that she told Mabel she intended to give up on New York and move permanently to New Mexico. Mabel's growing delight was cut short when she learned that Austin, however, had no intention of settling in Taos—where she'd been forced to trek to an outhouse to take care of necessary business. Instead, the author chose Santa Fe, where a rival artist colony was thriving.

For those who found Taos too remote and deficient in basic comforts, New Mexico's capital was proving to be a very appealing alternative. The old city, founded before any Pilgrim had sailed from England, retained a charming sense of antiquity. Santa Fe also boasted modern amenities Taos lacked: electricity, indoor plumbing, and a nearby railway station.

By 1920, Santa Fe had become the favored destination. Famous New York painters Robert Henri and John Sloan were summertime residents and celebrated writers such as Carl Sandburg and Willa Cather were known to pass through. The poet Alice Corbin Henderson, who'd first come to Santa Fe for her health in 1917, became a permanent resident along with her husband, the painter William Penhallow Henderson. They were joined by Gustave Baumann, a masterfully talented woodcut artist who had stayed briefly in Taos before choosing Santa Fe. Other locals included the prominent poet Witter Bynner along with Elizabeth Shepley Sergeant, a journalist friend of Mabel's who'd been wounded by a German grenade on the Western Front.

Santa Fe also attracted a younger generation of modernist painters, men in their twenties who were decidedly more experimental than the old-time Taos artists. Instead of trying to capture life, these rebels sought to create it, slashing bold strokes of color that nearly leapt off the canvas. Five of these outsiders banded together and called themselves Los Cinco Pintores. They built their own adobe homes in Santa Fe. Locals sometimes referred to them as the "the five nuts in mud huts."

Native fashions were the rage among the bohemian newcomers in Santa Fe. Turquoise jewelry and silver concho belts had become ubiquitous, along with moccasins and loose-fitting Navajo shirts. The local intelligentsia began championing nearby San Ildefonso Pueblo, home to painter Awa Tsireh and the potter María Martínez, already becoming famous for her black-on-black pottery. Beyond San Ildefonso, several more Pueblo settlements beckoned. Group visits to Native ceremonials became de rigueur among the smart set. "It was obligatory to go to every Pueblo dance," the writer Erna Fergusson observed. "Failure to appear on a sunny roof on every saint's day marked one as soulless and without taste."[7]

As Mabel sought to attract the world's "great souls" to Taos, she began to realize that the small house on her property was hardly adequate for the momentous task of transforming Western civilization. She would need to create a spectacular showplace to lure her targets and host them in necessary comfort and style.

She and Tony soon began work on the most ambitious building project

Figure 19. Los Gallos, ca. 1930s. Mabel Dodge Luhan Papers. Yale Collection of American Literature, Beinecke Rare Book and Manuscript Library.

seen in Taos since the construction of the original Pueblo almost a thousand years before. He took charge of the exterior, drawing up plans for a sprawling adobe palace while Mabel focused on the interior design. Tony hired and supervised work crews from the Pueblo along with local Hispanos. Whatever misgivings these men may have had about the relationship between Tony and Mabel, it was also true that the wealthy woman paid better wages than anyone else in the Taos Valley.

Mabel swelled with pride as she watched the hired help patiently mixing dirt, water, and straw to make adobe bricks. "Working with the earth was a noble occupation," she observed from her window. "To take the living earth from under their feet . . . and shape it into a house" seemed to involve a nearly spiritual transformation. "Money has very little to do with all this," she proclaimed.[8]

Yet Mabel's wealth announced itself with grandeur. The new home that rose from the earth was equipped with electricity and running water, two nearly unfathomable luxuries by Taos standards. For the interior, Mabel had her finest possessions shipped from New York and hauled overland to Taos: her ornate Louis XV–era furniture, antiques from China and Italy, and imperial paintings set in gilded frames. She combined this upper-class rococo motif with old, hand-carved chests from New Mexico's Spanish colonial era, bright Mexican serapes, Hispano santos, and pottery and baskets from Pueblo villages.

Soon a second-story suite was added to serve as Mabel's private bedroom hideaway. This offered her a balcony and an unobstructed view of Taos Pueblo's sacred mountain to the north. Other buildings started going up: guest houses, stables, barns, and a large gatehouse for use as the servants' quarters. Long, shaded porches connected many of the structures, knitting everything together. Mabel also commissioned original art, hiring San Ildefonso painter Awa Tsireh to paint a mural on an outside wall. Santa Fe artist William Penhallow Henderson created black-and-red floor tiles in a checkerboard pattern. After some discussion, Tony added a third-story sunporch above Mabel's bedroom. Here, she could have the privacy to sunbathe in the nude.

As a final decorative touch, Mabel bought brightly colored ceramic chickens from Mexico to set against the roof lines. The chickens gave the place its name, Los Gallos. This rambling compound of multistory adobe buildings began to seem very much a quirky, bohemian echo of the original Taos Pueblo—and it grandly announced the arrival of a new age in Taos.

CHAPTER II

THE REFORMER

1920–1921

John Collier had been a friend of Mabel Dodge Sterne's in New York, but he was getting damn tired of her unending letters from Taos, beseeching him to come and see the Pueblos. Collier had no time for Native Americans. He was a forward-looking man who saw the incoming waves of new European immigrants as the future. Indigenous people clearly belonged to the past. Their lingering populations, he believed, "were doomed to be swallowed up by the white world."[1]

A small, rumpled man with round spectacles and a boyish grin, Collier had been educated as a sociologist at Columbia. He also fancied himself a poet. Few had read his slender volumes of verse, but many in New York knew of him as a dynamic public speaker, a crusading reformer who delivered rapid-fire lectures lambasting industrialism's many ills. Working among impoverished immigrants, he viewed modern America, with its sweatshops and tenements and child labor, as a failed experiment.

Collier aimed to build a more cooperative, tolerant, people-centered society; one bound by a deep communion with art and nature. He saw the arriving immigrants, displaced from their native lands and seeking a new start, as fresh clay he could sculpt into this higher vision of humanity.

His results were underwhelming, but his messianic idealism resonated with other dreamers, progressives, and radicals—those alarmed by capitalism's excesses and horrified by the mass slaughters of the Great War. Collier's zealous advocacy of the downtrodden also brought him to the

Figure 20. John Collier, ca. 1920s. John Collier Papers. Yale Collection of American Literature, Beinecke Rare Book and Manuscript Library.

attention of Native welfare groups. Several times, they tried to recruit him to their cause, but he always refused to be swayed from his dedication to immigrants.

Mabel knew this, yet she kept sending him letters about Taos Pueblo. To Collier, her descriptions of "magical Indians" and their "magical habitation" sounded like fairy tales. Her appeals continued even after he and his family moved to California in 1919, where he had been hired to direct the state's immigrant education efforts.

It was easy for Collier to ignore Mabel's entreaties while everything was going well. His wife and children relished living in the Bay Area, with its balmy weather and nearby redwood forests. He buzzed about the state, making speeches and organizing new programs. Yet Collier soon discovered that California could be far more conservative than New York City. During the postwar Red Scare, suspicious legislators began denouncing his community-building ideas as Bolshevism. The legislature soon axed his budget, and he lost his job in the fall of 1920.

He didn't mind terribly much. After years on the front lines of various causes, he was burned out at age thirty-six. His wife, Lucy, came from a family of means and they had enough money saved to get by for a while. The Colliers took their three boys and the family dogs and headed south to Redondo Beach. He set up a tent and spent weeks decompressing, watching the waves and throwing sticks for his dogs. His family ate Thanksgiving dinner on the sand. Letters from Mabel continued to find him. She kept insisting that he see Taos. He wrote back, telling her they were going to Sonora, Mexico, where they planned to spend several more months camping out. A few days later, a fresh telegram came back: "You can detour here, and go on to Sonora so easily."[2] Mabel bought train tickets for the entire family, even the dogs.

In December 1920, Collier emerged from the Río Grande Gorge and saw Taos in the distance. A snowstorm was blowing down from the mountains as the setting sun lit the clouds on fire. The grandeur of the sight stirred him to poetry:

> *All day long the great winds lift on the mountain*
> *the snow in the clouds*
> *All day long on the mesas the changing color crowds,*
> *All day long;*
> *And duskly imagining worlds like these, the soul of man abides.*[3]

A few days later, on an icy January morning, Tony and Mabel took him to see Taos Pueblo's Deer Dance. Collier watched the intricate, ages-old drama in wonder: the elders chanted in rhythm as younger men, outfitted as deer and using sticks as forelegs, were lured from their winter lairs by beckoning women. These "deer" were drawn, through dance, ever-closer to the hidden hunters. When some deer fell, wounded and dying, their bodies were carried off by young boys and old men toward the kiva. Yet, as Collier observed, the hunters were careful to avoid injuring Father Deer or Mother Deer—and plenty of living animals were allowed to return to the forest.

To Collier, the performance was a revelation. This Native culture, which "had survived repeated and immense historical shocks" had somehow maintained a "beauty which suffused all the life of the group." He observed that "the community life is rich and great and that elusive, potent tradition of the Indian past has lost none of its vigor." He declared the ritual "the finest flower of the pre-history of the United States."[4]

Mabel, he realized, had been right about the Taos People.

Collier soon grew close to Tony Luján, who obligingly took him to the Pueblo whenever possible. Like other visitors before, Collier marveled at the communal work and the spare cleanliness of each individually maintained home. He agreed with Mary Austin that the Pueblo's women enjoyed a higher status than many females in mainstream America. "In the domestic sphere woman rules," Collier observed. "She is co-equal with man in those ritual activities which are the most solemn and creative parts of the tribe's life."[5]

He judged life at the Pueblo to be radically different from any other society he knew of. He found "no harshness or quarreling anywhere, among women or men." He never saw "a child whipped or struck or harshly scolded." Adolescents at Taos, he determined, were not rebellious or alienated from their families. Instead, they "are the most earnest and most sweet [and] seem the happiest bloom of Pueblo life."[6]

How could that be, Collier wondered? How had the Natives managed to shape the rocky adolescent years into such a joyous, life-affirming experience? He decided that Taos Pueblo's nature-worshipping religion, reinforced by its elaborate communal ceremonies, lay at the heart of its success.

Collier, like his fellow dreamer Mabel Dodge Sterne, was coming to regard the Taos People as a seedbed for American renewal: "A giver to the future of gifts without price, which future white man will know how to use."[7]

MARCH 10, 1921

Two blocks from the White House, the nation's brand-new Interior Secretary prepared to receive his first official visit from Native leaders—and he was ready to spar. Albert B. Fall had spent nearly a decade as a US senator from New Mexico. He'd become a whiskey-drinking, poker-playing pal of fellow senator Warren G. Harding. The easygoing Harding saw much to admire in Fall, the combative Westerner with a formidable intellect. When Harding got elected president, Fall expected to be named his Secretary of State. But Republican Party elders—aghast at the thought of the bellicose Fall as the nation's chief diplomat—intervened to block his appointment. So Fall had to settle for Interior, the very department he had once vowed to abolish. As a consolation, Harding promised him the first Supreme Court vacancy.

Fall, who'd made his political career railing against public lands and

Figure 21. Albert B. Fall. Harris & Ewing—Library of Congress Prints and Photographs Division. Harris & Ewing Collection. Call number: LC-H25-22472-D.

Indigenous people, would now oversee both. Conservationists and Native rights advocates were horrified. They had pleaded with Harding to nominate anyone else, but the new president would not be dissuaded. Harding described the New Mexican as "a star of a fellow" and "very much on the square." Others were not so sure. "God help the poor Indian," opined a nationally syndicated news story. The *New Republic* spoke for many when it described Fall as an "unspeakably bad appointment."[8]

Fall had been in office less than a week when the Native delegation arrived at the Interior Building. The group was composed of doctors, lawyers, educators and religious leaders representing several tribes: Cherokee, Sioux, Pawnee, and Chippewa. The men were outfitted in dark business suits, not tribal dress. They were led to the top floor, a redwood-paneled suite filled with portraits of Native Americans. The Interior Department's official seal, depicting the nearly extinct American bison, was displayed on one wall and two stuffed bald eagles were perched atop pedestals. The office nearly seemed to serve as a mausoleum for America's vanishing natural and cultural treasures.

The visitors were ushered into Fall's private chamber. They found him standing before his desk, which was already covered in papers and stacks of books. Fall greeted each man with an iron handshake. At age fifty-nine, his thinning hair was turning white and he was becoming jowly. But his hard, fiery eyes looked as ready to boil over as ever.

The Indigenous men presented their case. They asked that one of their own, Thomas L. Sloan, be chosen to head the Indian Bureau. Sloan, a member of the Omaha Tribe, was a prominent attorney who had argued before the Supreme Court. He also headed an organization of middle-class American Natives devoted to attaining full citizenship for all Indigenous people. The men in Fall's office told the Interior Secretary that over 80 percent of the Native tribes in the nation had endorsed Sloan.

Fall listened impatiently, chewing on a cigar. When the men finished, he responded forcefully. He had no interest in Thomas Sloan or any other Native man for commissioner. To Fall, the Indian Bureau had one simple job: "to eliminate tribal government and much of the old tribal customs."[9] Clearly, only a white man could carry out such a policy. When Fall finished speaking, the visitors were shown the door.

In New Mexico, Fall's appointment as Interior Secretary aroused great pride, for he had risen to the highest level of government anyone from the young state had so far achieved. Laudatory praise appeared in local newspapers: "For his extensive knowledge . . . and his uncompromising integrity, no man has ever assumed the office of Secretary of the Interior so splendidly equipped for its arduous and complex duties as Albert B. Fall."[10]

Yet Fall remained indignant that he didn't become Secretary of State. He tried to make the best of the situation, explaining to his wife that President Harding "thinks the Interior Department is second only to the State Department in importance." Harding also told Fall that he needed him to manage Interior because the department had "more opportunity for graft and scandal connected with the disposition of public lands . . . than there could be in any other department."[11]

Fall would soon prove Harding prescient, though not in the manner the president had intended.

Within weeks of taking office, Fall began eying two government-owned oilfields. One was at Elk Hills, near Bakersfield, California. The other was in Wyoming near a geological formation called Teapot Dome. These were two of the greatest oil discoveries in the world, representing countless barrels of oil. The US government had earlier set both areas aside as strategic reserves, to be saved for the US Navy's exclusive use in the event of war.

Fall soon persuaded a pliant President Harding to quietly transfer ownership of the reserves from the navy to his Interior Department. Then Fall gave away the entire oilfields in secret, sweetheart deals to the powerful oil titans Edward L. Doheny and Harry Sinclair. The men, already unfathomably rich, were guaranteed billions in new revenue. Doheny, after being awarded Elk Hills, dispatched his son with a satchel filled with $100,000 in cash to deliver personally to Fall. Sinclair, who received the rights to Teapot Dome, provided Fall with several gifts totaling some $300,000. (Fall's bribes amounted to over seven million in today's dollars.)

The assault on public lands was just beginning. Decrying "sentimental nature lovers," Secretary Fall called for opening national parks to mining, hunting, grazing, logging, and oil drilling. To the conservationists who challenged him, Fall retorted, "All natural resources should be made as easy of access as possible to the present generation. Man cannot exhaust the resources of nature and never will."[12]

Fall also brought a much harder edge to the Indian Bureau. His new Indian Commissioner became Charles H. Burke, a combative ex-congressman from South Dakota. Both Burke and Fall viewed Natives as vanquished enemies—people who had remained alive only at the mercy of a magnanimous victor. Burke considered Indigenous people "pathetically primitive." A pious ally of Christian missionaries, he lamented that so many Natives continued to live "without gospel privileges." As he was sworn into office, the new commissioner promised to work tirelessly "to hasten the time when all of the Indians in the country may become respectable, self-supporting, Christian citizens."[13]

John Collier and his family never did make it to Mexico. Instead, they stayed on in Taos with Mabel and Tony. Winter turned to spring, and then summer came. Collier had become a familiar sight at Taos Pueblo, where he had developed warm friendships and his children had many playmates. He wrote more poems, enough to complete a small book, which he titled *The Entry to the Desert.*

Tony Luján liked and trusted Collier. He and other Taos Pueblo leaders were also very much aware of the man's reputation as a highly regarded social reformer in New York. At the height of summer, a group of Pueblo men invited Collier to join them on a camping trip in the mountains. He eagerly agreed. On the appointed day, the party rode up to the timberline, their horses stepping delicately through the loose scree. As they emerged onto a high ridge, the Taos men pointed down below. Collier got his first look at Blue Lake.

That evening, sitting around a campfire at the lake, Collier's hosts explained that Blue Lake was the sacred source of their Pueblo's life and religion. The adjoining natural areas had long served as an open-air church, a place where Taos People performed necessary rites to keep the Pueblo's heartbeat alive. But now the US Forest Service was threatening to destroy their land and religion.

Conflict with the Forest Service had intensified during the Great War, when the agency, citing a national emergency, took away seven thousand acres of prime lands in the Blue Lake watershed from Taos Pueblo. Carson's Supervisor, Elliott S. Barker, gave new grazing permits to Anglo ranchers, friends of his, saying the outsiders would better utilize the range. Now the war was over, but the Forest Service refused to return the lands to the Pueblo. Meanwhile, those Anglos were running far too many cattle, overgrazing meadows, and fouling the sacred river that provided the Pueblo's drinking water.

Other Forest Service problems were also spiraling out of control. The agency's war of slaughter against indigenous birds and animals continued, emptying the forests of vital species that had lived alongside the Taos People for centuries. Meanwhile, Supervisor Barker decided to "improve" Blue Lake to make it more attractive to sportsmen. Over the Pueblo's objections, he began stocking the waters each summer with fingerling trout. Then the agency built a new hiking trail that led directly to Blue Lake and set up a picnic area on its shores. Now the Forest Service was promoting Blue Lake as a tourist mecca for the whites, drawing streams of outsiders to the Taos People's holiest place.

In the past, the Taos People could count on Special Attorney Francis Wilson to represent them, but Wilson had been eased out of his government post and returned to private practice in Santa Fe. Appointed in his place was Jacob Crist, the Democrat who had earlier fled New Mexico's Constitutional Convention after Albert B. Fall threatened to pistol-whip him. Crist barely made a ripple. The Indian Bureau, which earlier jousted with the Forest Service to help safeguard Blue Lake, no longer seemed to care.

The Taos men explained to Collier that what they wanted, more than all the world's riches or even their own lives, was for their people to regain custody of their sacred lake and its watershed. Without Blue Lake and its forests, their venerable nature-worshipping religion would surely perish, taking their people with it.

Beyond enriching himself at the expense of those government-owned oilfields and opening public lands to industry, Albert Fall had another major objective as Interior Secretary. He aimed to emphatically settle the vexing question of land ownership in New Mexico. The Pueblo People, as the earliest settlers, had naturally taken the choicest spots. The Natives had long ago established villages alongside the small streams that flowed from the mountains and provided life-giving waters that irrigated their productive desert farmlands.

Outsiders had steadily encroached on these areas over time. Some parcels had been granted to Hispano families that had lived peacefully alongside Pueblos for generations. Other tracts were swindled away and sold at rich profits to hapless outsiders who believed they'd acquired an honest title. Still more areas had been claimed in recent years by well-armed Anglo intruders. While legally termed "squatters," these were far from simple, homespun folks. They were calculating thieves who simply powered their way on to Native lands and remained there with the full backing of law enforcement and local courts.

The Pueblos' losses had been enormous, leaving their agricultural-based communities with ever-dwindling farm acreage to support their populations. Even Taos Pueblo, which had been resolute in repelling invaders, had seen outsiders gain nearly half of its irrigated lands. Other Pueblos fared even worse: Ohkay Owingeh lost 3,500 of its 4,000 irrigated acres. At San Ildefonso, fewer than 250 acres of arable land remained under Pueblo control.

Anglo intruders had long benefited from friendly New Mexico courts, which nearly always validated their unlawful possession. But the Supreme Court's bracing *Sandoval* decision in 1913—instigated by then-Pueblo Attorney Francis Wilson—changed everything. As wards of the federal government, no one could take Native lands without US government approval. The Pueblos, finally, had a legal weapon to fight back.

In the wake of the *Sandoval* ruling, the Pueblos began filing ejectment suits against the outsiders on their homelands. A crisis loomed as the cases entered the court system. Nearly 3,000 conflicting land claims were at stake, involving some sixty thousand acres of the most desirable, best-watered lands in New Mexico.

Figure 22. Ralph Emerson Twitchell. From Ralph Emerson Twitchell, *The Leading Facts of New Mexico History*, vol. 4 (Torch Press, 1917).

Albert Fall didn't believe for a moment that any Natives were entitled to that acreage. Now that he ran the Interior Department, he intended to convert those lands to white ownership. Yet he also understood the need to tread carefully because of that Supreme Court ruling. He decided to create a new government post: US Assistant Attorney General with Jurisdiction in Indian Matters. This innocuous-sounding position would in fact be the mechanism to provide legal cover for Fall's plan. The man he chose for the position was a close ally in Santa Fe: Colonel Ralph Emerson Twitchell.

The pompous Colonel Twitchell hadn't exactly won glory on any battlefield. He was a lawyer, not a soldier. But back in the 1890s, he'd been appointed judge advocate for New Mexico's territorial militia and was granted the honorary rank of "colonel." His tenure was brief and undramatic, but ever since he insisted on being addressed as "Colonel." A man inflated with pretension, Twitchell referred to New Mexico's capital city as "the mighty acropolis of Santa Fe."[14] He spoke with pride about the city's old Spanish colonial architecture even as he demanded "English-only" laws.

Twitchell, a dour-looking man in his early sixties, had published eleven books of New Mexico history. He wished to impress upon readers, as he wrote, "the fortitude, the courage, the suffering, and the martyrdom of those who first brought to New Mexico the banner of Christianity and civilization."[15]

Twitchell's masterwork was a four-volume set, *The Leading Facts of New Mexican History*, that totaled over two thousand pages. Though few people had read the entire work, its massive bulk served to confirm his status as New Mexico's preeminent historical authority. It was this quality of Twitchell's that Albert Fall most prized for the scheme he had in mind.

Twitchell's reputation among the Natives was less exalted. Taos Pueblo knew him as the scoundrel who helped conspire to secretly film one of their tribal dances, a private religious ritual closed to outsiders. Twitchell's son then screened the footage for thousands at the 1915 International Expo in San Diego, outraging the Taos People. Someone broke into Twitchell's office at the Expo and stole the film. Undaunted, the colonel had a backup print shipped from Santa Fe, then publicized the theft to drum up even more business.

None of the Pueblos were advised about the appointment of this new Assistant Attorney General with Jurisdiction in Indian Matters. That was part of Fall's plan. Twitchell would not actually *represent* any Natives, though it would appear so on paper.

The longer Collier stayed on in Taos, the more he began to see the very difficult challenges the Pueblo People faced. The average per capita income at Taos Pueblo was around thirty dollars—*per year*. Poverty was an immense problem, though one rarely acknowledged by the local artists. Nor was this unromantic reality addressed by Mabel, who insisted on portraying Taos as a paradise in order to attract noteworthy visitors.

Yet she clearly had a deeper reason for drawing the social reformer John Collier to Taos.

Collier observed malnutrition and he saw widespread diseases such as tuberculosis and syphilis impacting lives at the Pueblo. Many children suffered from trachoma, a painful eye infection that could lead to blindness. Medical care was uneven at best. Even a minor-seeming illness could quickly turn deadly, as Collier learned from Mabel, who told him about Tony's niece dying of pneumonia after contracting a common cold. Mabel railed against the injustice and described how she had filed an official complaint that led to nothing. She knew she was not equipped with the patience or the know-how to lead a long fight for government reform—but her friend John Collier had precisely those qualities, and in abundance.

Yet he demurred. He sympathized with the people at Taos Pueblo, but he had lost his appetite for activism. He simply wanted to live a quiet life. With fall approaching, a college in San Francisco offered him a job teaching sociology. Over Mabel's objections, he decided that his eight-month idyll in Taos had come to an end. Making apologies and vague promises to return one day, he and his family left for California.

CHAPTER 12

THE PLOT AGAINST THE PUEBLOS

1921–1922

After John Collier left Taos, Mabel Dodge Sterne became fixated on a new target: the English writer D. H. Lawrence. A coal miner's son who'd grown up near Nottingham, Lawrence had scandalized the British establishment with candid depictions of sexuality in his 1915 novel, *The Rainbow*. Authorities declared the book obscene, confiscating and burning all known copies. Lawrence's literary career was nearly ruined, but he persevered as a dedicated chorus of supporters praised him as a literary genius. Then his subsequent novel, *Women in Love*, published in 1920, was also attacked. A leading British journal condemned it as a "Loathsome Study of Sex Depravity."[1]

By that time, Lawrence had left England for Sicily. Joining him was his German-born wife, Frieda, who came from an aristocratic family related to the famed flying ace known as the Red Baron. Lawrence's novels were difficult to obtain in the United States, but Mabel read his work in *The Dial*, a literary magazine she subscribed to. She admired his prose and his seeming contempt for the machine age. She also approved of his call for American artists to reject Europe and embrace native influences. Then she read his new travel book, *The Sea and Sardinia*, and sensed a spiritual kinship.

"Here is the only one," she thought," who can really see this Taos country and the Indians, and who can describe it so that it is as much alive between the covers of a book as it is in reality."[2]

On impulse, she sent a letter inviting him to visit. She described Taos as a living oasis, an unspoiled Eden, "the dawn of the world."[3] She included some fragrant local herbs along with a necklace for Frieda, which Mabel promised carried good magic.

Charmed, Lawrence wrote back from Sicily. He asked practical questions about the cost of living. He told Mabel that he and Frieda did all their own cooking and housework, "because I loathe servants creeping around. They poison the atmosphere." The author also expressed wariness about Taos: "Is there a colony of rather dreadful sub-arty people?"[4]

After another exchange of letters, he sounded interested, but then wavered. He wrote to one friend, "I'm afraid there is a colony of New York artists in Taos. Evil everywhere." He and Frieda decided to leave Italy for Celyon (now known as Sri Lanka) instead. After a few months, the ever-restless Lawrence then traveled to Australia. Mabel refused to give up. She sent more letters and gifts. She concentrated her will on summoning Lawrence to Taos. She lit candles and aimed her thoughts at his mind, chanting, "Come, Lawrence! Come to Taos!"[5]

Albert B. Fall's ranch in southern New Mexico had never looked better. Electric lines crisscrossed his domain, thanks to his brand-new, privately built $53,000 hydroelectric plant. Automated irrigation wells watered orderly rows of apple, peach, and walnut trees. A paved road replaced the dirt lane leading to the main house. His range was now stocked with prized breeding animals, including a racehorse that had won at Belmont. Fall even purchased a neighboring ranch, making his down payment while ostentatiously flashing stacks of cash wrapped in $20,000 bundles. For a man who'd previously been ten years delinquent on his property taxes, the Interior Secretary's sudden turnabout in fortunes seemed remarkable.

Meanwhile, back in Washington, some were beginning to question how oil barons Edward L. Doheny and Harry Sinclair gained control over two of the nation's greatest oilfields. This unwelcome attention was just one of many headaches Albert Fall was giving his pal Warren Harding. The bombastic New Mexican was also constantly feuding with other cabinet members, often clashing with the Secretary of State over foreign policy. He alienated Harding's attorney general, a close friend of the president's, by snarling at the man during a cabinet meeting, "You don't know any law, and you can't learn any." Fall also provoked a crisis with Secretary of Agriculture Henry C. Wallace by attempting to wrest control of the US Forest Service away from Agriculture and transfer it to his own Interior Department—where he planned to gut the agency. Wallace managed to quietly outflank Fall while advising others not to get into "a pissin' contest with a skunk."[6]

Fall's policy ideas also proved controversial. His plan to open national parks to oil drilling sparked widespread protest, forcing him to abandon the move. He then pivoted to a new idea, declaring twenty-two million acres of Indigenous reservations to be "public lands." He called for opening the areas to oil and gas development, with not a penny of royalties going to any Native tribe. Fall also embarked on a quixotic mission to create a brand-new national park in southern New Mexico—an area surrounding his own ranch. Few believed that such a park was needed. Others seized on the clear conflict of interest, since Fall would personally benefit. Still, the Interior Secretary blustered ahead. At a heated congressional hearing, Fall lost his temper and shouted down his critics. After that, his park proposal was doomed to defeat.

Fall's stormy reign at Interior drew newspaper headlines, but far from the limelight, work proceeded quietly on his plan to pluck away the Pueblo People's lands. His handpicked US Assistant Attorney General with Jurisdiction in Indian Matters, Colonel Ralph Emerson Twitchell, prepared an appropriately murky historical analysis that delegitimized any Native claim to the contested lands. Then Twitchell began work drafting a bill that would set up an orderly process for legally transferring the lands to whites. To the public, he announced, "With a square deal assured to everyone," the Pueblo land controversies "are to be settled, definitely settled, with full regard for the rights of all parties."[7]

Even as Twitchell carried on his work, fresh tensions erupted over conflicting land claims. At Tesuque Pueblo near Santa Fe, a pair of wealthy ranchers with close ties to New Mexico's governor commandeered three thousand acres—including the stream that ran through the Pueblo. Ed Newman and E. B. "Dick" Healy installed two miles of barbed wire fence to seal their claim. A few days later, a group of thirty Tesuque men, led by twenty-three-year-old Martin Vigil, began dismantling the fence. Just like the Taos men in 1910 when they took down Lester Meyers's illegal fence, the Tesuque team was careful to not destroy any property. But the two trespassers became livid. Healy threatened "to shoot the hell" out of the Pueblo men. Newman called Governor Merritt Mechem and demanded he send the cavalry. While the governor tried to calm him down, Newman's wife grabbed the phone. "Those damn Indians are tearing up our fences and they will come after us next," she shouted. When her husband learned that the local Indian superintendent, Horace Johnson, had supported Tesuque Pueblo's actions, Newman threatened to shoot "that son of a bitch and every one of his god damned Indians."[8]

Both ranchers shot off telegrams to Charles Burke, the Commissioner of Indian Affairs. Burke immediately demanded an investigation—not of the intruders but, rather, of the Pueblo's superintendent for protecting the Natives under his charge.

A district judge in Santa Fe, Reed Holloman, surprised almost everyone by ruling that the two ranchers had illegally occupied Tesuque Pueblo land and had no right to erect fencing. His decision outraged many Anglos in Santa Fe, who filled the newspaper with letters of complaint. One suggested the turncoat judge should go live with the Natives. Another complained that he was a Bolshevik who should "paint himself red." One writer suggested the US government send "troops in to remove the Tesuque" before "Judge Holloman gives them all of the state."[9]

Among those upset by the judge's finding was Charles Burke, the very man most responsible for the Pueblos' welfare. The commissioner wrote to an Indian Bureau employee, "The decision made by Holloman was not in our favor and might lead to other Indians challenging authority . . . we will not permit such actions."[10]

Albert Fall soon ordered the superintendent, Horace Johnson, who had supported the Tesuques' rights, transferred to a remote outpost in the

Nevada desert. Fall then installed a new, more obedient Pueblo superintendent in his place.

Colonel Twitchell, still crafting his legislation, arranged to meet with the aggrieved Tesuque trespassers. He also conferred with A. B. Renehan, the attorney representing many Anglo squatters seeking to claim Pueblo lands. In the past, Renehan had often sparred with former Pueblo Attorney Francis Wilson, who'd tried to get Renehan disbarred.

While Colonel Twitchell huddled with the white interests, he avoided meeting with any Puebloans or their representatives. Occasionally he would agree to an appointment with a Native advocate, only to cancel. Rumors began circulating about Twitchell's legislation, but little information was forthcoming. The colonel would only say that "Indians and settlers on adjoining lands are to receive full legal protection and exact justice, so far as humanly possible."[11]

In May 1922, Indian Commissioner Burke arrived in New Mexico on an official inspection tour. A group of leaders from Laguna Pueblo, concerned about Col. Twitchell's work, came to the Bureau's office in Albuquerque to see the commissioner. They waited outside his door for eleven hours. Burke granted them ten minutes. During the brief meeting, he told them not to worry, that they would receive fair treatment from Twitchell and Interior Secretary Fall.

A few weeks later, Fall summoned Twitchell to Washington, along with squatters' attorney A. B. Renehan. The men joined Fall in his office to hash out the final version of the legislation. Renehan was there to represent the Anglo intruders; Twitchell on behalf of the Pueblos. Secretary Fall viewed himself as the impartial judge who would bring both sides together in the spirit of compromise.

The resulting document was nearly three thousand words long and contained sixteen sections. In essence, it resolved the disputes by awarding all the contested lands to the trespassers. Under its provisions, occupiers such as the two men who'd attempted to steal three thousand acres of Tesuque Pueblo land would be granted full legal title to their claims. The Pueblos would be compensated with a paltry cash payment or vague promises of comparable public lands—which, of course, were bone-dry and therefore did not exist. As a Pueblo superintendent noted, "The public domain adjacent to the pueblos, if any, would scarcely reimburse the cravings of a hungry jack rabbit."[12] In rare instances, the Pueblos might be allowed to retain their tribal lands—but the burden of legal proof in every case would be on the Natives, not the invaders who had stolen their land.

Indian Commissioner Burke, invited to review the document, agreed with Fall that the bill was "the very best that can be hoped for"[13] in protecting the Pueblos. No one would breathe a word of this legislation back in New Mexico. Burke's employees at the Indian Bureau were forbidden from even mentioning the bill to the Pueblo People.

New Mexico senator Holm Bursum, who had assumed office after Fall became Interior Secretary, agreed to sponsor the necessary legislation. In July 1922, Bursum introduced the bill, telling his colleagues that the measure "is recommended by the Interior Department and by the Commissioner of Indian Affairs, and also is agreed to by the parties."[14] Albert Fall sent an official letter to the senate, describing the bill as a routine administrative measure. The legislation was referred to the Public Lands Subcommittee for review.

Back in New Mexico, a single newspaper carried a celebratory account of Bursum's measure, noting that it would afford "complete relief" to settlers. The paper credited Colonel Twitchell and attorney Renehan for their good work. It assured readers that "passage is predicted."[15]

At Isleta Pueblo, south of Albuquerque along the Río Grande, tribal leader Pablo Abeita saw that news story. He'd been aware that some legislation was in the works, but this was the first he'd heard of any bill being filed. Abeita was no stranger to politics. At age fifty, he'd met with every US president since Grover Cleveland. He came from a prominent family and had a college education and ran a successful business. Abeita enjoyed renown as a brilliant orator and was widely considered the most influential Native American in New Mexico. Many believed he could have been elected the state's governor had he been born white.

In an attempt to find out was going on, Abeita drove to Santa Fe and showed up at Colonel Twitchell's office to confront him in person. Twitchell brushed Abeita off, calling him "an ungrateful Indian" who failed to appreciate the colonel's efforts.[16]

Abeita responded, "If that's all you can do for us Pueblos, then as far as I'm concerned you can go straight to hell!"[17]

Abeita began sending letters to various Native rights organizations, denouncing Bursum's bill and asking for help fighting it. He received sympathetic responses, but precious little action. Still, some letters of opposition reached Senator Irvine Lenroot, who chaired the subcommittee considering Bursum's Bill. Lenroot queried Interior Secretary Fall about the matter. Fall, in a written response, described the bill as a compromise that couldn't make everyone happy. He conceded that it may not be perfect, but he could not "suggest an amendment to perfect it." When Lenroot raised concerns that the Pueblo People had not been consulted, Fall lied in response. He told Lenroot that Col. Twitchell had represented the Pueblos "by their own choice."[18]

Fall's response satisfied the chairman. The measure was reported out of committee with no hearings. On September 11, 1922, Bursum's Bill passed the senate by unanimous consent. Inside his office at the Interior Department, Albert Fall lit a victory cigar.

After leaving Taos, John Collier rented a house in Mill Valley, a forested hideaway north of San Francisco. He took the ferry across the bay for the classes he taught at San Francisco State. Even though he had been too controversial for state government, Collier remained in demand as a public speaker. Many people wanted to hear his ideas on how to improve society. He began hitting the lecture circuit again to give talks about immigration. But he couldn't stop thinking about Taos Pueblo: "My thought of the Indians, and my concern in their life, grew day by day."[19]

He knew that the Taos People faced so many challenges: not just the pressing issue of public health, but also guarantees of civil rights, conservation of their tribal lands, preservation of their culture and religion, and the need to regain their sacred Blue Lake. In his public remarks, Collier began talking less about immigrants, and more about Indigenous people. He blasted "400 years of oppression," charging that the United States "has wiped its boots on the soul of the first Americans."[20]

"I lived among the Indians," Collier told audiences. "I never saw a child struck or humiliated before his fellows. I never saw an adult made to feel himself an outcast, the old lack of respect, nor a widow left in want." Out of the Natives, he said, "might flower art forms and spiritual beauty of which the white man never dreamed."[21]

His increasingly strident lectures soon brought him to the attention of Stella Atwood. She belonged to the General Federation of Women's Clubs, a service organization two-million strong, composed primarily of prosperous, socially conservative women. She'd grown up among the Chippewa in Minnesota, an experience that had given her a lifelong sympathy for Native Americans. In California, Atwood got herself appointed to work on "Indian welfare" for the Women's Clubs. The leadership likely expected that this "welfare" would conform to the standard missionary outreach of the times. But Atwood didn't believe Natives needed more Bibles—she thought they needed more respect and support for their existing cultures. She threw herself into the work, pestering politicians on Indigenous issues and personally lobbying Indian Commissioner Charles Burke. She also cornered Interior Secretary Fall at a California hotel, demanding he do more for Natives. When Atwood heard John Collier give a speech, she introduced herself and the two quickly became allies.

By May 1922, Atwood found a wealthy patron who agreed to fund Collier for a two-year assignment as a "research agent" for the Federation of Women's Clubs. His task would be to investigate Puebloan living conditions and recommend specific actions to improve matters. Collier resigned from his teaching position at San Francisco College. He knew exactly where he wanted to begin his new work: Taos, New Mexico.

Collier always traveled light, just a small, battered suitcase containing a couple of changes of clothing. After a brief layover in Santa Fe, he caught the Chili Line heading north toward Taos. On the way, he stopped in at Española to meet with Pueblo Superintendent H. W. Leech.

Very little news about Bursum's legislation had seeped into the public. Yet many Pueblo leaders were already registering alarm. Pablo Abeita of

Isleta Pueblo had drawn up a petition opposing the bill and presented it to Leech. This superintendent was the more docile overseer Albert Fall had installed after transferring Horace Johnson to Nevada. Yet even Leech became discomfited after realizing the devastating impact of Bursum's Bill. He forwarded the Pueblos' petition to his boss, Indian Commissioner Charles Burke, with a note that the Natives "have what appears to be good grounds"[22] for opposition. Burke ignored the appeal.

In Española, Collier announced himself at Leech's office. During their conversation, the superintendent mentioned the Bursum Bill. Collier knew that some sort of legislation was in the works, but he had no idea a bill had already been filed and sailed through the senate unopposed. Leech provided Collier with a copy of the text, explaining that it was "an act of insubordination"[23] for him to do so.

As Collier examined the bill, it struck him like a "body blow." Clearly Albert Fall had outmaneuvered everyone by surrounding the Puebloans with overwhelming legal firepower, a "legislative monster" that would "pulverize all Indian property and Indian group life." This attack would not be a bloody massacre like Sand Creek or Wounded Knee, but it would be similarly devastating. Quickly, Collier wired ahead to Mabel Dodge Sterne in Taos: "This will mean the ruin of the Pueblos. I am sicker at heart than anything has ever made me."[24]

CHAPTER 13

"GOING INDIAN"

1922

Mabel Dodge Sterne, after nearly a year of wooing, had finally snared her prize catch. Sitting in the back seat of the Cadillac driven by Tony Luján was the world-famous British writer, D. H. Lawrence. To bring Lawrence to New Mexico, Mabel had to promise that he wouldn't have to meet any of the Taos painters. "I feel I never want to see an artist again while I live," Lawrence had written to Mabel. "The Indians, yes; if one is sure that they are not jeering at one. I find all dark people have a fixed desire to jeer at us."[1]

Lawrence and his wife, Frieda, had docked in San Francisco after sailing to the United States from Australia. He wired Mabel to tell her they only had twenty dollars to their name. She promptly sent them train tickets to Santa Fe, where she and Tony met them. Now, traveling along the bumpy dirt road toward Taos, she could see what an odd pair they made. Lawrence was tall and gangly, a nervous man with stooped shoulders. His burning blue eyes peered from a face mostly hidden by a bushy red beard. Frieda, stout and hearty, spoke with a growl, a lit cigarette dangling from a corner of her mouth. Mabel, uncharitably, noted she "had a mouth rather like a gunman."[2]

The two quarreled violently while Tony drove, shouting curses at each other. Yet soon after the squall passed, they fluttered over each other like young lovers. Later Lawrence yelled at Tony about his driving, calling him a fool. If Tony heard the Englishman, he gave no indication.

Figure 23. D. H. and Frieda Lawrence, 1925. Pictorial Press Ltd/Alamy Stock Photo.

On September 11, 1922—Lawrence's thirty-seventh birthday and the same day the US Senate passed the Bursum Bill—Tony steered them out of the dark Río Grande cañon on to the sunlit Taos plain. Clouds boiled over the mountains like angry fists. Then a jagged streak of lightning bolted across the sky. Seconds later, a ferocious storm exploded. The travelers crawled into Taos as hailstones pounded the roof of the car. For Mabel, it was hard not to read dark portents into this bruising arrival.

Lawrence barely had time to get acclimated before Mabel asked Tony to drive him 120 miles to attend an Apache ceremony. Tony made a face, but complied. The two men were gone for five days. When they returned, Lawrence saw that another guest had arrived at Mabel's. John Collier had taken up residence, and all anybody could talk about was the Bursum Bill.

~

As John Collier paced the floor in Mabel's living room, the situation looked bleak. The House of Representatives was even more conservative than the Senate, and the Bursum Bill's passage seemed a foregone conclusion. Collier realized that the Pueblos' only hope lay in sparking a vigorous public resistance. Yet there was no national movement for Native justice. Advocacy groups such as the Indian Rights Association existed, but they were missionary-oriented. They would not be invested in a battle to safeguard Pueblo lands.

Any protest movement would need to start from scratch. Tony Luján arranged for Collier to meet with Taos Pueblo's governing council. Collier entered the sanctum, holding his creased copy of the Bursum Bill. He shook hands with the governor, Tony Romero, and each of the two dozen other men present. Governor Romero, a bulky man, had attended boarding school and was proficient in English. He translated for the others as Collier spoke.

Collier explained the bill in detail. He pointed out that it legitimized a bogus boundary survey commissioned by white trespassers. A New Mexico court would be authorized to make decisions based on that survey. In addition, all water rights would be transferred to the victors. Beyond stealing the Pueblos' land and water, Collier pointed out, the bill targeted tribal sovereignty. It reassigned jurisdiction of Pueblo matters to a New Mexico court. If that happened, Taos Pueblo's duly elected ruling council would become powerless.

Collier sat quietly while the governor and council conferred among themselves in Tiwa. Each man was granted an opportunity to speak, and the discussion lasted long into the night. Finally, Governor Romero addressed Collier in English. Taos Pueblo, he said, would join all efforts to oppose the Bursum Bill. It would also provide him with letters of introduction so that he could approach the other Pueblos for support.

Tony then drove Collier to Picuris, about 25 miles south of Taos. Anglo and Hispano settlers had already surrounded most of the fading pueblo. The Picuris People maintained only forty irrigated acres from their original 17,000-acre land grant. Here, too, tribal leaders pledged to join the fight against the Bursum Bill.

Next, Collier and Tony drove to Cochiti Pueblo, southwest of Santa Fe along the Río Grande. The Cochiti People knew of the Bursum Bill, but they had not yet been fully advised of its devastating consequences. Alarm spread during the meeting. Then Governor José Alcario Montoya rose to speak: "We must call all the Pueblos together. We must organize as we did long ago, when we drove the Spaniards out."[3]

Governor Montoya was referring to the great Pueblo Revolt of 1680, which humbled the mighty Spanish Empire and led to significant reforms in the crown's treatment of Natives. Collier instantly agreed that convening all the pueblos would be the best way to organize—and would offer a dramatic symbol of resistance. Letters went out to all nineteen Pueblos in New Mexico, inviting each to send emissaries for an All Pueblo Council—the first such official gathering in more than two hundred years.

While Collier and Luján worked to organize the Pueblos, Mabel Dodge Sterne roused white opposition to the Bursum Bill. In Taos, artists Ernest Blumenschein and Walter Ufer offered their services. Bert Phillips, painfully aware that he had once been on the other side of this very issue, also pledged support. Mabel also sent letters and telegrams to New York, soliciting eminent writers, artists, and others she believed could help. "They are the ones who want Indian life saved, for they get much from it," she observed.[4] Among those she contacted was Mary Austin—"God's Mother-in-Law"—who was just finishing her new book on Natives called *The American Rhythm*. Mabel also reached out to her friend, the prominent anthropologist Elsie Clews Parsons, who promised to help round up support among the scientific community.

Mabel also wrote and telephoned people in Santa Fe, hoping to enlist them in the battle. Among those she reached was Francis Wilson, the former Pueblo Special Attorney. Wilson was flourishing in private practice after leaving his government post, but he agreed to join the fight. Word of the Bursum Bill spread rapidly through the city. On September 22, the *Santa Fe New Mexican*, which had earlier praised Colonel Twitchell's efforts, published the entire text of the Bursum Bill, noting "we do not gather that it is giving the Pueblos any of the best of it."[5] Two days later, thirty people in Santa Fe gathered at a Canyon Road home to hear more about the bill. A larger meeting soon followed with presentations from John Collier and attorney Francis Wilson. Among those listening were several local artists along with the poets Witter Bynner and Alice Corbin Henderson. The Santa Feans quickly formed their own group in opposition, calling themselves The New Mexico Association on Indian Affairs. They closely coordinated efforts with Mabel and Collier in Taos, rallying together under the slogan, "Let's Save the Pueblos!"

A letter-writing campaign began aimed at senators and congressmen. Witter Bynner drafted text for a joint declaration to be signed by all writers and artists opposed to the Bursum Bill. Mabel worked to round up signatures for the petition. Among those she hoped to persuade was her houseguest, D. H. Lawrence. The famed writer, however, loathed all the commotion about the Bursum Bill.

Lawrence had come to Taos to make art, not embroil himself in a political dispute. He'd hoped to write a book about Mabel, telling the story of how she and Tony met and fell in love. Mabel, of course, was delighted by such a prospect and eagerly agreed to cooperate. On their first day of work together, Lawrence reported, as instructed, to her second-story bedroom suite. There he found Mabel wearing only a white bathrobe.

"I don't know how Frieda's going to feel about this,"[6] the author said, looking very uncomfortable. He suggested it might be better if they worked together at his guest house, in full view of his wife. That plan didn't work any better, as Frieda made her displeasure known by slamming doors and interrupting constantly. After a few tense days, the book project was abandoned.

Mabel and the Lawrences had better luck with horses. Tony kept several and showed the guests how to saddle and handle the animals. Then he and Mabel took Lawrence and Frieda on long rides, enjoying the crisp fall air and the heart-lifting views of golden aspens splashed against the blue mountains. Mabel could see the tension melt away from the couple as they fell into a quiet, loping rhythm, surrounded by a beauty that even Lawrence couldn't jeer at. The famous writer was becoming seduced, if not by Mabel, then at least by Taos: "In the magnificent fierce morning of New Mexico, one sprang awake," he wrote, "a new part of the soul woke up suddenly and the old world gave way to the new."[7]

At Mabel's urging, Tony began taking Lawrence to Taos Pueblo and showing him around. The Englishman was a striking presence, with his

Figure 24. D. H. Lawrence, Santa Fe, New Mexico, 1922. Photograph by Witter Bynner. Courtesy of the Palace of the Governors Photo Archives (NMHM/DCA), Negative Number: 200135.

awkward height and red beard. As he spent more time at the Pueblo, Lawrence began to gain some measure of Pueblo life and its significance:

"While a tribe retains its religion and keeps up its religious practices . . . there is a tribal integrity and a living tradition going back far beyond the birth of Christ, beyond the pyramids, beyond Moses. A vast old religion which once swayed the earth lingers in unbroken practice."[8]

"You can feel it, the atmosphere of it, around the pueblos," he wrote. "Not, of course, when the place is crowded with sight-seers and motor-cars. But go to Taos Pueblo on some brilliant snowy morning, and see the white figures on the roof: or come riding through at dusk on some windy evening, when the black skirts of the silent women blow around the white wide boots, and you will feel the old, old root of human consciousness still reaching down to depths we know nothing of: and of which, only too often, we are jealous."[9]

Lawrence became a familiar sight at the Pueblo, and the Taos People began calling him "Red Wolf," a name that flattered the author very much.

In October, the appeal on behalf of the Pueblo People was ready for distribution. THE PROTEST OF WRITERS AND ARTISTS AGAINST THE BURSUM INDIAN BILL condemned the "great wrong" that threatened the Pueblos. Declaring the legislation "grossly unjust to the Indians," the signers called upon the American people to join them in protesting, "as a test of national honor."[10]

The proclamation, which appeared in newspapers across the nation, was signed by forty-eight luminaries, including most of the founding Taos artists (Ernest Blumenschein, Bert Phillips, Joseph Henry Sharp, and Walter Ufer), along with their compatriots from Santa Fe: Gustave Bauman, John Sloan, Robert Henri, and many others. Mary Austin, Mabel Dodge Sterne, and Elsie Clews Parsons added their names, along with other notables Mabel had rounded up, including painter Maxfield Parrish and poet Carl Sandburg. The Western novelist Zane Grey, who'd killed countless Natives in his fiction, was among the well-known writers to announce his support. And in a major coup, the manifesto also boasted the name of D. H. Lawrence, who had at last agreed to sign.

On the first Sunday in November, 121 delegates from all 19 New Mexico Pueblos converged at Santo Domingo Pueblo. Among the representatives was Pablo Abeita from Isleta, who'd been among the first to raise alarm about the Bursum Bill. Joining the meeting was John Collier, who'd ridden with Tony Luján and several other Taos men, including Governor Tony Romero. Most other delegates also arrived by automobile, though some rode on horseback from neighboring Cochiti and San Felipe Pueblos. Other invited guests included attorney Francis Wilson and members of the newly formed New Mexico Association on Indian Affairs.

Snow had fallen the day before and a brisk wind chilled the air. Everyone crowded into the underground kiva and found a place to sit cross-legged. A small fire helped warm the room. The Puebloans passed around a bag of tobacco, and every man rolled his own from a stack of corn husks. Smoke floated into the air and the first official All Pueblo Council in 242 years began.

For the next two days, delegates listened to speeches and readings of prepared statements. Much time was spent on translating, for at least three distinct Pueblo languages—Keresan, Tanoan, and Zuñian—were spoken in addition to Spanish and English. A strong consensus emerged to issue a united proclamation on behalf of all the Pueblos. Nine Pueblo leaders crafted the language, and John Collier typed everything into the form of a resolution. The final text was read before the assembled delegates in each language. When the vote was called, all 121 men rose to their feet to approve.

AN APPEAL BY THE PUEBLO INDIANS OF NEW MEXICO TO THE PEOPLE OF THE UNITED STATES proclaimed that the Bursum Bill "will destroy our common life and will rob us of everything we hold dear—our lands, our customs, our traditions. Are the American people willing to see this happen?"[11]

This message from the Pueblos brought sympathetic news coverage and a wave of denunciatory editorials. Collier published several articles himself, many with alarming alliterative titles: "Plundering the Pueblo Indians," "Politicians Pillage the Pueblos," "The Plot Against the Pueblos." Collier also worked with attorney Francis Wilson to publish a devastating legal analysis of the Bursum Bill, titled "Shall the Pueblo Indians of New Mexico Be Destroyed?" Mabel had copies mailed to every member of Congress. In New Mexico, the *Santa Fe New Mexican* turned against the Bursum Bill, joining the opposition. In New York, Mabel's friend Elsie Clews Parsons circulated a petition signed by the nation's leading anthropologists. Parsons also persuaded major museums and scientific organizations to issue resolutions condemning the bill. In California, Stella Atwood raised hell through the General Federation of Women's Clubs, galvanizing an organization that represented two million women who now had the power to vote.

Protests poured into Congress and the Department of the Interior. Even the Campfire Girls and the Boy Scouts got into the act, raising pennies for the cause and sending postcards bearing crayon notes of protest. At the Office of Indian Affairs, Commissioner Charles Burke was deluged with letters and telegrams. As the wave of opposition grew, even the chairman of the Indian Bureau's advisory board, a prominent attorney named George Vaux, was moved to send a letter to Commissioner Burke. Vaux took pains to mention that he was not allied with "the extreme agitators," yet he pointed out, "I do feel that they are on the right track in endeavoring to have the Bursum bill modified."[12]

All the while, Mabel Sterne kept pestering D. H. Lawrence, asking him: "Won't you use your great genius at this time to help get something out to the world?" At last, he grudgingly agreed to write a tract against the Bursum Bill, which the *New York Times* published as a guest column. In it, a clearly annoyed Lawrence complained, "I wouldn't know a thing about it if I needn't. But it's Bursum, Bursum, Bursum! The Bill, the Bill, the Bill! Twitchell, Twitchell, Twitchell!, O Mr. Secretary Fall, Fall Fall, you bad man." He went on to lambaste the legislation for executing "the Wild West scalping trick a little too brazenly."[13]

John Collier became increasingly viewed as the man in charge of the opposition. The reformer was seemingly everywhere, working twenty-hour days. He met with countless writers and editors in New York to enlist them in the cause. He also became a fixture in Washington, where he made a special effort to his keep his one good suit cleaned and pressed while lobbying Capitol Hill. He also frequently returned to New Mexico to help organize local opposition.

To the growing cascade of criticism, Secretary of the Interior Albert Fall refused comment, declaring, "Unfortunately, we have no publicity agent, no publicity bureau, in the Department of the Interior. It has been my custom since I have been in the office of Secretary to confine myself to official utterances . . . We have submitted in silence to any abuse which might be heaped upon us, confident that sooner or later the matter would right itself."[14]

Fall's Indian Commissioner Charles Burke expressed no such reluctance, taking his case to the press. "Prior to the passage of the bill by the senate we received no protests at all," Burke argued, ignoring the fact that the bill's provisions had been kept secret and Pueblo leaders had earlier registered alarm. The commissioner added, "The Indians were perfectly satisfied until some of these organizations . . . stirred them up."[15]

On November 21, the day after Congress returned from its summer recess, Senator William Borah of Idaho rose to speak about the Bursum Bill. Its "terms were quite misunderstood when it passed the senate,"

Borah argued. "As I understand the bill now, it is an outrageous piece of legislation . . . one of the boldest raids on Indian lands ever attempted in Congress."[16] With that, Borah made a stunning announcement. He was recalling the bill from the House of Representatives, ordering that it be returned to the senate for further consideration.

Back in Taos, Mabel Dodge Sterne joined in the jubilation. She and her friend Mary Austin exchanged joyful letters. For so long they had dreamed that America might learn from its Native Peoples. Now, they were witnessing a spirited campaign that brought everyone together in support of the Pueblos. Mabel's dream of building a bridge between cultures seemed to be coming true. Writing to Austin, she enthused, "The country almost has seemed to *go Indian*."[17]

CHAPTER 14

THE INDISPENSABLE VILLAIN

1923

The Senate's recall of the Bursum Bill from the House of Representatives rattled its backers, who realized they now faced a high-stakes political brawl. Indian Commissioner Charles Burke accused John Collier and his allies of doing "more harm to the Indian problem than anything that has ever transpired in my recollection." Burke still refused to believe that Pueblos had the capacity to act on their own in opposing bill. He complained that outside agitators were at work, lamenting that it was "so easy to deceive these primitive people and destroy their confidence in the Government that is their protector."[1]

Interior Secretary Albert Fall bemoaned that "sworn officials of this Government, under oath to perform their duties, and charged by law with the duty, are being abused every day in the public press." Fall added, "If we are to have a Government by propaganda, the present conditions in Soviet Russia would constitute a political paradise . . . compared to what we might have here."[2]

Fall ordered government investigations of his opponents and he issued a public threat: "Special agents," he vowed, were pursuing "interesting matter concerning certain of the particular individuals who are now, under the cloak of protection to the Indians, engaged in misleading statements . . . some of them in defamatory statements concerning officials of the Indian Bureau and this department."[3]

John Collier realized what Fall was up to. He told Mabel, "They are letting it be known in advance because they think they can scare us. The one necessity is that they should not scare us. But likewise they really do not know how to fight any other way, we must be wary."[4]

Collier was Fall's most tempting target. The often-disheveled, high-strung activist certainly *looked* the part of a radical. Yet a wide-ranging probe turned up little dirt on the squeaky-clean organizer. Finally, an employee of the Indian Bureau in New Mexico volunteered to provide damaging information. Questioned further, the source could only say that Collier "smelled badly."[5]

Fall had struck out with Collier, but he found another tempting target: the wealthy woman in Taos with a long history of radical connections. Mabel Sterne had consorted with birth control advocates, feminists, socialists, and long-haired artists. Now, Albert Fall had reliable information from Colonel Twitchell that this married woman was carrying on an illicit affair with a Native man from Taos Pueblo. Further, this Pueblo lover was actually *living* in her house. Exposing this adulterous liaison might prove a bit tricky, given President Harding's own rampant infidelities. But gathering hard evidence and unleashing it at the right moment might shatter Fall's opponents.

Even as the Interior Secretary remained on the attack, persistent questions about Teapot Dome kept eroding Fall's standing in Washington. More critics were asking why he had given away the nation's most valuable oil fields, which had been reserved for the US Navy, to private interests at rock-bottom prices. "Many are the charges whispered in the corridors of the Senate and House," the *New York Times* reported. President Harding defended his Interior Secretary, saying, "If Albert Fall isn't an honest man, then I'm not fit to be president of the United States."[6]

Yet the Senate, in a rare show of bipartisanship, voted unanimously to authorize an investigation. The chamber also demanded to see all of Fall's documentation relating to the controversial oil leases. Talk of a possible scandal grew and the embattled Secretary was forced to announce, "I have not resigned, I have not been asked to resign, and I am not thinking of resigning."[7]

John Collier viewed the developments with glee. "It is plain that Fall is wusser'n than we thought even," he reported to Mabel. Collier understood the marquee value of a notorious adversary. Though the bill bore Holm Bursum's name, Collier saw the New Mexico senator as merely a "dull tool." It was Albert Fall who Collier considered "the indispensable villain."[8]

Senate hearings on the Bursum Bill were scheduled for January 1923, and the All Pueblo Council intended to send a delegation to Washington to testify against it. Collier and Mabel enthusiastically agreed, believing that the publicity value of such a visit would be tremendous. Collier envisioned a full-scale East Coast speaking tour that would dramatize the Pueblo's cause while raising funds for the movement.

Yet Collier saw a problem with the Pueblo leaders. Most of those who attended the All Pueblo Council had worn jackets and ties and several kept their hair cut short. Many had been educated in American schools and spoke excellent English. These men did not resemble the image Collier had been playing up in the press, portraying the Pueblos as the last living vestiges of an ancient golden age. If these modern Natives showed up in Washington looking like they were already assimilated, it could undermine their cause. Collier knew what people wanted to see: the living, breathing manifestations of the romanticized Pueblo paintings that appeared in the Santa Fe Railway's corporate advertising. If the Puebloans were going to travel east and gain valuable publicity, *they needed to put on a show.*

Mabel heartily agreed. "We must select them ourselves," she said. "They always vote that their smart, short-haired Americanized ones shall go: just the wrong ones."[9]

Collier and Mabel discussed how to choose the right men for the journey. At the top of Collier's list was "Someone who can talk—simply as the typical Indians talk, not artificially the way Pablo Abeita talks." He also wanted "impressive or attractive looks" along with the "Ability to sing together [and] Ability to dance together."[10] Collier and Mabel had an ideal Pueblo type in mind: handsome, dignified Tony Luján, who majestically embodied the old ways.

Mabel's guest in Taos, the writer D. H. Lawrence, had little regard for the activist Collier, who he considered "utterly out of balance." Lawrence had already endured endless discussions about the Bursum Bill, and his patience was running low. When he learned of Mabel and Collier's plans to join a contingent of Pueblo men east, he jeered at her: "You as an aesthetic Buffalo Bill!"[11]

Mabel ignored Lawrence's scorn, viewing the upcoming publicity tour as a personal triumph. She had orchestrated much of the artists' and writers' responses to the Bursum Bill, and she would arrive in New York at the head of one of the most fashionable reform movements the country had seen in ages.

Yet even as she and Collier arranged appearances in Chicago and New York, strangers were snooping around Taos. These outsiders were asking locals probing questions about Mabel and Tony Luján. One day, a suspicious-looking man was spotted lurking outside the gates of Mabel's estate.

Collier realized what was happening. Albert Fall's "special agents" were investigating the relationship between Mabel and Tony. At first, Mabel refused to believe such a thing could be happening. But others saw what the Interior Secretary was up to. In New York, Mabel's friend Mary Austin learned that newspaper and magazine editors were being approached by Fall's men, who promised a sensational scoop. She wrote to warn Mabel of a "determined effort to push you into newspaper publicity."[12]

Collier made it clear: If Mabel accompanied the Puebloans to the East Coast, she would be walking into a trap.

D. H. Lawrence had decided that "Taos is about the best place in the U.S.A.," but that didn't mean he was enjoying life with Mabel. In a letter, he described her as "little loved—very clever for a female [who] likes to play the 'patroness.'" Although Lawrence had insisted from the beginning that he wanted nothing to do with Taos's artist colony, which he condemned as "smoking, steaming shits," he became upset that Mabel didn't host parties in his honor. The Lawrences did deign to attend a few social occasions in town, but their appearances were often marked by murderous quarrels. At one party, everyone looked on in astonishment as Lawrence yelled at his wife: "Take that dirty cigarette out of your mouth! And stop sticking out that fat belly of yours!" She shouted back, "You'd better stop that talk or I'll tell about *your* things."[13] A few moments later, he and Frieda were seen strolling arm and arm, nuzzling each other like young lovers.

By Thanksgiving 1922, Lawrence and Frieda had retreated from Mabel's compound, taking a log cabin at a ranch in the nearby mountains. Shortly thereafter, they decamped to Mexico with a couple of Santa Fe poets. He sent Mabel a letter:

> Don't trouble about the Indians. You can't "save" them: and politics, no matter what politics, will only *destroy* them . . . In your lust even for a Saviour's power, you would just destroy them. The same with Collier. He will destroy them. It is his saviour's will to set the claws of his own White egotistic *benevolent* volition into them. Somewhere, the Indians know that you and Collier would, with your salvationist but poisonous white consciousness, destroy them . . . I tell you, leave the Indians to their own dark destiny. And leave yourself to the same.[14]

Pueblo leaders swiftly overruled Collier's and Mabel's recommendation that only "picturesque" types make the journey east. Instead, they chose those who would best represent their interests—most prominently Pablo Abeita from Isleta Pueblo. Maybe Abeita's hair was too short and he was too loquacious to please Mabel and Collier, but as far as the Pueblos were concerned the eloquent, college-educated Abeita was the most respected voice of the Pueblo resistance.

Collier's directive that the Puebloans needed to provide "showmanship" to attract attention was offensive, but most Pueblo leaders were well aware of the need to "play Indian" for the whites. They preferred to be regarded as statesmen for their people, rather than exotic curiosities—but if singing and dancing in ceremonial regalia was needed to protect their lands they were willing to do it.

The only problem was, not every modern-day Pueblo man still owned the old traditional wardrobe. As the group prepared to depart, Sotero Ortiz from Ohkay Owingeh Pueblo drove his car to Tesuque Pueblo, where he gratefully accepted the loan of buckskin leggings, a vintage blanket, and a pair of beaded moccasins. Then he sped on to join the others.

On a sunny, unseasonably warm January afternoon, the small railway station outside Santa Fe was crowded with Pueblo leaders, their white allies, and a handful of watchful agents spying for the Indian Bureau. Seventeen Pueblo men had been selected for the journey. Some were "progressives" with close-cropped hair who'd embraced Christianity. Others were keepers of traditional religions. A few, notably Pablo Abeita, were experienced at statecraft and had traveled to Washington before. Others were boarding a train for the first time in their lives. The delegation included old Santiago Naranjo, the revered Santa Clara governor with long, flowing white hair. The youngest man was twenty-four-year-old Martin Vigil, who'd earlier led the Tesuque Pueblo men in taking down the white intruders' fences. Underscoring the consequential nature of this trip, several of the leaders carried the carefully preserved, silver-tipped ceremonial canes that Abraham Lincoln had earlier presented to each Pueblo as a symbol of America's pledge to respect their land rights.

Taos Pueblo's representatives included Tony Luján, who'd been deemed too important to leave behind despite the risk of exposing his affair with Mabel Sterne. Not only was he impressive-looking, but he was also an excellent musician and a natural leader. He would be in charge of organizing the singing and dancing performances.

Attorney Francis Wilson, nattily dressed as always, joined the Pueblo men at the train station. Wilson had been hired by the General Federation of Women's Clubs to represent the Pueblos before Congress. John Collier had helped raise the funds to bring Wilson aboard, even as he balked at the extravagant fifty dollars a day per diem Wilson required for his services. Collier himself was used to living on less than three dollars a day while on the road.

As the train departed, the lead agent from the Indian Bureau wired a telegram to a displeased Commissioner Burke, informing him that the Pueblo delegation was on its way.

At Chicago, several of the Pueblo men exchanged their wingtips for moccasins. They donned buckskin and wrapped themselves in tribal blankets. They also slipped on full, feathered headdresses. If some had been skeptical about John Collier's idea for them to appear in such a fashion, the reception in Chicago proved the activist correct. The Pueblo men were mobbed by enthusiastic admirers everywhere they went. In a whirlwind tour, they sang and danced and made speeches at the Chicago Women's Club and the Union League. They also spoke to civic leaders at the prestigious Cliff Dwellers Club, atop the Symphony Center with its unspoiled view of Lake Michigan.

In New York City, the Pueblos received an official welcome from Mayor John F. Hylan, who posed for photographs with Zuñi Pueblo's High Priest, Waí-hu-si-wah. Newspapers featured photographs of the Pueblo men striding down Fifth Avenue. The group was feted all over town and even took in a Broadway show. At Cooper Union, Tony Luján led some of the men in a Corn Dance and then others, including Taos Governor Tony Romero, gave passionate speeches against the Bursum Bill. Joining the Pueblo leaders onstage was Mary Austin, who proclaimed the Pueblos "a national asset . . . from which we have much to learn."[15]

At the Explorer's Club, the Pueblo men, in full headdresses, joined elderly matrons for a tea and cake reception. News accounts marveled at how the Natives sipped from the fine china "politely and with considerable social grace."[16] From there the contingent visited the People's Institute, where John Collier had once worked among new immigrants. The Pueblos were greeted by hundreds of working-class men who thronged among the visitors, shaking hands and wishing them luck.

With Mary Austin's help, an appearance was arranged at the New York Stock Exchange. On the appointed morning, the Pueblo men paraded along Wall Street toward the great temple of American capitalism. Inside, they were led to the terraced visitors' gallery overlooking the immense trading floor. Buyers and traders began pointing up to the Puebloans, and the frenzied shouting began to quiet. Soon the only sound was the clatter of unattended stock tickers. Tony Luján raised his drumstick high, then began pounding the Pueblos' heartbeat. The others joined him in singing "The Morning Song." When the performance ended, the floor erupted in cheers and whistles. Mary Austin wrote to Mabel that "the Exchange simply got up on its hind legs and howled."[17] From Wall Street, a deluge of telegrams flooded Washington, calling on Congress to "Kill the Bursum Bill."

CHAPTER 15

WE PUEBLO INDIANS DEMAND JUSTICE

1923

JANUARY 15, 1923

On this morning of senate hearings on the Bursum Bill, the Pueblo delegates ascended the steps of the US Capitol. At the building's front entrance, two foreboding statues stood guard. At left was "The Discovery of America," depicting a triumphant, ten-foot-tall Christopher Columbus, standing over a Native woman crouched in submission. At right was "The Rescue," which showed a white frontiersman overpowering a tomahawk-wielding Native who'd tried to murder a white woman and her baby. The sculptor, Horatio Greenough, said his work was meant "to convey the idea of the triumph of the whites over the savage tribes."[1]

The ominous greeting did little to ease concerns about what measure of justice might await the Pueblo men inside the capitol. Senator Bursum was said to be furious and anxious to confront his foes. Interior Secretary Fall was scheduled to testify, along with Indian Commissioner Burke and Colonel Ralph Emerson Twitchell. While the Pueblo men had been making public speeches for days, none had been granted permission to speak at this committee hearing. Instead, they would have to rely on their attorney, Francis Wilson.

The Pueblo envoys filed into the hearing room, accompanied by John Collier, Stella Atwood, and other white allies. Everyone took seats in the visitors' section. No feathered headdresses were worn on this occasion.

Figure 25. Pueblo leaders in Washington, DC, 1923. Pablo Abeita is seated front and center. Tony Romero, governor of Taos Pueblo, is seated at the right. Courtesy of the Field Museum of Natural History, Chicago and Palace of the Governors Photo Archives (NMHM/DCA), Negative Number: 098640.

Most of the Pueblo men dressed in jackets and ties and several carried the silver-tipped canes bestowed by President Lincoln. Tony Luján was nowhere in sight, as Collier made sure he avoided presenting himself as a target to their opponents.

Chairing the session was Republican Senator Irvine Lenroot of Wisconsin, joined by Holm Bursum of New Mexico and other committee members. Indian Commissioner Burke was already present, ringed by

Figure 26. Indian Commissioner Charles Burke, 1921. Library of Congress, Prints & Photographs Division, LC-DIG-npcc-03854.

aides from his agency. Burke and the other Indian Bureau officials glowered at the Pueblo men.

Burke was allowed to testify first. He settled in at the witness table, and Senator Bursum of New Mexico took the lead in questioning. In a bit of rehearsed stagecraft, Bursum asked the Indian Commissioner: "I notice that there are several Pueblo Indians here at this time. In that connection I desire to ask the commissioner whether they were here at his direction or with his permission or acquiescence or knowledge in advance of their coming?"[2]

Burke turned his hard gaze on the Puebloans. "We have had nothing whatever to do with it," he responded. "We were not consulted. I have no knowledge whatsoever about how they came here or who is paying the expense, except as I hear a rumor."

Bursum, too, looked over at the Natives, feigning astonishment. "And for what purpose? Are they here to testify before the committee?"

Burke continued staring at the Pueblo delegation. He wanted everyone to understand that these were renegades who'd defied the Indian Bureau. "I have no knowledge, Mr. Chairman and gentlemen, as to why they are here."

The commissioner then began presenting his prepared statement. The man, Collier realized, had the poised instincts of a professional assassin. He retained a calm-seeming demeanor while expertly slipping a sharpened knife between his opponents' ribs. He spoke of his sincere regret that decent people—who he granted had perhaps "the very best of intentions"—had allowed themselves to be "bunkoed" by a "paid publicity agent."

In case anyone doubted who Burke might be referring to, the commissioner produced a copy of a letter that John Collier had sent earlier to a congressman. With obvious distaste, Burke began reading Collier's words:

> I am pretty familiar with the type of so-called white man who spends his life stealing everything the Indians have, and from what I have seen, I am unable to admit that the Bursum Bill can possibly be converted into anything but a piece of the lowest kind of thievery, no matter how much it is remodeled. It is just the kind of legislation to be expected from some of the ex-mule skinners and fur dealers, and so forth, that sometimes acquire a smattering of law and appear at Washington as Senators.

Burke set the letter down and turned to face the senators, affecting a deeply aggrieved expression. "I do not know to whom he refers, whether it is the honored Senator [Holm Bursum] who sits at this table, or whether it is the distinguished Secretary of the Interior, who was his predecessor in the Senate. But this shows, Mr. Chairman, the character of communications that are being sent."

Francis Wilson was stunned. He knew that Collier was a firebrand, but he had no idea that the man had written such needlessly insulting letters about the body of lawmakers presiding over their case.

Commissioner Burke continued, charging that the Puebloans could not have written the All Pueblo Council's widely circulated protest against the Bursum Bill: "I want to say that did not come from the Indians. It does not represent the sentiment of the Pueblo Indians." Pointing again to Collier, he declared, "They were inspired to adopt a declaration of that kind upon being exhorted, and misstatements being made to them."

The Indian Commissioner's testimony continued for two days as the assembled senators listened with respect. No one interrupted or contradicted him at any point. This was a very bad sign, the Pueblos and their advocates realized.

On day three, Colonel Ralph Emerson Twitchell approached the witness table. Twitchell's calculated pomposity had been carefully cultivated over the years to make him appear larger, yet here in this Senate hearing room, he seemed somehow very small. Guided by Senator Bursum, the colonel spent hours establishing the elaborate historical context that justified the reasoning behind the bill. It all seemed so innocuous. Twitchell, in his woolen suit and buttoned vest, seemed to truly believe his frequent protestations that he wanted a "square deal for everyone." Of the Puebloans, he maintained, "I was doing everything I could to protect these people in their rights."

He wound up with a heartfelt plea against "people who would impugn the motives of sworn officers of the Government." Then Twitchell considered himself finished.

Yet Senator Irvine Lenroot was just beginning. As chairman of the committee and a capable attorney in his own right, Lenroot began prying away Twitchell's platitudes, focusing on the bill's actual provisions. Lenroot's questioning intensified and the brave colonel began to melt. Glancing at the clock, and knowing that the committee had adjourned at noon the previous two days, Twitchell pleaded, "It is now about the noon hour, Mr. Chairman."

Everyone stared at Twitchell. Was the witness asking for mercy? Twitchell stammered on: "I think that a part of this explanatory business should devolve on some of these other lawyers here."

Lenroot didn't miss a beat. "I think you should explain it."

Still, the chairman was not without compassion. He agreed to a recess until the following morning.

On day four, Lenroot methodically led Colonel Twitchell through the bill, step by step. The colonel was forced to concede, time after time, that each provision was in fact extremely injurious to the Pueblo People. "Really that feature of it had not occurred to me," Twitchell protested after one criticism. He began backpedaling from the legislation he had spent more than a year working on. "I am not wedded to that provision," he responded after another Lenroot challenge. When the chairman objected to another section of the bill, Twitchell replied, "I was opposed to the idea, to start with, and only consented . . . believing that the interests of the Indians were safeguarded."

As the pressure mounted, Colonel Twitchell, in alarm, pointed again to the clock on the wall. "It is now nearly 12 o'clock, Mr. Chairman."

Lenroot replied steadily, "We will run until a quarter of 1 today." Twitchell sagged in defeat.

By the time Francis Wilson was allowed to testify on the fifth day of the hearings, Senator Lenroot and Colonel Twitchell had already done most of his work for him. Still, Wilson's presentation was a tour de force. He demolished what was left of the Bursum Bill, pointing out that the survey Colonel Twitchell had relied on to establish Pueblo boundaries was actually a recent creation, made solely for the benefit of Anglo trespassers. The survey had no valid historical justification and Twitchell had no honorable defense for having used it. When Wilson finally concluded, both Colonel Twitchell and Senator Bursum looked very pale.

Wilson then asked for a special dispensation. He explained that the Pueblo leaders had sat through several days of testimony and had not been allowed to say a word. "When they return to their respective pueblos they will be asked what they did. If they are not able to show that they made some statement before the committee, their people are going to consider it a very peculiar thing, because their habit is for each member of every council, when they are brought together, to make a statement about the matter before the council. We do not ask that they all be heard, but we would like to have a statement in the record by each delegation."

Chairman Lenroot paused. He and the other senators weren't convinced that any of these Natives could have written their own statements. Still, he agreed to add them to the record.

Wilson then pressed further. Considering that Commissioner Burke had been allowed to speak for two days, he requested that one of the Pueblos be granted fifteen minutes. Lenroot obliged.

Then Pablo Abeita, the prominent Isleta Pueblo leader, came forward to be sworn in as a witness.

As Abeita took his place before the US Senators, Holm Bursum from New Mexico saw his chance to regain the offensive. Before Abeita could

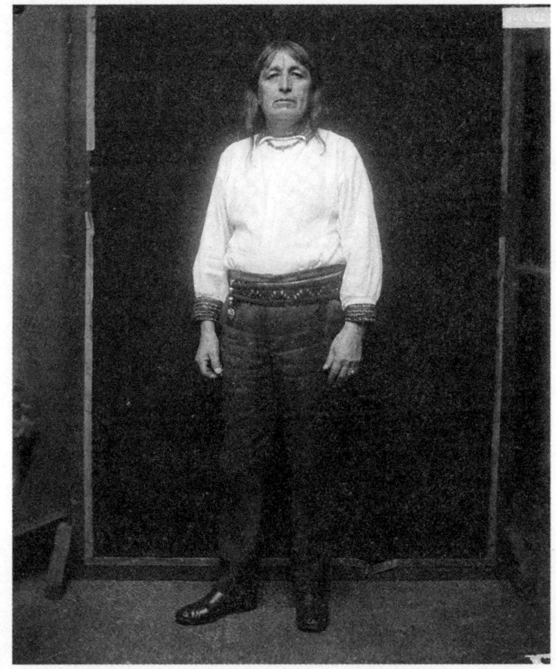

Figure 27. Pueblo leader Pablo Abeita in Washington, DC, 1923. National Anthropological Archives, Smithsonian Institution, NAA INV 06338400.

begin speaking, Bursum leaned in with a question: "Have you some Mexican blood in you? Are you part Mexican?"

Abeita responded, "Not that I know of."

Bursum: "Spanish?"

Abeita: "Not that I know of."

Chairman Lenroot interrupted, halting Bursum's hectoring so that Abeita could make his statement. The Pueblo leader spoke in a steady, measured voice, but there was no concealing his outrage:

> Mr. Chairman and gentlemen of the committee, it is only once in a great while that we are privileged to appear before you like today here, and in most every case that we come before you we come to beg, to plead. . . . This time, gentlemen, we have a far greater mission than ever before, and in our mission we have a few things that we will not beg, but will demand. It has come to a point, to a time, where we Pueblo Indians have to raise our voices and demand justice.

Senator Bursum and others were shocked. They had expected deference from this man. Instead, Abeita's authoritative voice shook the room as he displayed a fiery resistance.

Abeita continued: "Way down in New Mexico civilization was in full bloom when Christopher Columbus's great grandparents were murdering and massacring each other. We need not say any further about this civilization. It was, but is dying out today, and why you may ask? We point the finger at you white people. We were civilized and lived as such until you came in to disrupt and corrupt our method of civilization. Today what few are left are clamoring for protection."

Abeita told the senators: "Gentlemen, I could go on for hours telling you just what destruction your people have done to us Indians. . . . You have taken and gobbled our all, land, water, game. You first took them away by force, later by playing friendship, with means illegal[3], and now you want to make it legal." The Bursum Bill, he added, takes "away from us part of what little land we have left."

But Abeita made it clear that he was not speaking as a supplicant: "You need not think that we come here as mere beggars; we come here as people who believe we are entitled to more consideration and justice." He then spoke of the Pueblos' contributions during the Great War: "We sent some of our boys across the ocean to help stain that land with that precious blood of our blood. We gave our pennies to the Red Cross, war-work fund, and bought Liberty bonds as far as our means allowed. . . . We have cast our lot with you till Kingdom come."

He wound up his oration by posing a deceptively simple question that exposed the Bursum Bill's true intent: Why was it necessary to force the Pueblos off their long-established homelands with a pledge to reimburse them? Abeita asked. Instead, "why not reimburse the non-Indian trespasser and make him get off?"

After he finished, Senator Lenroot asked, "Did you write all that yourself?

"Yes," Abeita responded.

"Nobody helped you in your language?"

"No, sir."

"It is all your own language?"

"Yes."

Senator Bursum, swelling with indignation, could contain himself no more: "I want to ask Mr. Abeita a few questions." The chairman nodded for him to proceed.

Bursum scowled at the Pueblo leader. "Your children are being generally educated by the Government, are they not?"

Abeita: Yes.

Bursum: Do you think that is a good policy, a good thing for your people?

Abeita: Yes.

Bursum: You think it is a good thing for them to acquire that education?

Abeita: Yes.

Bursum: Do you not think that the Government is doing something for you which is of lasting benefit in providing this education?

Abeita: Yes, but nothing in comparison to what the Government has taken away from us.

Bursum: This Government has not taken anything whatever away from you. This Government has been giving to you.

Abeita: I cannot agree with you, outside of what you mentioned as to schools; but as far as land is concerned, there is no man can convince me that he has given me this land.

Bursum: All the title which you have now is by reason of what this Government and Congress have done. Is there any other title?

Abeita: The Government has simply given us the papers, but the land was always ours.

At this, Senator Bursum launched into a long harangue, arguing that the government was so helpful to the Pueblos, "equipping your children to meet the problems of life so as to make you independent, it seems to me is a policy for which you people should feel very grateful and highly appreciative. . . . Don't you think that is fine and liberal treatment on the part of the Government to do that?"

Abeita responded: "It is a fine thing that the Government is doing, and we are not complaining about what it has done. We are complaining about what it is *trying* to do."

On the ninth and final day of the hearings, the Secretary of Interior strode into the Senate committee room.

"I am here simply," Albert Fall announced, "to assist the committee in formulating its judgment." If the Interior Secretary was troubled by new developments in the Teapot Dome affair, he didn't show it. Yet the oilman Harry Sinclair, who had secretly paid Fall over $300,000, had just been subpoenaed by the Senate with a demand to turn over his financial records. A day of reckoning was approaching for Fall, who would become the first US cabinet member convicted of a felony and sentenced to prison.[4]

The Interior Secretary presented both himself and Indian Commissioner Burke as martyrs for having suffered "the most unjust and absolutely false statements and propaganda." He proclaimed, "I have long since learned to see the words I have uttered twisted by knaves to make a trap for fools." If anyone in the room doubted who Fall might be referring to, he named the chief villain: "Mr. Collier—I believe that is his name."

Fall then spoke of his high personal regard for Pueblo People, noting that his Interior Department had devoted significant funds to Native welfare over the years: building and maintaining schools, drilling wells, and providing salaries to Indian Bureau employees. Fall went on for more than an hour, launching a virtual filibuster as he cited everything from the number of patients successfully discharged from a Jicarilla Apache hospital to the purchase of a rock crusher for Laguna Pueblo. The intent behind the piles of data was, of course, to obscure the issue at hand—the land grab he had orchestrated. Instead, Fall maintained that the entire purpose of the Bursum Bill was "to work out something for the benefit of these Indians."

Pueblo attorney Wilson spoke up. "I would like to ask the Secretary some questions," he said.

Fall recoiled in horror. "Mr. Chairman, am I to submit to a cross-examination from this man? I object!"

Fall's objection was upheld. The Interior Secretary then let loose with his own carefully planned ambush against Wilson. Armed with a stack of papers from government archives, Fall spoke regretfully of "Mr. Wilson's conduct of affairs while he was Pueblo attorney." He cited an earlier land case involving Pojoaque Pueblo in which the Natives had been cheated—and he said that Wilson was responsible. Holding up a piece of paper as "evidence," Fall made an incendiary allegation. He accused Wilson of a "conspiracy to defraud the Government and the Indians out of their lands." Fall stared at Wilson and thundered, "He should be prosecuted for the same."

The Secretary's last-ditch effort to blow up the hearings with this diversion worked—for a brief spell. Chairman Lenroot soon discovered that Fall was simply rehashing old charges from a failed effort to discredit Wilson back when he'd been the Pueblos' Special Attorney. Wilson had long since been exonerated. The senate committee's own investigator reported back: "It is clear that the charges made against Mr. Wilson are without basis in fact or law, and that a grave injustice has been done to him and the organizations he represents by the statement of Secretary Fall."[5]

Wilson never got to ask Fall any questions under oath, but it did not matter in the end. The increasingly embattled Interior Secretary resigned from office, and the Bursum Bill was soundly defeated by the US Senate.

CHAPTER 16

SODOM AND GOMORRAH OF THE MODERN WORLD

1923–1924

APRIL 16, 1923

Mabel Ganson Evans Dodge Sterne Luhan's first wedding had been a lavish affair, drawing Buffalo's leading families. By the time of her fourth marriage, Mabel opted for a simple, private ceremony. She and Tony exchanged vows in a Taos clergyman's adobe home, joined by two witnesses. Knowing that her English-speaking friends would have trouble correctly pronouncing "Luján," she decided to spell her new last name phonetically: she became Mabel Dodge Luhan.

When the news hit Buffalo, it made the front page: FORMER BUFFALO SOCIETY GIRL MARRIES AN INDIAN. Other papers across the nation ran a full-page, illustrated feature: WHY BOHEMIA'S QUEEN MARRIED AN INDIAN CHIEF. The article explained that Mabel, "fascinated by paintings of savage life," found "its reality so much more delightful." The story continued:

> When Antonio Lujan, a full-blooded Pueblo, very red of skin and long of hair, fell in love with her and begged her to let him be her fourth husband, it is thought she had no hesitancy about flinging herself into his muscular arms and allowing her "Yes" to be smothered by his kisses.[1]

Tony's previous wife, the report noted, "generously consented to remove herself from the picture by applying for a divorce." That wasn't exactly true. In reality, Mabel had been paying Candelaria Luján a thirty-five-dollar-a-month stipend in exchange for surrendering Tony. Because divorce proceedings involving Taos Puebloans were so rare, the judge presiding over the case refused to act—until attorney Francis Wilson exerted considerable pressure on Mabel's behalf.

Even after Tony's divorce, Mabel hesitated before going through with the wedding. Intermarriage between Natives and whites was outlawed in many states, though not New Mexico. More than any social opprobrium, Mabel was mostly concerned about her mother. Sara Montague helped sustain her daughter with a $1,000 monthly allowance, and Mabel feared she might cut her off if she married Tony.

In the end, Mabel's mother kept the money flowing. Tony's own relations at Taos Pueblo didn't fare nearly so well. Many people, including members of his own family, were angry at him for marrying the white woman. He was expelled from his religious kiva and was no longer permitted to sing and play the drum at Taos Pueblo's ceremonial dances. At age forty-four, he was barred from all community worship.

In all his years taking on impossible causes, John Collier had never known such success. He'd helped build a new movement, and its momentum seemed unstoppable. But there was more to do. Everywhere he looked he saw other crises confronting Indigenous people. Poverty and poor health care were rampant, and the Indian Bureau seemed unable and unwilling to meet those challenges. Beyond the agency's failings loomed an even graver threat: cultural extinction and forced dispossession remained official US government policy, as codified in the 1887 Dawes Act. Collier told Mabel, "The job is a heap more than beating the Bursum Bill."[2]

He told her about his plans to expand the movement into a larger battle for reform: "We shall have to establish our right to dictate Indian policy," he said, "and get ourselves strongly 'on top' politically. . . . <u>After</u> our power is established, then we can get the fundamental changes needed."[3]

Indian Commissioner Charles Burke was furious at the Pueblos for defying him and allying with the radical John Collier to oppose the Bursum Bill. Burke intended to punish this challenge to his authority, and he quickly found a rationale. Ever since taking office, he'd been hearing complaints from Christian missionaries about the Pueblos' ceremonial dances. The rituals often symbolized nature's fertility, a matter vital to agricultural societies. But opponents discerned something far more sinister. Matthew Sniffen, head of the missionary-dominated Indian Rights Association, charged that Pueblo dances were nothing more than "a carnival of promiscuous carnal indulgence."[4]

Sniffen had spent years collecting "evidence" to prove his claims, often from dubious sources. His efforts were supplemented by reports from an Indian Bureau investigator, Reverend E. M. Sweet, along with William E. "Pussyfoot" Johnson, a former chief special officer for the Indian Bureau.

Together, Sniffen, Sweet, and Pussyfoot compiled a thick binder of malicious gossip that came to be known as the "Secret Dance File." The pornographic particulars, Sniffen claimed, were "too filthy to be described in public print . . . of so vile a character that they are not permitted circulation in the mails."[5] Yet the reports were freely shared among government officials, including members of Congress and the new Interior Secretary, Hubert Work.

The Secret Dance File alleged that the Pueblo People, regarded by many as paragons of personal modesty, were in fact "grossly immoral" and engaged in "the most disgusting practices." The Natives were said to enjoy "dancing naked and going through the motions of fornication." An Indian Bureau employee reported that "at one of their dances the men have the privilege of sucking any woman's teats, which they do in the most promiscuous fashion in the plaza and the streets of the pueblo." Another described how Pueblo women would "squat like a hen or bend over like a cow or sheep. The man would bend over the woman and hold her tight in his arms exactly as a stallion, a ram or a dog would do in the act of sexual intercourse . . . keeping up the performance for hours." Another overheated witness swore that he saw "Indians fucking like goats, burros and horses fucking—many men and women."[6]

The katsina clowns were condemned as the instigators of many of the outrages. Several informants reported clowns who displayed oversized penises made of wood. Others claimed that, during the secret dances, every woman stopped to kiss a clown's penis. Another swore, "I seen a squaw suck a buck's prick." The Secret Dance File's judgment was devastating: the Pueblos were "the Sodom and Gomorrah of the modern world."[7]

Commissioner Burke had no firsthand knowledge of Pueblo ceremonial dances. He had considered them primarily tourist bait, "weird and picturesque spectacles for the study of artists or a relief to the ennui of surfeited pleasure seekers."[8] Burke likely knew that many of the missionaries' accusations were ludicrous. Still, the Secret Dance File gave him the means to strike back at the Pueblos.

On February 14, 1923, just three weeks after the Bursum Bill failed in the Senate, the vindictive Burke issued new orders to his Indian superintendents. Among his directives:

- That Indian dances be limited to one in each month in the daylight hours of one day in the midweek.
- That none take part in the dances or be present who are under fifty years of age.
- That a careful propaganda be undertaken to educate public opinion against the dance and to provide a healthy substitute.[9]

In New Mexico, the reaction was swift. The *Santa Fe New Mexican* blasted "the utter injustice of misrepresenting their ceremonials as evil and foolish, harmful and depraved." Mabel Dodge Luhan protested that the Pueblos possessed "a well-balanced, natural and usual sex life. . . . Furthermore they have not got sex on the brain like the missionaries."[10] When Mary Austin learned that Burke favored the Maypole Dance as a "wholesome" substitute, she contemptuously pointed out that maypole ceremony was itself a relic of archaic fertility rites in Europe.

Pueblo leaders called another All Pueblo Council. They sent an appeal to Commissioner Burke: "We have inherited and kept pure for many ages a religion which, we are told, is full of beauty even to the white persons. To ourselves, at least, our religion is more precious than even our lives." The Pueblo leaders explained "One way of worshiping our God is by dancing and singing. . . . We do not hold or have any dances, races or other tribal customs merely for the fun there is in it. It all has a solemn meaning to us."

The appeal ended by asking Burke to rescind his orders, concluding: "There is no future for the race of the Indians if its religion is killed."[11]

The commissioner refused to budge.

John Collier paid scant attention to the brewing dance controversy, for he was distracted by a new crisis. The Bursum Bill had been replaced by a compromise authored by Senator Irvine Lenroot. The new bill promised nearly everything Collier had been seeking. Especially important, it guaranteed that New Mexico's crooked courts would not adjudicate the land claims. Instead, a three-person federally appointed tribunal would settle the cases.

Attorney Francis Wilson helped negotiate this compromise while Collier had been away from Washington, raising much-needed money in California. On only one point did Wilson fail. He agreed to waive all Native claims against long-tenured Hispanos, those families who'd lived alongside the Pueblos for generations, sometimes centuries. Among them were many citizens of the Hispano village of Taos, which was originally founded in 1615 on land that belonged to Taos Pueblo.

Yet when Collier learned of Wilson's concession, he became apoplectic. Unbeknownst to Wilson, Collier anticipated using the new bill as a means to help Taos Pueblo recover its sacred Blue Lake. His saw the Pueblo's historic claim to the city of Taos as valuable leverage. His plan was for Taos Pueblo to put up a fight for the city's land, and then ultimately agree to relinquish its claims in exchange for the return of Blue Lake. Now Wilson had given away that vital negotiating asset.

Collier, railing about Wilson's "treachery," returned to New Mexico and confronted the attorney in Santa Fe. Then he followed up with a blistering letter: "A fact which you seem not to realize any longer, or perhaps never realized vividly, may be called to your mind. The stake in this Pueblo struggle is the life or death of the Pueblo communities."[12]

Collier had no interest in Hispano welfare, caring only about justice for Indigenous people. If Hispanos suffered for that to happen, so be it. But attorney Wilson saw a more nuanced situation. Like many in Santa Fe, he was as sympathetic to New Mexico's venerable Hispano culture as he was to the Pueblo People. He had no intention of putting longtime Hispano families at risk. In this, Wilson was joined by the Santa Fe writers and artists who had organized to "Save the Pueblos" and founded the New Mexico Association on Indian Affairs.

The frustrated Wilson wrote to Collier: "Your egotism and supreme belief in your own infallibility, characteristic of people like you, is such as to make open minded discussion with you impossible."[13]

Collier then fired Wilson as the Pueblos' attorney and formed a new advocacy group, the American Indian Defense Association. Meanwhile, the Santa Feans continued to back Wilson. This set off a mad scramble as the opposing groups vied for Pueblo support. In August 1923, another All Pueblo council meeting was called. At issue was the Lenroot compromise bill, but the real choice was between Collier and Wilson. Once again, the delegates met at Santo Domingo Pueblo. Wilson was there, joined by other members of the New Mexico Association on Indian Affairs. Among them were Witter Bynner and Alice Corbin Henderson, two Santa Fe–based writers who had each helped lead the charge against the Bursum Bill. Taking the other side was John Collier, accompanied by Tony Luján and Mary Austin.

Mabel Dodge Luhan had friends on both sides. She stayed away.

When the meeting began, Collier stood and attacked Wilson for usurping his authority. He asked the Pueblos if they had ever granted Wilson the power to negotiate a compromise bill. The men responded, "We never did!"[14]

Collier, getting wound up, charged that Wilson had "gone over to the opposition."[15] He urged the Pueblos to reject any concessions and to demand full compensation for *all* land claims. Wilson and the other members of the New Mexico Association protested, but to no avail. The Pueblo delegates voted overwhelmingly to support Collier. With that, the losing side left the Pueblo.

Collier had alienated most of his white allies in Santa Fe, but thanks to the national reputation he'd built in defeating the Bursum Bill, his new organization, the American Indian Defense Association, soon boasted some 1,700 members across the country. He marshalled intense opposition to the Lenroot Bill, attacking it and Francis Wilson as mercilessly as he'd earlier gone after Albert Fall and the Bursum Bill.

In the end, Collier prevailed, defeating the Lenroot Compromise. In its place came the Pueblo Lands Act, of which he and the Pueblos approved. This new legislation included the provision Collier insisted on—full compensation for all Pueblo claims, including the entire Hispano village of Taos.

To Collier, the bruising fight with Wilson and the Santa Feans had been unfortunate, but ultimately necessary for justice to prevail. If he could win Blue Lake back for Taos Pueblo, all the lost friendships in the world would be worth it.

While Collier spent his time focused on political battles, Charles Burke and the missionaries expanded their campaign to drum up outrage over Pueblo dances. They recruited "progressive" Natives who had embraced Christianity and adopted white ways. One such ally was John Dixon of Cochiti Pueblo, who denounced those who "howl like coyotes in savage dances, jump up and down like madmen, have feathers and fuzz sticking out from the hind end of our pants, sing dirty, nasty songs, do many other things too vile to describe, too obscene to be permissible in Dante's inferno."[16]

No Pueblo seemed to rankle Commissioner Burke more than

Taos—known for its devotion to traditional culture along with its close ties to John Collier. The commissioner dispatched Matthew Sniffen from the Indian Rights Association to ramp up an investigation into Taos. Sniffen sought out Pueblo men who might denounce the native religion like John Dixon had done at Cochiti. One of those he interviewed was Manual Mondragón, a respected elder nearly sixty years old. Mondragón, also known as Sun Elk, had been Bert Phillips's friend and model many years earlier. Over time, Mondragón had curtailed his family's participation in tribal dances.

To Sniffen, Sun Elk complained that the time-consuming religious devotionals often interfered with academic progress, and he wanted his children to "compete with the white man." Sniffen pressed him to talk about the obscenity. Weren't the secret dances full of sexual depravity? Sun Elk responded, "I don't know of any immorality connected with them."[17]

Sniffen ended the interview, disappointed. But in the manner of a visiting anthropologist, he kept poking around Taos Pueblo until he eventually found what he wanted to hear. He resurrected the bogus charge of human sacrifices, claiming that Taos Pueblo slaughtered two boys every four years "as a sacrifice to the Water God."[18] But even more important from his perspective, Sniffen finally uncovered what he believed to be the deepest, darkest evil at the heart of Taos Pueblo's holiest religious ritual: The annual pilgrimage to Blue Lake was in actuality a gathering for a tribal orgy.

Missionaries and Indian agents had long spread fantastic rumors about Blue Lake. To their minds, something so secretive must by necessity conceal great perversity. Pussyfoot Johnson, the former Chief Special Officer for the Indian Bureau, had blustered that Pueblo "boys and girls are stripped naked and herded together entirely nude and encouraged to do the very worst that vileness can suggest."[19]

Even members of the Taos art colony were taken in by rampant gossip about Blue Lake. One was Blanche Chloe Grant, a recent arrival who published a book on Taos Pueblo. In it, Grant claimed that the ceremony amounted to ritualized sexual assault: "Girls and childless women are forced to go to the mountain" she wrote, where they must "submit to this ceremony imposed upon them by the older men." Grant quoted a local Anglo who said, "with a sorry shake of his head, 'I have seen the girls come back looking like wilted flowers.'"[20]

In truth, many people from Taos Pueblo returned from Blue Lake physically drained, for they'd made a four-day, fifty-mile round-trip journey through rugged mountain terrain while participating in ceremonies that included all-night dancing and singing. Taos Pueblo's most holy gathering was not a tribal orgy, nor a pedophilic deflowering ritual, but rather the culmination of strict religious training for young men at the Pueblo.

For centuries, Taos elders had identified future leaders during childhood. These boys underwent a rigorous program that could last as long as eighteen months. They were taken away from their family and friends to live in an underground kiva. Religious leaders instructed them, teaching them the history of their people and the uses of various plants for healing. The pupils were required to memorize intricate religious instructions word for word and in exact order—up to eighteen thousand words in all. They underwent difficult endurance rituals and other physical challenges. At the end of their training, these boys emerged from underground to be reborn as young men and future tribal leaders—with the final crowning ceremonies taking place at Blue Lake in August.

In Spring 1924, Taos Pueblo requested permission to temporarily withdraw two boys, aged nine and twelve, from the Indian Bureau's local school for this religious training. In years past, such requests had been routinely honored and the children resumed their school studies after kiva training was completed.

This time, Commissioner Burke was in no mood to be conciliatory. His Pueblo superintendent advised that granting the Taos' request would "almost mean a surrender of our attempt to educate these Pueblos in our Christian civilization." Burke agreed that the time had come to "give the Taos Indians a lesson, that sooner or later the Pueblos have got to learn."[21] He notified Taos leaders that the boys could only miss two weeks of school.

Tribal leaders duly removed the children from the classroom. After two weeks passed the boys remained absent. Taos Pueblo had no intention of surrendering.

A standoff ensued as missionary activist Pussyfoot Johnson railed against the Pueblo. Certain that the Taos Peoples' religion was based on perverted sexual practices, Pussyfoot stoked widespread outrage, charging that the two boys were being kept out of school for "a two year course in sodomy."[22]

Commissioner Burke then decided to go to Taos and confront the Pueblo directly. Interior Secretary Hubert Work, who had replaced Albert B. Fall, was reported to be incensed by the charges against Taos Pueblo. He agreed to join Commissioner Burke for the showdown in Taos.

CHAPTER 17

SUPERSTITIONS

1924–1925

APRIL 17, 1924

On this Thursday before Easter, an icy blast of winter greeted Indian Commissioner Burke and Interior Secretary Hubert Work as their government sedan steered toward Taos. Traveling with them were other Bureau employees along with the author of the Bursum Bill, Colonel Ralph Emerson Twitchell. Their announced intention was an "inspection tour" of Taos Pueblo.

The men reached town at dusk and took rooms at the Columbian Hotel, a low-slung adobe on the plaza. The fledgling Taos Chamber of Commerce had arranged a banquet in honor of the visiting dignitaries. Before the dinner, the men went to observe the Holy Thursday ceremony in the city, joining hundreds of others who lined the streets in the bitter cold. At the head of the procession, a man held aloft a large cross adorned with a blood-streaked Christ. Parading behind him was a long line of pious men, their heads bowed, carrying lanterns and torches. These were the Penitentes. Tomorrow, on Good Friday, the Hermanos de Sangre would retreat into the mountains to carry out their secret ceremonies to honor Christ's martyrdom.

Over at Taos Pueblo, the Easter season meant something very different. The Natives weren't immune to the drama of Christ's suffering, but more important was the fact that growing season had arrived. Instead of fasting or lashing themselves, the Puebloans kept busy cleaning out irrigation ditches. On the Saturday before Easter, everyone would gather to help clear the village of invasive weeds. In the days to follow, a ceremonial dance would be staged to welcome the sprouting corn.

On the morning of Good Friday, the US government officials motored into the Pueblo, proceeding directly to the small, wood-plank schoolhouse where the Taos Tribal Council awaited. The Puebloans had been barred from having any outside representatives on hand for this showdown.

Introductions were made amid grim handshakes. Then Interior Secretary Hubert Work began his remarks. Work, a medical doctor and a devout Christian, was as honest as Albert Fall had been corrupt. Dr. Work had little sympathy for Native cultures, but he did possess a sincere desire to combat infectious diseases such as tuberculosis that ravaged many Indigenous communities. He vowed "energetic action"[1] to improve Native health and welfare. The Taos men remained unmoved. They had heard such promises before.

Then Commissioner Burke came to the front of the room, pacing the floor and staring at the Taos leaders. An interpreter translated Burke's words into Spanish, but there was no softening its content. He complained that the Taos artists and bohemians were harming the Puebloans by encouraging their outdated tribal traditions. He demanded that the men stop consorting with such immoral influences.

Burke then pivoted into an attack on the Pueblo's religion. Native religious ceremonies took up too much valuable time, he declared. Time that could be better spent plowing fields. As his harangue continued, Governor Tony Romero spoke up to defend the Pueblo. Burke snapped at him: "I don't want to hear what you have to say. You have nothing to say. You do what I tell you."[2]

Then the commissioner issued his demand: Those two boys who'd been removed from school for kiva training had to be back in the classroom by next Monday. If not, the Indian Bureau would file criminal charges against every Taos tribal leader. All of them would go to jail. To back up his threat, Burke began citing cases of other Natives who'd been imprisoned for years after violating such government orders.

The men in the schoolhouse grew restive, muttering among themselves. Interior Secretary Hubert Work rose and stood by Burke's side. The Secretary had expected submission from these people, not defiance. His temper flared. He denounced the Pueblo's cacique, its religious leader, Justo Concha, calling him a "pagan dictator." He said the Taos People had no legal right to indoctrinate their children in "pagan rites." Then Work issued a threat. If the tribal council refused to follow orders, he would see that Taos Pueblo was dissolved, terminated by the US government. How would they like it, he asked, if they were turned over as private citizens to the state of New Mexico?[3]

The muttering among the Taos men grew louder. The Interior Secretary raised his own voice in response. "The artists [would] rather see you wild, like an animal, so that they could get better material." Work was practically shouting now. The Taos People, he bellowed, were "half-animal."[4]

The room fell silent. The government officials left without shaking hands.

As word spread in Taos about the encounter, the artists sprang into action. Bert Phillips, Ernest Blumenschein, and Walter Ufer collected statements from witnesses to turn over to John Collier's American Indian Defense Association. Mabel Dodge Luhan sent off telegrams to Collier on the West Coast, and he quickly returned to Taos to help organize the resistance.

Taos Pueblo soon drafted a letter to Commissioner Burke, defending its beliefs: "This religion is many thousands of years old among our people and is more important to each one of us than money, horses, land or anything else in the world. It teaches us about God and the earth and about our duty to God, to earth and to one another."

The Taos leaders pledged, "We shall not offer any violent resistance because we have always been peaceful." Yet they vowed to defy the

Indian Bureau: "We cannot comply with this order, no matter what the penalty may be, because this order would violate our religion and also destroy it."[5]

They warned Burke to expect a new publicity campaign and reminded him of the successful fight to defeat the Bursum Bill: "Will the American people not come to our rescue now, when it is proposed to take away our very souls?"[6]

The letter was signed by the governor and twenty-eight other tribal leaders. But Commissioner Burke saw it as the work of one man—John Collier. He sought a federal injunction against Collier, aiming to banish the activist from any tribal lands to keep him from "exciting insurrection as he has done on other occasions."[7]

The fiery Collier was positively gleeful at the prospect of battling Burke on the issue of religious freedom. He considered the commissioner a "damfool" who'd played right into the reformers' hands. As Collier saw it, Burke's dictatorial overreach promised to galvanize even more broad-based support for Native rights, thus emboldening his larger campaign.

Collier and Tony Luján helped whip up fresh opposition from the All Pueblo Council. While Tony wasn't allowed to participate in religious ceremonies, his value as a political asset kept him on the Pueblo's ruling council. While he and Collier worked together, Mabel Dodge Luhan again lobbied influential writers and editors. Many of the Santa Fe-based Pueblo advocates, setting aside their differences with Collier for the moment, also joined the new cause. In New York, Mary Austin threw herself into the battle, rounding up support from national experts on Indigenous matters who condemned the Secret Dance File as "the grossest misinformation." The *New York Times* and other papers ran editorials lambasting Burke's "grossly unjust" crusade.[8] Meanwhile, the commissioner's plan to ban Collier from the Pueblos collapsed after government attorneys informed him the directive would never hold up in court.

The testimonials from the nation's leading authorities got the attention of Interior Secretary Hubert Work. He, too, was a man of science and he was greatly displeased to learn that he'd been bamboozled by missionary propaganda. Dr. Work also kept an eye on the political winds. Originally appointed by the anti-Native Harding, he was now serving under Calvin

Coolidge, who harbored mild sympathy for Indigenous people. Work's support for Burke's inquisition faded.

The Indian Commissioner backpedaled. He conceded that his earlier threats to jail Taos Pueblo's leaders were "seized by our critics . . . to bring about an embarrassing situation." He notified Bureau employees, "The time has arrived when the Indians must be dealt with in a manner different from that of twenty years ago."[9]

Finally, Burke announced that he had never actually "ordered" Taos Pueblo to return its children to school, insisting that he had merely "requested" such an action. He claimed that the entire affair had been "a tempest in a teapot which could have been amicably settled without Collier."[10]

The high-profile battles to protect Pueblo lands and religion added new luster to Taos's growing mystique. Mabel's compound in Taos attracted a constant swirl of artists, writers, and Greenwich Village bohemians. Although Prohibition remained in full force, the parties flowed freely at Los Gallos. The favored cocktail was orange juice mixed with Taos Lightning. Some of the more adventurous guests also dabbled in peyote, although Mabel remained opposed—and made sure her husband stayed away from it, too.

In the spring of 1924, D. H. and Frieda Lawrence returned to Taos, taking up residence in one of Mabel's guest houses. The famous author had made amends with Mabel by letter. "Yes, I was pretty angry," he wrote to her from Mexico. "But now let us forget it. At least I will forget, forget the bad part. Because also I have some beautiful memories of Taos."[11]

Yet before long Lawrence was clashing with Mabel again. He particularly despised how she extolled Taos Pueblo as a model society while in the next breath issuing sharp orders to her Native servants. Lawrence suggested she couldn't be fully liberated until she learned how to bake her own bread and get down on her knees to scrub floors.

Mabel had no interest in common housework. Instead, she had begun writing her autobiography on the advice of her therapist. During one evening gathering, she had a friend read aloud passages from her memoir-in-progress. Lawrence listened, glowering. When Mabel asked him what she should do with the manuscript, he snarled, "Take a boat out to the middle of the Atlantic and sink it."[12]

Later, he lashed out at her: "Well, I can't stand a certain way you walk."

"Oh, oh," she cried, sobbing, "You want to *kill* me, that's what you want!"

"No—o," he replied, in a hesitating voice. "Not exactly."[13]

Despite the rancor, or perhaps because of it, Lawrence was writing prolifically in Taos. Mabel didn't wish to see him leave, especially under bad terms again. "The genius is there," she told a friend, "buried under the small meannesses, & the unhappiness & the conflicts."[14]

Wanting to keep him around but knowing it was impossible for them to live near each other, she decided to give the Lawrences her 160-acre Kiowa Ranch, located about twenty miles north of Taos. The proud author would not accept such a gift, but Frieda worked out a solution. She pressed a box into Mabel's hands. Inside was a manuscript draft of Lawrence's early novel, *Sons and Lovers*, written in the author's neat, exacting hand. In return, Mabel gave Frieda the deed to the ranch.

Mabel considered Lawrence's book a masterpiece, but she was never sure what to do with the manuscript. Finally, when her psychoanalyst in New York presented her with a large bill, she handed over the stack of papers as payment.[15]

One of Mabel's new guests was a bohemian intellectual she and Tony had met from California. Jaime de Angulo, with his long, kinky hair and rope-soled sandals was the sort of free-spirited soul who gave Indian Commissioner Charles Burke nightmares. The peripatetic de Angulo had earned a medical degree but also pursued a range of eclectic interests: anthropology, linguistics, and astronomy, among them. Most notably, he had studied with the world-famous psychologist Carl Jung in Zurich. He believed that Jung's developing theory of a collective unconscious might have natural affinities with Native American religious beliefs.

In Taos, de Angulo appreciated Mabel's generous hospitality, though he noted, "in a subtle way she manages to impose her will on everyone." He gravitated more toward Tony Luján, with whom he developed a strong bond. Tony, for his part, seemed to appreciate that de Angulo didn't require a constant buzz of conversation and he never pestered people with questions. One of Tony's tasks was to escort the flocks of Mabel's guests to tour Taos Pueblo, but with de Angulo he made sure it was just the two of them who went together. At the Pueblo, the outsider could see that, while Tony still had many friends and seemed to feel at home, his banishment from tribal religious ceremonies "hangs over him like a black cloud."[16]

Through Tony, de Angulo met an impressive young Pueblo leader named Antonio Mirabal. The slightly built Mirabal was known to be an exceptionally strong-willed person. As a child he'd only had a few months of schooling, but he went on to become proficient in English by tenaciously studying a secondhand dictionary. Now a voracious reader, he subscribed to a range of contemporary publications, becoming one of the Pueblo's best-informed men about the outside world. Mirabal often impressed Anglos with his bristling intelligence and his fluid ability to converse in English. One of John Collier's associates, intending to compliment

Figure 28. Antonio Mirabal, ca. 1920s. Courtesy of the Palace of the Governors Photo Archives (NMHM/DCA), Negative Number: 043705.

Mirabal, exclaimed that he spoke "with perfect clarity just as a white man might."[17]

Despite his seeming comfort with whites, Mirabal remained intensely devoted to Taos Pueblo's traditional culture. His Native name, translated as Mountain Lake, was itself an homage to the Pueblo's sacred Blue Lake. Mirabal's range of abilities, combined with his assertive personality, helped him emerge as a tribal leader despite his relative youth. Only in his thirties, he'd already been elected Taos Pueblo's lieutenant governor.

Mirabal and Jaime de Angulo quickly hit it off. Among de Angulo's many current projects was an ongoing linguistic study of various Native Peoples, research funded in part by his mentor, Carl Jung. He and Mirabal soon agreed to cooperate on an analysis of Taos Pueblo's language, carefully conducted to safeguard privileged tribal information.

The two men spent several weeks working together, developing a warm intellectual rapport that extended well beyond linguistics. Eventually, de

Figure 29. Carl Jung, ca. 1935. ETH-Bibliothek Zürich, Bildarchiv © Wikimedia/Creative Commons.

Angulo returned to Berkeley to write up his report. It was there, on New Year's Day, 1925, that he received a surprise telegram from Carl Jung.

The Swiss psychologist was on a whirlwind tour of the United States and had arrived in New York three days before Christmas. Ironically, Mabel Dodge Luhan was in New York at the very same time, visiting her Freudian analyst. From New York, Jung traveled west by train in the company of two wealthy benefactors: Fowler McCormick, who was John D. Rockefeller's grandson, and George Porter, heir to a Chicago railroad fortune. The group arrived at the Grand Canyon on New Year's Day. Jung enjoyed the scenery, but above all he desired to see some Native Americans. He knew just the man to ask.

Jaime de Angulo raced to meet Jung and the others at the Grand Canyon. He wrote to Mabel and Tony, "You can imagine my excitement. I made up my mind that I would kidnap him if necessary and take him to Taos."[18]

Jung's millionaire companions expressed doubts about de Angulo's idea for Jung to visit Taos Pueblo. There was no train to Taos, and the great man's time in the United States was very limited. But de Angulo kept insisting. Finally, the foursome took to the road in a rented Chevrolet. De Angulo wired ahead to let Antonio Mirabal know that he was coming with Jung. Mirabal understood the stakes. He would have a unique opportunity to possibly influence one of the greatest thinkers that European civilization had produced.

On January 6, de Angulo brought Jung and the others to Taos Pueblo. They arrived just in time for the Buffalo Dance. Jung, a burly man nearly fifty years old, wore round wire spectacles and had a bushy gray moustache. He and the other visitors were bundled against the cold in heavy overcoats. To the thumping heartbeat of the drums, they watched as dozens of Taos men filed into the plaza, each outfitted as a buffalo. In years past, the dancers wore actual bison heads, which had been skinned and cured for ceremonial use. But as the buffalo disappeared, the Taos People had to adapt. Now they wore imitation heads made of cow horns and leftover bear fur.

The costumes may have lost their authenticity, but there was no mistaking the power of the mythology on display. As Jung watched the dance, he saw a people "much nearer to the primal vitality, the archetypal world of the unconscious."[19]

After the ceremony, Mirabal led the psychologist up a series of ladders until they reached the top of the Pueblo, five stories above the ground. Here they held a commanding view of the village and surrounding mountains. Above, the blazing sun helped warm them in the frosty air. Then they began an extended conversation.

Jung grasped that Mirabal was shrewd, but he had no idea how well prepared this Taos man was to receive him. They began speaking of the differences between white men and Indigenous people. Mirabal talked about how "the whites always want something; they are always uneasy and restless. We do not know what they want. We do not understand him. We think they are mad."

Jung asked him why they struck him as mad.

"They say they think with their heads," he replied.

"What do you think with?" Jung asked.

"We think here," Mirabal said, pointing to his heart.[20]

With that, Jung fell into a long meditation as Mirabal sat quietly beside him.

As the sun rose higher, Mirabal pointed to the sky: "Is not he who moves there our father? How can anyone say differently? How can there be another god? Nothing can be without the sun."

Jung, thinking of Western religious traditions that had separated God from nature, asked whether the sun might simply be "a fiery ball shaped by an invisible god."

Mirabal had little regard for such distinctions. He replied, "The sun is God. Everyone can see that."

The Taos man began speaking about the attacks on the Pueblo religion. "Why do the Americans not let us alone? Why do they want to forbid our dances? Why do they make difficulties when we want to take our young people from school in order to lead them in the kiva? We do nothing to harm the Americans!"

He told Jung, "What we do, we do not only for ourselves but for the Americans also. Yes, we do it for the whole world. Everyone benefits by it."

Jung realized that Mirabal, who had made it clear he would never reveal any tenets of the Pueblo's religion, was now prepared to at least discuss its significance. The psychologist asked, "You think, then, that what you do in your religion benefits the whole world?"

Mirabal replied, "Of course. If we did not do it, what would become of the world?" He pointed to the sun. "We are a people who live on the roof of the world; we are the sons of the Father Sun, and with our religion we daily help our father to go across the sky. We do this not only for ourselves, but for the whole world. If we were to cease practicing our religion, in ten years' time the sun would no longer rise. Then it would be night forever."[21]

As Jung considered what had just been revealed to him, he began to realize that the West's dismissiveness of Native "superstitions" had everything backward. Scientifically speaking, the Taos People's belief that the sun was the source of all life was far more rational than a virgin mother giving birth to a demigod who demanded belief in his existence as the primary qualification for heavenly salvation. Yet the whites arrogantly presumed "that Christianity is the only truth."[22]

Superstitions were in the eye of the beholder. "Out of sheer envy we are obliged to smile at the Indians' naiveté and to plume ourselves on our cleverness," Jung decided. "For otherwise we would discover how impoverished and down at the heels we are." As the psychologist saw it, the Taos People had successfully resolved humanity's chief concern: "Am I related to something infinite or not?" The Indians' "tranquil composure," he judged, came from a life that is "cosmologically meaningful."[23]

The Swiss psychologist returned to Taos the following day. He stood by the small, icy river, the Río Pueblo de Taos, which flowed down from Blue Lake and ran through the middle of the Pueblo. Suddenly he heard a man's deep voice, "vibrant with suppressed emotion," speaking to him from behind: "Do you think that all life comes from the mountain?"[24]

Jung turned to see an old Taos man. He had no idea who this gentleman might be, but he understood that he was being asked to consider a profound question. Jung thought about what Mirabal had said about the sun, and he looked at the ice-crusted river, its mountain waters slipping past him. He had heard about the Puebloans' sacred lake, and he was aware of their annual pilgrimage. He looked at the Taos man and replied, "Everyone can see that you speak the truth."[25]

~

Carl Jung, like many outsiders, viewed the Pueblo People as living in harmonious splendor. Yet divisions and factions existed at all Pueblos, just as in every human society. The increasing pressures of modernization were only making things worse. Almost every Pueblo was ensnared in conflict as pro-assimilationist, Christianized "progressives" challenged the resolute traditionalists who favored the old ways. The situation at Taos was different, for there were relatively few Christian progressives. Instead, Taos Pueblo's rebellious minority had become the peyote-using members of the Native American Church.

The "Peyote Boys," as they were called, were often those who'd gone off to boarding schools. They'd come home more Americanized and more independent. They continued to participate in the Pueblo's communal ceremonies while also seeking out the more individualized religious experience provided by peyote.

For years, Taos's tribal elders had harassed peyote users, raiding ceremonies and stripping away kiva memberships. Still the movement endured and kept gaining more followers. As their numbers grew, the Peyotists increasingly confronted the tribal leadership.

In early 1925, just a few weeks after Carl Jung's visit, two young Taos peyotists appeared at a ceremonial dance. One was José Sandoval. The other was Juan Gómez, whose father, Geronimo Gómez—Star Road—had earlier posed for Ernest Blumenschein's painting depicting the coming ascendency of the peyote movement. In a direct challenge to the Pueblo's religious leaders, Sandoval and Gómez refused to conform to the required traditional regalia. Instead, they wore jeans and boots. The council swiftly decreed its punishment: the men could pay a one-dollar fine or be subjected to lashes on the back.[26]

In the old days, public whippings had been a common way of enforcing order in the Pueblo. It was nearly unheard of in modern times. The two Peyote Boys chose the lash. They wanted to dramatize the injustice.

On the appointed day, Sandoval and Gómez reported to the governor's quarters to receive their punishment. Lieutenant Governor Antonio Mirabal raised the leather bridle and applied the strokes.

The Peyotists immediately filed a complaint with the Indian Bureau. They pointed out that Taos Pueblo's tribal council had made much-publicized appeals for religious freedom but were now denying those same freedoms to their own people.

Commissioner Burke was hardly sympathetic to peyote use. Yet the prospect of punishing Taos Pueblo's leaders proved irresistible. Burke waited until mid-August, when everyone at Taos Pueblo, including the Peyotists, was preparing for the upcoming pilgrimage to Blue Lake. On August 14, government cars squealed into the Pueblo, raising clouds of dust. Armed agents from the Indian Bureau poured out of the vehicles, looking for members of the ruling council. When they found the governor, Guadalupe Lucero, they handcuffed him. Lieutenant Governor Antonio Mirabal was also taken into custody along with seven others. All nine men were chained together, like animals, and driven to jail in Santa Fe. Bond was set at $500 each, more than ten times each man's annual income.

None of the Taos leaders would spend a night behind bars. Mabel Dodge Luhan immediately provided the bail money, and John Collier's American Indian Defense Association dispatched attorneys to argue their case. The judge in Santa Fe was not impressed with the Indian Bureau's overzealous actions. He ruled, "The Pueblo Indian chieftains have the right to regulate tribal customs, costumes, and affairs." Then he said, "Take these men home."[27]

CHAPTER 18

MABELTOWN

1925–1926

Mabel knew that D. H. Lawrence was busy writing, but she didn't realize exactly what he was up to until he sent her the pages of a new story. Titled "The Woman Who Rode Away," it described a ridiculous, wealthy woman who becomes obsessed by a sun-worshipping Native tribe. Lawrence wrote: "She felt it was her destiny to wander into the secret haunts of these timeless, mysterious, marvellous Indians of the mountains."[1]

In the story, the woman learns that the Natives she admires have been losing power to white invaders. There was only one way to change course and save the tribe. "When a white woman sacrifice[s] herself to our gods," a Native man tells her, "then our gods will begin to make the world again, and the white man's gods will fall to pieces."

As Mabel read on in horror, Lawrence's tale came to its inevitable conclusion. On the day of the Winter Solstice, the tribe's aged cacique, "naked and in a state of barbaric ecstasy," presides over the ceremony as the Natives cut out the white woman's heart and offer it to their sun god.[2]

Lawrence, unable to destroy Mabel in person, had done so on the page. And while living at the ranch she'd given him.

"It is D. H. who is evil at times, witchlike & full of hate!" Mabel railed. "As for opposition!!! He dies of opposition."[3]

Lawrence, in fact, nearly died soon after finishing the story. He journeyed back to Mexico and became sick with malaria in Oaxaca. When his condition worsened, the gravely ill author was taken to Mexico City. A chest X-ray revealed that he was suffering from advanced tuberculosis. The doctor gave him "a year or two at the most."[4] He and Frieda retreated to their New Mexico ranch and its high, dry air. He avoided Mabel—and Taos, which he derided as "Mabeltown."

Mabel was finally ready to admit that bringing Lawrence to New Mexico had been a failure. Still, she continued to believe that other evolved minds could readily appreciate Taos's cosmic significance. She published a new appeal, "A Bridge Between Cultures," in a highbrow arts magazine. "The life force is at high tide in the idealists," she intoned. She called on America's most ambitious artists to reject the chains of New York and come west to "that land of crystal space, among the higher altitudes." In Taos, she prophesied, they might "develop art that would draw the world to them."[5]

The "movers and shakers" kept coming and Mabel's sprawling estate became overrun with painters, poets, journalists, feminists, social reformers, and various hangers-on. People who were "a little different from the horde," Mabel boasted. She described them as "the great and the semi-great and the lovers of the great. They had a deeper awareness, more capacity, a larger dimension. Potentiality."[6]

Not everyone agreed. "It's a queer mix-up of artists and would-be artists and Indians," observed Jaime de Angulo, who had brought Carl Jung to Taos. To de Angulo, Mabel's visitors weren't pursuing spiritual renewal or social change. Instead, the picturesque locale simply provided a fresh stage for the same old diversions: "Here they are, talking about the grandeur of the landscape, so immense and bare. And straightaway they proceed to put frills and laces on it with their chatter, their bric-a-brac, their picnics, their rushing about on horseback rides, gossiping, painting, talking of the wonderful Indian and in their heart laughing at his superstition—and every last one of them believes in chiropractics!"[7]

In the evenings, the guests at Mabel's gathered around the piano to sing popular songs. Sometimes they played mah-jongg or charades. Mabel often hired dancers from the Pueblo to provide entertainment while Tony thumped his drum and sang. Mabel's husband was always happy to make music, but he had little interest in the ongoing parties and hours of aimless conversation. On many nights when the revelry filled Mabel's great room, voices raising higher and higher as the Taos Lightning took hold, Tony could be found slumped over in his wingback chair, fast asleep. "They talk and talk and talk," he confided to de Angulo. "And the more they talk, the harder I sleep."[8]

Mabel's high-profile marriage to Tony was crucial in attracting cultural luminaries to Taos, yet many onlookers struggled to make sense of their relationship. Everyone could see how handsome and well-built Tony was, but his interests were practical and he possessed none of the intellectual vitality that Mabel clearly craved. Mabel explained to anyone who would listen that Tony was her rock in life. She credited him for having "awakened my heart & my altruism & who had kept it alive so that it is alive for good."[9]

Still, many who knew Mabel kept questioning her marriage—and more than a few were known to ridicule it. Mary Austin, with withering candor, informed Mabel that few in their social circle had "ever treated Tony with respect." She added, "I should explicitly tell you that not only is he a

Figure 30. Mabel Dodge Luhan and Tony Luján. Photograph by Carl Van Vechten, 1934. Mabel Dodge Luhan Papers. Yale Collection of American Literature, Beinecke Rare Book and Manuscript Library. © Van Vechten Trust.

joke,—a good natured and occasionally ribald joke—but still a joke to most people who come to your house." In a moment of self-pity, Mabel wrote a poem, "Inevitable," in which she mourned "What incomprehensible aloneness for the white woman / Who crossed over into the Indian heart."[10]

Mabel and Tony's marriage was difficult to maintain under the best of circumstances. He had sacrificed so much, including his religion, to be with her. Mabel's family back east, including her son and her mother, remained dismayed by her decision to marry him. Their symbolic union, that living "bridge between cultures," often seemed on the verge of collapse. The problem wasn't so much their different cultures as a deeper quality Mabel and Tony shared: neither was particularly well-suited for monogamy.

Mabel had always been drawn to younger men, and her passions ripened as she aged. Nearing fifty, she engaged in numerous flirtations. The young Taos Pueblo men employed as her servants were not immune from her advances. Mabel was also attracted to Eastern artistic types, and in New York she openly consorted with an ambitious young writer, denounced as a "callow youth"[11] by one of her literary friends. More consequentially, she became infatuated with the magnetically dashing Jean Toomer, whose book *Cane* helped spark the Harlem Renaissance. Though Toomer was sixteen years younger, Mabel pursued him with reckless abandon, driving Tony mad. Toomer deftly resisted committing to Mabel while simultaneously soliciting $14,000 (more than $200,000 in today's dollars) from her, ostensibly as a loan to establish a new spiritual center in Taos. Toomer's mesmerizing spell over Mabel broke only when she realized there would be no center and she would never see her money again.

Tony Luján, meanwhile, enjoyed romantic liaisons with many of Mabel's female guests, who he viewed as "fresh fruit." In addition, he kept long-running mistresses in Taos and he also returned to the Pueblo to sleep with his first wife whenever Mabel went away. Mabel often suffered from crushing jealousy, even as she conceded her inability to prevent such liaisons. "He's so attractive to women & women to him there is always something in the air!"[12]

Mabel portrayed Taos as a Shangri-la to outsiders, but in reality the small village remained a work in progress. Almost everyone in town used outhouses, and many peoples' water wells had become polluted. Creaky wooden wagons wheeled in fresh spring water from farther up Taos Cañon. Locally hunted rabbits were the major source of fresh, unspoiled meat. Milk and vegetables—when available—were delivered by horse and buggy from surrounding farms. Convicts had built a new highway from Santa Fe, but local roads turned to mud every spring. Electricity had finally arrived, but only in the form of gasoline-powered generators. Each evening, as darkness fell, the quiet was broken by the sputtering sounds of machines rumbling to life.

Mabel believed that if Taos was to stage a great American revival, improvements were necessary. She couldn't do much about the endemic poverty, but she sought to smooth some of the town's rougher edges. One problem that caught her eye was the growing pile of discarded tin cans alongside the highway approaching Taos. No one knew who'd started this informal dump, which had grown into a rusting hill, but it hardly presented an inspiring welcome. Mabel launched a campaign to remove the eyesore, organizing a "Tin Can Dance." She recruited local artists to create posters promoting the community-wide event. Art pieces made from tin cans were auctioned off, and enough funds were raised to finally clean up the dump.

"It would be nice in a way to keep lovely Taos hidden away in her verdant mountain valley," the *Santa Fe New Mexican* opined in the summer of 1925. "Difficult of access, a prize you have to work for."[13] But the enthusiastic publicity Mabel helped to inspire attracted increasing throngs of visitors. In 1926, the Fred Harvey Company moved to capitalize on the opportunity. Over the decades, Harvey Houses had become synonymous with the Santa Fe Railway's tourism campaign. Its hotels were clean and comfortable, and the famed "Harvey Girls" served as well-trained, knowledgeable guides. Taos, inaccessible by rail, had previously been beyond the reach of the Harvey empire. But now, with highways supplanting rail lines, chartered bus tours began rumbling into Taos.

These "Indian Detours," Harvey promised, were "The newest way to see the oldest America."[14] For prices beginning at fifty dollars ($750 today), sightseers received a three-day tour aboard a company bus, guided by bright young women. In years past, the Harvey Girls resembled Puritan maidens with their long black dresses and starched white aprons. Now, they were outfitted in the Native-bohemian style. Draped in turquoise jewelry and wearing loose-fitting Navajo blouses and silver concho belts, they looked as though they'd just wandered over from Mabel Dodge Luhan's compound.

These employees treated their customers "not as tourists to be bundled about," the Harvey corporation pledged, "but as part of a little group off on a private exploration where one of the party knows and loves the country and is going to do her utmost to make you revel in every hour you spend in it."[15]

Upon arriving in Taos, travelers were escorted to see the famous painters working in their studios. Few visitors were able to pay several hundred dollars for large, museum-quality paintings, so the artists adapted. Each began making what they called "suitcase paintings:" small, quickly executed works designed for the tourist trade. Not every artist appreciated the interruptions. Walter Ufer was known to hang a sign on his studio door when he wanted to be left alone: KEEP OUT, TNT EXPLOSIVE.

Venerable Taos Pueblo was the main attraction. People at the Pueblo were also adapting to the tourist boom. Some turned their homes into part-time curio shops, selling drums and bows- and arrows. Others performed, for a fee, the new-fangled hoop dance, a vaudevillian display that quickly caught on as a prize attraction. The Pueblo also boasted a well-known artist, Albert Looking Elk, who'd been inspired by the Taos art colony and made his own plein air paintings of the Pueblo. Whenever the tour buses arrived, Looking Elk could be seen standing before his easel, selling paintings along with photo postcards of himself.

Amid the growing commercial clamor, one of the Pueblo's young entrepreneurs, Albert Luján, suggested to the governing council that they could begin charging each visitor a dollar to enter the Pueblo. Most of the tribal elders were devoted farmers and held old-fashioned views. They did not believe for a moment that anyone would pay a dollar simply to walk on to the Pueblo's grounds. Luján kept asking. Finally, he was granted permission to try his plan for a week. After the seventh day, he reported back to the council and dumped a bag full of cash onto a table. After that, entrance fees at Taos Pueblo became standard.

Even as Taos gained mass appeal as a tourist destination, Mabel kept insisting that the Puebloans offered a spiritual model capable of radically transforming America. She and others in her elite circle imagined themselves to possess an enlightened, special kinship with the Taos People. But as thousands of middle Americans began descending on the Pueblo in smoke-belching buses, it was hard to ignore the fact that the only utopia being created was for sightseers. The incoming hordes didn't give a damn about sacred, timeless knowledge. Instead, they wanted to see a hoop dance. As one of Mabel's allies from the Bursum Bill fight archly observed, "So we've saved the pueblos for Fred Harvey."[16]

CHAPTER 19

THE DOUBLE CROSS

1926

AUGUST 23, 1926

Slouched in the saddle of the horse he'd borrowed from Taos Pueblo, the bespectacled John Collier looked something like a cowboy professor. Alongside him, mounted on a trim white pony, was Antonio Mirabal, the strong-willed tribal leader who'd earlier parleyed with Carl Jung. The animals were loaded with food and camping supplies. It had rained earlier in the day, and the clean scent of sagebrush wafted in on the fresh breeze. Up ahead, the riverside trail disappeared into the dark woods.

Earlier in the day, hundreds of people from Taos Pueblo had followed this route—men, women, entire families. Some were on horses while many others chose to walk. The difficult journey would cover twenty-four miles and take two days. The pilgrims' destination was Blue Lake.

No white man had ever been permitted to witness Taos Pueblo's most holy and secretive religious ceremony. Now, John Collier was set to become the first.

Collier's presence on this trip had everything to do with Charles Burke and the Indian Bureau. The commissioner had developed a seeming pathological hatred of Taos Pueblo. Last year he'd arrested nine Taos leaders on the eve of the Blue Lake rites. With summer approaching again, Burke renewed his charges of obscenity and spoke darkly of retribution. Pueblo leaders worried that he would find a pretext to disrupt or even use force to try and stop their religious pilgrimage.

After much discussion, Taos leaders decided to take an unprecedented step. They invited Collier and another white man to accompany them to Blue Lake, believing that the presence of prominent outsiders would deter any government interference. The tradition-breaking decision was not made easily, and many at the Pueblo remained opposed.

On the morning of the journey, the people at Taos Pueblo washed their hair with river water and yucca blossoms. The men twisted their long ponytails into chignon buns, and women arranged their hair into two side whorls. Everyone wore their best turquoise and silver and packed their finest clothing for the trip, vintage garments and accessories handed down for generations.

Collier was told to remain behind as the main body of travelers departed. With him was James Webb Young, an advertising executive and wealthy benefactor of Collier's American Indian Defense Association. Young had not been Collier's first choice, but others he had approached, including two US senators, had turned him down. Still, Young was a powerfully connected public relations genius. Collier knew he would be a perfect foil should Commissioner Burke try to interfere.

After waiting several hours at the Pueblo, Antonio Mirabal and another man finally led the two whites on to the trail. Collier did his best to remain composed, but the magnitude of the occasion was overwhelming. Just as the Taos People worshipped nature, he in turn worshipped the Taos People. "They are the expression," he thought, "perhaps the last expression in this, our modern world, of the unifying import of the common source and common destiny of life."[1] To be granted access to their most holy religious ritual was an honor beyond measure.

As the men climbed higher into the mountains, a light rain began to fall. Once the sun set, the skies cleared and a full moon rose. The forest path was dim, but the horses knew the route well. Finally, near midnight, Collier could see the glow of campfires ahead.

In a large grassy meadow where bison once foraged, the Taos People had set up their overnight camp. A hush fell over everyone as the two white men rode in. Collier saw many people he knew, but no one acknowledged him. Mirabal led the outsiders to a spot at the edge of the glade, near a cluster of trees. The men quietly unsaddled their horses and built a fire. They could hear conversations around them quietly coming back to life, but tension filled the air.

Tribal leaders summoned Mirabal for a conference. While the council huddled, another nervous silence fell over the camp. Collier and Young sat by their campfire, smoking cigarettes. Finally, Mirabal returned with bad news. Many people were objecting to the white men's presence: not just the tradition-minded cacique but also the renegade peyote users. All agreed that the outsiders would desecrate the sacred ceremony.

Collier and Young began preparing to withdraw. Mirabal asked them to wait and then left for another long conference. When he finally returned, he said that they would be permitted to stay for this first night. They could leave in the morning.

With the impasse settled, the encampment came back to life. Fresh logs were added to fires. The flames climbed higher and the drumbeats began. Then a chorus of men's voices rose in song. Everyone came together in the meadow, dancing and singing—old women and children, religious leaders and peyote users, mothers holding babies. All night long the festivities continued, "an incomparable splendor of dance and an uninterrupted, glorious song from hundreds of singers,"[2] observed the mesmerized Collier. Finally, in the gray light of predawn, a lone man strode into the middle of the meadow. He looked into the sky and lifted his voice. No drum accompanied him. His song ended just as the first streaks of sunlight lit the mountain peaks above.

Then it was over. Everyone began breaking camp. Antonio Mirabal and the other Taos People continued their journey to Blue Lake while Collier and Young turned their horses back toward the Pueblo.

By 1926, Collier had moved his family to Washington, DC, where he kept expanding the battle for Native reforms. His American Indian Defense Association boasted wide membership and prestigious board members, but Collier dominated everything. He stalked the lumbering Indian Bureau like a lone wolf. He took on the cause of the Navajos, whose reservation had been opened to oil and gas development without a penny of royalties going to the tribe. Over Commissioner Burke's objections, Collier lobbied Congress to provide the Navajo People their fair share. Ultimately, he amassed enough support among influential senators to carry the day.

The activist then threw himself into opposing a new Burke-backed bill that would greatly expand the Indian Bureau's powers. The legislation authorized the agency to imprison Native people for up to six months without a trial. Collier labeled it "A Bill Authorizing Tyranny." He rounded up other foes, including members of the more conservative, missionary-oriented Indian Rights Association. In blistering congressional hearings, Collier denounced the measure as "absolute ruthless, even fantastic, oppression and enslavement."[3] Once again, he prevailed over Burke.

The sixty-five-year-old commissioner hardly knew what to make of his young adversary. Burke had come of age in South Dakota, on the front lines of the nineteenth-century wars of conquest—when many whites believed "the only good Indian is a dead Indian." The commissioner viewed surviving Native Americans as subjugated people whose only hope for salvation was to become absorbed into white culture. For that to happen, they needed to be ruled with iron discipline.

But Collier, at age forty-two, held completely different views. He not only valued Indigenous culture; he also believed Natives had the right to rule themselves. And everywhere Collier looked, he saw an Indian Bureau harming Indigenous people. He accused Burke and his Bureau of following the "original military policy which regarded the Indian as an outlaw and danger to society."[4] Previous generations of reformers had criticized the Indian Bureau for being too ineffective. For Collier, the problem lay much deeper: The Bureau was the enemy.

His American Indian Defense Association fired off dozens of official complaints against the Indian Bureau, pointing out that the mortality rate of Indigenous people had increased nearly 50 percent since Burke took over as commissioner. When Collier discovered that Burke had suppressed a Red Cross report revealing dire health conditions on Native reservations, he published scathing stories in the national press. After one such article, *The Survey* magazine asked Burke to respond. The commissioner could only reply, "It is impossible to conceive of seventeen pages of typewritten matter that could contain so much that is untrue, misleading and ridiculous."[5]

But Collier had already moved on to attack boarding schools: "One of the reasons for the high mortality rate is the policy pursued toward Indian children," he argued. "Children in many tribes are taken away from their parents, in some cases as early as at six years, and sent away to boarding schools, where violent efforts are made to 'Americanize' them."[6]

Collier pointed out that many of the students were forced to provide manual labor even as they were denied enough food to eat. This "was a bleak life," Collier said, "and a hungry life." He accused Burke of presiding over "slow starvation and heartbreak."[7]

The commissioner defended his agency, maintaining that pupils were "well-nourished and are receiving food that is up to the standards of similar institutions."[8] But Collier soon uncovered the evidence proving the terrible truth: Native schoolchildren were allocated less than twelve cents a day for food—starvation rations.

Burke had no answer for that, but soon thereafter a series of attacks appeared in the press targeting Collier. The activist was reported to be a Soviet agent, "paid $10,000 annually by Moscow for his activities on behalf of the Indians." Collier's ultimate aim, readers were told, was "to create disturbance and revolution."[9]

Burke disavowed planting the libelous accounts, but the stories were eventually traced back to him. At the same time, Collier's fresh revelations about the Indian Bureau were stirring more US senators to action. Interior Secretary Hubert Work, who possessed a genuine humanitarian concern for Native welfare, became worried that his Indian Bureau might be failing at its core mission—keeping its charges alive. He agreed to a senate proposal to authorize a full, independent investigation of conditions among Natives in the United States. Indian Commissioner Burke was forced to pledge cooperation—even as everyone understood that his handling of Native affairs would be on trial.

As the battles between Burke and Collier raged, the Pueblo Lands Board prepared to descend on Taos. Collier considered this board his greatest success as a reformer. The original Bursum Bill would have granted New Mexico's courts the authority to decide whether the contested Pueblo lands belonged to the Natives or outsiders. Collier had insisted on this federally appointed commission, which he believed would be more impartial and thus more fair to the Puebloans. With the passage of the Pueblo Lands Bill, he had prevailed.

President Coolidge, Attorney General John Sargent, and Interior Secretary Hubert Work had each appointed a member to the new board. Collier had hoped to influence the selections but got shut out. He was not especially pleased with how things turned out. The chairman, selected by the Interior Secretary, was H. J. Hagerman, a millionaire's son who'd once been New Mexico's territorial governor. Hagerman had earlier worked with Albert B. Fall to open Navajo lands to oil exploration. Like Fall, Hagerman did not believe the Natives merited any royalties for oil found on their lands. He and Collier had sparred over the issue on Capitol Hill, and hard feelings remained.

For eighteen months, Hagerman's board had conducted hearings throughout New Mexico. More than a thousand claims had been argued, but precious few decisions had been announced. The commission was not tipping its hand yet, and Collier remained suspicious of how it would rule. Yet when it came to Taos, Collier knew the Pueblo had an iron-clad claim. Much of the Hispano village of Taos was indisputably on the original Pueblo land grant, recognized in the seventeenth century by the king of Spain and confirmed by the US government in 1848.

The historical record was clear: The Taos People could make the case that the town of Taos legally belonged to them. Over two hundred individual claims awaited, many stretching back centuries. At stake were a thousand acres of prime real estate worth hundreds of thousands of dollars.

Collier had clashed with Francis Wilson earlier because the attorney had been willing to relinquish those town claims. No one believed for a moment that the Pueblo would actually regain the city lots in Taos—most of which had been granted or sold to Hispano settlers hundreds of years ago. The Taos People had always been clear that they had no wish to evict these longtime residents.

But Collier had recognized Taos Pueblo's leverage as a valuable bargaining chip. His zealotry had split New Mexico's pro-Pueblo alliance and ensured him the lasting enmity of Wilson and other Santa Feans. But Collier didn't care. Now, with the Pueblo Lands Board due to arrive in Taos, he could at long last move forward with his plan to regain Blue Lake.

In September 1926, just a few weeks after Collier's abandoned trip to Blue Lake, the activist called on H. J. Hagerman, chairman of the Pueblo Lands Board. There was no love lost between Hagerman and his visitor, yet the former governor was a politician who knew how to make deals. Hagerman listened with growing interest as Collier outlined his proposal: The Taos People were willing to surrender all their claims to the town of Taos—in exchange for expanding their government reservation to recover the Blue Lake watershed. Collier pointed out that the Blue Lake area was appraised at $30,000. In contrast, the Pueblo claims in town were valued at ten times as much. This would be a sweet, easy, profitable deal for the US government.

Figure 31. Herbert J. Hagerman, 1904. From Fayette Alexander Jones, *New Mexico Mines and Minerals: World's Fair Edition* (New Mexican Printing Company, 1904) © Wikimedia/Creative Commons.

Hagerman liked what he heard. In one move, he could clear two hundred cases while saving taxpayers a lot of money. He immediately notified Commissioner Burke, pointing out that such a swap could save "a tremendous amount of work for the Board [and] a great deal of trouble and expense to the people of Taos." Hagerman also suggested that the Indian Bureau would benefit by having Blue Lake become part of Taos Pueblo's reservation, for it would give Burke's Bureau greater control over the annual Blue Lake pilgrimage. Hagerman noted, "This age-long discussion about the ceremony, with all its accompanying gossip, rumor, dark hints of murder and other things, could be settled."

Hagerman's recommendation was clear: Collier's deal, he said, "would be a good thing to do."[10]

Commissioner Burke remained unmoved by Hagerman's practical arguments. Instead, he saw a chance to inflict maximum damage on John Collier and the Taos People. He suggested a far different course of action.

In October 1926, the Pueblo Lands Board arrived in Taos. The people of Taos Pueblo, with Collier's encouragement, made their offer. The board sounded sympathetic. "We have no objection to the Indians having Blue Lake," said Charles Jennings, appointed by the US Attorney General. "I would be glad for them to have it." Princeton lawyer Lucius C. Embree, appointed by President Coolidge, concurred: "I want to say that I feel disposed to do anything I can to secure the Blue Lake region to the Indians."[11] H. J. Hagerman missed the meeting, but he put out word that the Interior Department and the Indian Bureau also supported the idea.

Yet there was a catch. The Pueblo Lands Board was only authorized to settle claims. It did not have the authority to make land swaps or grant any other outside deals. An act of Congress would be required to expand the Taos reservation. The best the board could do would be to note Taos Pueblo's concessions in its report and officially recommend that Blue Lake be returned to the tribe in exchange. This endorsement from the high-level federal appointees would presumably persuade Congress to take appropriate action.

Collier and the Pueblo's leaders were faced with a difficult choice. Could they accept these earnest guarantees of goodwill? Would justice be served?

In the end, the chance to regain Blue Lake could not be passed up. Collier addressed the Pueblo Lands Board. He told them that the Taos People "understand that if the Board and the Secretary of the Interior are in a position to recommend to Congress vigorously . . . I think it could be said that the Indians are willing to take a gambling chance to relinquish whatever claims they may have in return for the assurance that they will have help."[12]

Collier had played right into Commissioner Burke's hands. Now that the stage was set, the double cross was executed in merciless fashion.

Hagerman informed Burke in a letter, "I will advise against saying anything about Blue Lake in our report, and have no doubt but that my associates on the Board will be very willing to adopt my viewpoint."[13]

The Pueblo Lands Board duly accepted Taos Pueblo's offer to waive $300,000 worth of land claims in the town of Taos. In return, the board did nothing. In its final report, as Hagerman promised Burke, it neglected to even mention that the Pueblos' concession had been conditioned on the return of Blue Lake.

For compensation, Taos Pueblo received a thousand acres of sagebrush desert where rabbits could occasionally be hunted. Essentially, the trade amounted to what the original Bursum Bill would have provided had it passed Congress. Collier had not only failed; he had been crushed. On his advice, Taos Pueblo had surrendered $300,000 for a few bowls of jackrabbit stew.

Afterward, Hagerman gloated to a pleased Commissioner Burke: "It does not seem as if the Taos Indians were getting into a very enviable position. [They] are pretty bitter against Collier. I do not know what will happen to him if he goes back. He probably won't go back for awhile."[14]

PART III

THE INDIAN NEW DEAL

CHAPTER 20

A NEW COURSE

1926–1928

NOVEMBER 16, 1926

Tribal leaders from all nineteen Pueblos assembled at the invitation—some would say the *orders*—of the Indian Bureau. The government was calling this a friendly powwow. The Pueblo men who gathered on the campus of the Santa Fe Indian School were not so sure.

Leading this meeting was H. J. Hagerman, now appointed a "Special Commissioner" for the Indian Bureau in addition to chairing the Pueblo Lands Board. Hagerman was joined by several other high-level officials, including US Senator Andrieus Jones of New Mexico. Also present were missionary leaders and representatives from the more conservative Native rights groups—those opposed to John Collier.

On this day, a blustery northwest wind whipped across the land. Everyone gathered inside the library on the Indian School campus. The new building, crowned with a towering brick chimney, had become a distinctive addition to Santa Fe's modest skyline. Pablo Abeita of Isleta Pueblo, who'd earlier sparred in Washington with Senator Bursum, spoke for many of the Pueblo representatives: "We came here like blind men, not knowing the meaning of this meeting. What is the real object of this council?"[1]

Hagerman spoke reassuringly. He said the Bureau fully supported the Natives' initiative in holding their own All Pueblo councils. Now, the government wanted to help the process work even better. "It is the object of this [new] council to become the connecting link between you and the government," Hagerman said. He told the assembled men, "You will get better and quicker results by dealing directly with the government than through other channels."[2]

Abeita knew what Hagerman meant by "other channels." He was talking about Collier and his American Indian Defense Association. But the Isleta man kept quiet for the moment.

Hagerman continued, proposing that this new arrangement be called the "United States Pueblo Indian Council." Then, in a show of democratic inclusion, he called for a vote on the suggested nomenclature. The Pueblo men duly voted in favor. Then Hagerman appointed a man from Laguna Pueblo as the chairman. No vote was offered for that decision. The man Hagerman chose was a Christian activist who favored assimilation.

Abeita and the others understood what was happening. The government was trying to undermine their All Pueblo council and break their alliance with John Collier. Outside, the winds picked up and dust swirled. The building's windows began rattling.

Over the rising noise, Abeita parried back. He said he had "no doubt of the good intentions of both Mr. Hagerman and Charles Burke." But then Abeita added, "We do not want to lose our privilege to go to our friends for help—those who have done so much good for us."[3]

Hagerman responded smoothly, "You always have the right to appeal to your friends, but we are trying to do away with the roundabout methods to get results. You can now deal directly with the government."[4]

A Taos Pueblo representative, Joe Luján, had heard enough. He made a motion to adjourn the meeting. He was ignored. Hagerman and the other government officials kept talking.

The winds were howling now. Many of the Pueblo men glanced around uneasily. This had become a powerful gale. The entire government building seemed to be shaking on its foundation. Undaunted, one of the other white men began talking. More noise swelled, and a suddenly a powerful boom was heard as the storm snapped the massive chimney. Falling bricks and mortar crashed through the roof and poured into the room. Shouts flew as people scrambled for cover. When the air finally cleared, several Pueblo men were lying wounded. Pablo Abeita was among them, his head bleeding from a fallen brick. Wind and dust whipped through the broken building as the fallen were rushed to a nearby hospital. Somehow, the Pueblo men sourly noted, the whites had all escaped injury.

Despite its luckless beginning, Burke and Hagerman believed their new, government-controlled Pueblo council could reset Native governance on a more pliable course. What they didn't count on was the Pueblos' refusal to abandon John Collier. He may have failed in his attempt to win back Blue Lake, but the Taos People didn't blame Collier—they blamed the US government. Taos and the other Pueblos knew of no other white man who would fight so relentlessly for them.

A new All Pueblo Council was called, and Collier was invited to speak. To no one's surprise, he advised them to boycott the government-sponsored council, saying they "could not trust" the Indian Bureau.[5] Pueblo leaders swiftly agreed. The next time the government called a meeting of its United States Pueblo Indian Council, only a handful of assimilated Christians from a few Pueblos showed up.

Collier had refused to retreat after the Pueblo Lands Board debacle. Though he and Taos Pueblo had been humiliated, Collier focused on the larger picture. He saw that many of the board's rulings were clearly tilted toward the Anglos. They not only won most of the judgments; in the rare instances when they did lose, their compensation amounts were far higher than those paid to the Natives. Collier threw himself back into the battle. His American Indian Defense Association began filing federal lawsuits against the Pueblo Lands Board, accusing it of cheating the Pueblo People.

The flurry of legal action soon drew attention from the Senate Committee on Indian Affairs, which began looking into the matter. At this crucial moment, the Taos People were buoyed by the re-emergence of an old supporter.

The painter Bert Phillips, now nearly sixty years old, had always maintained that the purpose of the national forest was to protect Taos Pueblo's ancestral rights. Now Phillips volunteered to testify before the Senate committee and explain the truth. He argued that the Forest Service should now return the Blue Lake watershed and its sacred forests to Taos Pueblo: "We feel they should own that country. It adjoins their land. They have used it for many years, for centuries, for ceremonial purposes."[6]

The stakes for Blue Lake were higher than ever. The Forest Service had begun logging blue spruce and Douglas fir in the watershed, and no one could stop them. Even more threatening, a new mining boom had erupted and hundreds of prospectors were digging into the mountains above Taos Pueblo. Blue Lake and the Rio Pueblo de Taos were directly in the path of mining tailings and runoff. Taos leaders were stunned to learn that the Forest Service endorsed such ecologically harmful activity. By decree, the agency encouraged mining in national forests. Water quality was secondary.

Taos Pueblo leaders, in their ongoing fight to regain control of Blue Lake, coordinated with Bert Phillips to gain a helpful new ally. This was a young attorney in Taos, Floyd Beutler, who was engaged to the painter's daughter, Margaret. Beutler had been a junior staffer on the Pueblo Lands Board when the double cross was executed against Collier and Taos Pueblo. He'd been powerless to prevent that, but now he wanted to help. Beutler held a potent connection to Interior Secretary Hubert Work, who was an old family friend. Beutler soon sent Work a personal appeal:

"I am presuming on your friendship with my father in writing you this letter with reference to the claim of the Taos Pueblo to that portion of the Carson Forest Reserve known as the Blue Lake region," Beutler explained. "It has been used by them in their religious ceremonies for hundreds of years and is an intrinsic part of their annual tribal ceremonies, being regarded by the Indians much as we regard our churches."[7]

Then Beutler stated his case: "Recently a number of prospectors and timber men have entered this region, much to the alarm of the Indians who feel that if this section of the country is open to the public that the ceremonial life of the Pueblo will be shattered and their water supply ruined by mining and timber operations."[8] He closed by pleading for the Secretary's help to return Blue Lake to Taos Pueblo's control.

The Interior Secretary had come a long way since that encounter two years earlier when he'd denounced Taos Pueblo's tribal leaders as "half-animal." He agreed to support them: "This Department would like to do anything that is practicable in their behalf."[9]

Work navigated Washington's political thickets, looking to expand Taos Pueblo's reservation. He found some support in Congress, but a major obstacle remained. Agriculture Secretary William M. Jardine remained opposed, for the Forest Service considered the Blue Lake watershed one of its most prized assets.

Jardin's opposition killed any hope of expanding Taos's reservation. Yet not all was lost. An odd alliance came together as Secretary Work joined John Collier and some US Senators to apply pressure on the Forest Service to recognize Taos Pueblo's historic rights and continuing religious use of the Blue Lake Watershed.

After much negotiation, the Forest Service and Taos Pueblo eventually signed a Cooperative Agreement in September 1927. The new arrangement set aside 31,000 acres of land in the Blue Lake watershed for special treatment—"for the purpose of conserving and protecting the water supply of the said Pueblo."[10] No commercial logging would be allowed, and only Pueblo stock could graze.

The accord also gave Taos Pueblo authority to regulate access to Blue Lake. Any tourist who wanted to hike or camp in the area would be required to have permits signed by Taos Pueblo's governor. Most significantly, the agreement protected the Pueblo's annual ceremony at Blue Lake: "For a period of three days during the latter part of August of each year . . . exclusive use and occupancy of said area is hereby accorded to the Indians of the Pueblo of Taos for the purpose of conducting religious ceremonials."[11]

This landmark agreement was followed by an executive order from President Coolidge, which banned mining in the Blue Lake region. At long last, after more than twenty years of struggle, the Taos People appeared to regain some control over a portion of their sacred heartland.

Taos Pueblo's new Blue Lake agreement invigorated John Collier's ever-widening campaign to revolutionize federal Native policies. He crisscrossed the country in his battered old car, armed with a portable typewriter, churning out new appeals and articles. He consulted with various tribes in identifying strategies to help empower them. He organized legal challenges to the US government's long-standing policy of billing Native tribes for public work projects that mostly benefitted white interests. He drew the progressive journalist, Vera Connolly, to Taos and inspired her to conduct a six-month investigative report into the state of America's Native People. Her resulting series appeared in *Good Housekeeping*, sparking moral outrage and rattling Indian Bureau leaders.

Collier continued publishing wave after wave of his own incendiary articles, highlighting abuses against Native Americans. He also gave countless public talks. In a speech to the Campfire Girls of America, he described Dickensian scenes at government boarding schools. He told the young girls that Native children their own age were kept chained to beds in rat-infested basements, where they were repeatedly whipped for minor offenses.

In New Mexico, Collier's "fantastic lies" and "balderdash" were ridiculed by newspapers and political leaders. The idea that any Pueblo People had been cheated or abused seemed preposterous. US Senator Octaviano Larrazolo from New Mexico assured his colleagues, "I am here to tell you, gentlemen, that there is no lot of people in the United States better treated or better used than the Indians are, and I am in a position to know what I am talking about." The *Santa Fe New Mexican* mocked Collier's charges of Pueblo suffering: "If you see any San Ildefonso Indian in the act of starving please report it at once to John Collier!"[12]

The fiery reformer remained unwelcome among the Santa Fe intelligentsia. The artists, writers, and others who formed the New Mexico Association on Indian Affairs viewed Collier's zealotry with disdain. They never forgot that in his single-minded devotion to the Pueblos he had been willing to sacrifice Hispano families. Collier's vision of restoring the Pueblos to a pristine, preconquest status struck many of the Santa Feans as hopelessly naïve, and more than a bit messianic.

The Santa Fe crowd sought to marginalize Collier in every possible way. The president of the New Mexico Association on Indian Affairs, Margaret

McKittrick, eagerly joined H. J. Hagerman's ill-fated United States Pueblo Indian Council simply because she saw it as a means to punish Collier. The Santa Fe poet, Alice Corbin Henderson, put together an anthology of New Mexico poetry she called *The Turquoise Trail*. Every local writer of note was represented, even Mabel Dodge Luhan, who no one considered a serious poet. Collier, meanwhile, had authored four volumes of poetry, including one devoted to New Mexico. He'd hoped to be recognized but was left out, much to the Santa Feans' delight. They not only disagreed with Collier politically—they also judged him a bad poet.

In 1928, the US government's independent commission to study Native welfare released its findings. Called the Meriam Report, it proved a stinging rebuke of Commissioner Charles Burke and the Indian Bureau. The investigation exposed an agency that was ill-organized, incompetent, and often hostile to Native people. The report revealed appalling health conditions on reservations across the country, as well as widespread abuse at boarding schools. Compiled by sober-minded authorities of unquestioned integrity, the Meriam Report validated most of what John Collier had been saying for years. Burke's support on Capitol Hill quickly collapsed. The commissioner lashed out in a senate hearing, alleging a conspiracy to "destroy me and the Indian Service." Ultimately, Burke decided to resign as Indian Commissioner. He had no comment for reporters other than to say he was "very happy indeed to get out."[13]

In November 1928, Herbert Hoover's election as president was celebrated by Native rights activists as a triumph. Hoover had spent months as a boy living on an Osage Reservation and he appeared sympathetic to Native Americans. His new Indian Commissioner, Charles Rhoads, had once headed the missionary-directed Indian Rights Association. Rhoads pledged to implement the massive reforms called for in the Meriam Report.

The writer Mary Austin, who counted Herbert Hoover and his wife, Lou, as personal friends, hailed the Rhoads appointment as "a good omen both for the Indian and for our own credit as an enlightened people." John

Collier had doubts about a missionary directing Native policy, but he agreed that the appointment was a good one, praising Rhoads as a "revolutionary type from the standpoint of the Indian Bureau old-guard."[14]

At long last, a new era seemed to be dawning. The nation's approach to Native affairs appeared to be tilting toward benevolence, rather than punishment. And whether people supported or reviled John Collier, nearly everyone was forced to agree that he, more than any other individual, had been responsible for pushing the government in this new direction.

CHAPTER 21

INDIAN DETOURS

1929–1930

MAY 1, 1929

An Indian Detour bus crammed with tourists bounced along the rutted dirt road. Its destination was San Felipe Pueblo, which was staging its annual corn dance on this spring day. Among the passengers was a forty-one-year-old painter. She was a slender, ascetic-looking woman in a long black skirt and a white shirt. Her long, dark hair was pulled back into a tight knot. She lived on the thirtieth floor of a New York hotel and painted views of cityscape from her window, though she was best known for her erotic-tinged depictions of billowing flowers. Recently, a set of her paintings of calla lilies sold for a $25,000, a record sum for a living American artist.

Georgia O'Keeffe had briefly visited New Mexico in 1917 and had been trying to get back ever since. Yet her husband, the famed photographer and art gallery dealer, Alfred Stieglitz, refused to let her go.

A few months earlier, O'Keeffe had seen Mabel Dodge Luhan in New York. Mabel encouraged her to come west. She'd even offered O'Keeffe a guest house and a private studio at her Los Gallos estate. O'Keeffe wanted to say yes. She knew her work was beginning to stagnate in New York. Her much older husband, who was getting rich selling her art, was forced to agree that she needed fresh inspiration. Reluctantly, he allowed her to make the trip.

Figure 32. Georgia O'Keeffe, 1930. Photograph by Alfred Stieglitz. Metropolitan Museum of Art, New York.

Sitting on the Indian Detour bus next to O'Keeffe was her close friend, Rebecca Strand. The sad-eyed, chain-smoking "Beck" also wore a black skirt and a white blouse, though she rarely bothered with the top few buttons. A painter herself, she was married to the photographer Paul Strand. Beck, too, had seen Mabel in New York and was also offered a Taos guest house. But she'd heard stories from her husband that Mabel could be a domineering hostess. So O'Keeffe and Beck decided against visiting Taos. Instead, they would tour New Mexico on their own.

As their bus lumbered into San Felipe Pueblo, the tour guide, a young woman outfitted in Native-bohemian splendor, reminded everyone that photographs were not permitted. The plaza was already crowded with white visitors. As O'Keeffe and Strand peered out the bus window, they were shocked to see a familiar face. Mabel Dodge Luhan was there, along with her husband, Tony. Mabel had spotted them and was waving furiously.

The next morning, O'Keeffe and Beck were on their way to Taos with

Mabel and Tony. They weren't exactly captives, but Mabel had given them no other option. O'Keeffe was seated in the front alongside Tony as he smoothly navigated the winding road, singing as he drove. "He is a very good driver," O'Keeffe reported to her husband. "He is very grand."[1]

Whatever misgivings O'Keeffe might have had about staying with Mabel vanished when she arrived in Taos and took in the landscape. "Well! Well! Well!" she exclaimed. "This is wonderful. No one told me it was like *this*." She wrote to Stieglitz: "I wish I could tell you how alive I feel—I really never felt better in my life."[2]

Mabel put O'Keeffe and Beck in the Pink House, where Willa Cather once stayed while working on *Death Comes for the Archbishop*. O'Keeffe woke to the sound of birds singing every morning. Prairie dogs often nosed outside her door. Other guests discovered a nest of rattlesnakes under their porch, but O'Keeffe was unfazed. She was entranced by the views across the desert to looming Taos Mountain. "I feel full to bursting for work," she wrote to Stieglitz, "and I feel it is going to be good."[3]

She was quite taken by Tony Luján. "I must say that Mabel picked one of the prize men of the tribe," she observed. "I like him very much—and I wouldn't like Mabel nearly so much if it wasn't for Tony." She worked in the art studio Mabel provided, and she spent long hours watching Taos Mountain. She asked Tony if he also liked the mountain. He smiled and replied, "That's why I'm here."[4]

Before long, Tony was escorting O'Keeffe around Taos in his Cadillac. She preened when others at Mabel's exclaimed that they had never seen Tony "so nice to anyone."[5] He showed her the Pueblo, the river full of rushing snowmelt, young willow trees in bloom, and the still-silvery cottonwoods, nearly ready to leaf into spring. High above everything rose the granite, snow-covered peaks.

"I seem to be hunting for something of myself out there," the painter told her husband. "Something in myself that will give me a symbol for all this—a symbol for the sense of life I get out here."[6]

In Santa Fe, the bathtub gin parties at the poet Witter Bynner's house were

Figure 33. Ansel Adams, ca. 1950. 1950 Yosemite Field School, National Park Service © Wikimedia/ Creative Commons.

enlivened by a recent visitor from San Francisco, a twenty-seven-year-old classical pianist with a bushy black beard and a hearty laugh. Ansel Adams delighted everyone with his performances, though not in a manner the great composers had intended. "I grandly played my spoofs," Adams recounted, "of a Chopin etude with benefit of an orange in my right hand and Strauss's 'Blue Danube' performed both with my fingers and, for the emphatic chords, with my derriere."[7]

The rambunctious Adams had planned to become a professional concert pianist ever since teaching himself to read and play music at age twelve. Yet he also loved the outdoors and developed a growing interest in photography. He began making pictures of Yosemite for the Sierra Club that drew attention. A wealthy arts patron in San Francisco decided that Adams's larger talent lay in photography, not music. That millionaire, Albert Bender, also admired Mary Austin, who he considered "the greatest writer in the West."[8]

Two years earlier, in 1927, Bender brought Adams to Santa Fe to meet the great lady. On that visit, the aging, often dour Austin grudgingly agreed to sit for new publicity photographs. Adams later mailed her the images with a note: "I have selected several of the best pictures of you . . . I am anxious that you be utterly pleased."[9]

Instead, Austin rebuked him. "I dare say you can take away that dreadful smirk, and the drawn look about the mouth," she responded. "But the carriage of the head, with the face thrust down and forward, and the slumped shoulders are not only not characteristic of me, but contradict the effect it is still necessary for me to make on my public."[10]

The young photographer was chastened, but did not give up. With the promise of financial assistance from Bender, the ingratiating Adams soon persuaded Mary Austin to collaborate with him on a new book. She would write the text, and he would provide the photographs. Their subject: Taos Pueblo.

Now, in the summer of 1929, Adams was in Santa Fe with his wife, Virginia. Austin had invited them to stay at her Spanish colonial-style home, Casa Querida. At age sixty, Austin was in poor health, battling heart and stomach ailments along with high blood pressure. She continued working feverishly to maintain her many obligations and had just returned from a grueling lecture tour. She was putting the finishing touches on a new novel, *Starry Adventure*, and had begun her long-awaited autobiography. The enterprising Austin also wrote marketing copy for Fred Harvey's Indian Detours and published intellectual essays in high-brow journals. She also, notably, penned a blistering rebuttal to *Harper's* magazine after it carried an article referring to New Mexico as "the backwash of Spain."[11]

In her spare time, Austin continued championing Native American causes. Though she was not wealthy, she donated much of her money to the effort. She also worked to honor New Mexico's Hispano culture. She cofounded the Spanish Colonial Arts Society in Santa Fe and she had recently helped preserve a sacred old adobe church at nearby Chimayó.

It was easy for Ansel Adams to feel intimidated by her. A recent newspaper story had praised Austin as "the most intelligent woman in America."[12] She certainly agreed with that assessment and never hesitated to let others know. While her poor health made her more irritable than usual, she warmly tolerated Ansel and Virginia Adams, treating them kindly while they stayed with her.

In between the parties in Santa Fe, Austin and Adams mapped out their work for the Taos Pueblo book. The younger Adams made sure to describe the project as "*your book*" in his conversations with her. He agreed that Austin's writing would be "the dominant feature of the book."[13]

Mary Austin concurred. She regarded the young man as merely her illustrator. When they discussed possible publishers, she informed him, "In the first place, you must realize that the illustrator is always a secondary consideration with the publisher. The contract is made with the author."[14]

After Austin arranged for Mabel Dodge Luhan to host Adams, the photographer and his wife traveled to Taos. Upon arriving, he wrote to friends back in California: "Jezuz Krize but this is a great place. Such MOUNTAINS!!!!"[15]

As he unpacked his new camera equipment at Mabel's, Adams could see that the compound was overrun with visitors. The Irish poet Ella Young was living in one guest house, and author Neith Boyce in another. John Collier's son, Charles, was spending the summer while readying for his first year of college at Columbia. A journalist friend of Mabel's from New York, Hutchins Hapgood, had sent along his wife and children, who settled into the big house. And then there was Georgia O'Keeffe and Beck Strand, sharing the Pink House.

Adams still had no real assurance that he would even be allowed to photograph the Pueblo. Yet Mabel prevailed upon Tony, who obligingly called together the tribal council. He then made an appeal on Adams's behalf. After some deliberation, the leaders agreed, charging Adams twenty-five dollars for the privilege. The photographer also promised to provide the Taos People with a copy of the finished book. He and his tripod soon became a familiar sight at the Pueblo.

Before long, another artist arrived at Mabel's. John Marin was a California modernist who created abstract landscapes with watercolors. Looking for a chance to peacefully commune with Taos Mountain, he instead was interrupted by Ansel Adams, "laughing, stamping, making a noise." Just as Marin decided he didn't like this boisterous young man, a group of people pushed Adams toward Mabel's piano. "He sat down and struck one note," Marin observed. "One note. And even before he began to play, I knew I didn't want him to go away. Anybody who could make a sound like that I wanted for my friend always."[16]

Marin might have been charmed, but Georgia O'Keeffe remained aloof. She had little use for Adams's music and absolutely no regard for him as a photographer. In a letter to her husband Alfred Stieglitz, the grand man of American photography, O'Keeffe neglected to even mention that Adams was a photographer. Instead, she described him as a young man "from California sent here for the summer to cure a bad sinus."[17]

Georgia O'Keeffe also received permission to paint at Taos Pueblo, thanks to Tony Luján. During the summer of 1929, O'Keeffe and Adams shadowed each other's artistic efforts, even as she kept her distance from him. To Adams, O'Keeffe's haughty reserve came across as "imperial cool."[18] While he photographed the terraced Pueblo with its sacred mountain rising in the background, O'Keeffe made a painting with a similar view. Adams also photographed the bulky adobe church at Ranchos de Taos. O'Keeffe, too, made her own painting of the building.

Unlike Adams, O'Keeffe became increasingly fascinated by the large, weathered Penitente crosses she could see in the mountains from her studio. She began painting those, as well, putting huge, black crosses in the foreground of her landscape paintings. She also got Tony to drive her up to see D. H. Lawrence's ranch, though the couple had long since returned to Europe. Tony showed her the Ponderosa Pine that Lawrence used to sit against while he wrote. Looking up from the trunk of the tree into the starry sky, O'Keeffe created another masterpiece, titling it "The Lawrence Tree."

The artist continued to delight in Tony Luján's warm presence. "Tony wears wonderfully," she wrote to her husband. "He is really fine." Tony had made it clear over the years that he had little regard for the paintings outsiders were making in Taos. Yet when he saw O'Keeffe's new works in her studio, he lit up with pleasure. He told her, "Just like it."[19]

For Mabel Dodge Luhan, the summer of 1929 seemed a culmination of the vision she'd had for Taos from the beginning. Two of the nation's most acclaimed painters were working out of her home, and a luminous young photographer was busy making pictures at Taos Pueblo for a book with Mary Austin. On the political front, her friend John Collier had vanquished the old regime at the Indian Bureau. New leaders were pledging reforms to benefit the Pueblos. And all the while, Taos's fame continued to spread. Newspapers across the country carried stories of the picturesque artists' retreat and its nearby Pueblo. A typical headline read: TAOS, A WONDERLAND IN NEW MEXICO.[20] The state highway department handed out thousands of free tourist maps to automobile travelers. For those who arrived in New Mexico by rail, Fred Harvey's Indian Detours to Taos were booked full. New hotels, restaurants, and curio shops opened in town. One of Mabel's guests commented to Tony that he must be pleased to see all the people returning to enjoy summer in Taos. Tony replied, "Yes, pretty soon flies will be back too."[21]

In her more reflective moments, Mabel realized that, despite the buzz Taos generated, few of her guests were expanding their consciousness in response to the Pueblo. Nor were many volunteering to aid the Puebloans' political battles and social needs. Mabel knew that Georgia O'Keeffe would sell her Taos canvases for huge sums while the typical Taos Pueblo resident continued to subsist on less than thirty dollars per year. The artists were really not so different from the mining companies extracting ore from the nearby mountains. Mabel's original vision of Taos was sliding away. Instead of transforming Western civilization, Taos was being co-opted by it. The art colony was becoming just another way to make money.

She thought often of her failure to persuade D. H. Lawrence to write the great book about Taos. If only he had applied his perception in the way she had asked, it could have changed everything. He would have given "a voice to this speechless land."[22] Lawrence had left for good in September

Figure 34. “Indian Detours.” Etching by John Sloan, 1927. Crystal Bridges Museum of American Art, Bentonville, Arkansas, 2013.25. Photography by Edward C. Robison III.

1926, exactly four years to the day after he’d arrived. He and Mabel were not on speaking terms when he departed, but afterward they began exchanging letters. They soon found that, from afar, they could enjoy a warm, devoted friendship. He even dedicated his new book of essays, *Mornings in Mexico*, to her.

Through her relationship with Lawrence, Mabel came to understand that she should not rely on someone else to tell her story. She needed to grow beyond simply regarding herself as other peoples’ muse or catalyst or a famous hostess. Now at age fifty, she needed to become an artist herself—a writer.

Though Lawrence had earlier castigated her attempt at an autobiography, he now encouraged her to tell her life's story. Unsure of her talents as a stylist, Mabel concentrated on the one advantage she knew she possessed—unflinching honesty. She poured out hundreds of pages, recounting her privileged but loveless childhood in Buffalo, her long sojourn in Italy, her heady Greenwich Village days, and, finally, her arrival in Taos, where she fell in love with Tony and her spirit awakened. The more she wrote, the more she found to reveal.

To her delight, Lawrence responded very favorably to her manuscript. "It's the most serious 'confession' that ever came out of America," he wrote to her. "Perhaps the most heart-destroying revelation of the American life-process that ever has or will be produced." The great writer offered her only one major piece of advice: "Why oh why didn't you change the names!"[23]

In his frequent letters, Lawrence spoke often of his hope to return to New Mexico. He also described how his newest novel, *Lady Chatterley's Lover*, had been declared obscene and was confiscated by British authorities. Though he kept up a cheery sense of brio, his communications were increasingly pockmarked by references to his ill health. The tuberculosis was taking its toll. In August 1928 he wrote to her, "If only I can get a real start, to shake off this accursed cough, I ought to come along all right." As Mabel played host to Georgia O'Keeffe and John Marin and Ansel Adams, Lawrence promised, "If I was really well again . . . I'd dearly love to come to New Mexico for a year or so." Frieda then sent along her own note, telling Mabel, "L's health is frail as a blue bird's egg!"[24]

In the summer of 1929, Mabel suffered her own health crisis. Felled by terrible stomach cramps, she retreated to bed. Tony took her to doctors in Albuquerque, but no one could figure out what was wrong. Though she appeared gravely ill, Mabel pleaded with her guests to continue enjoying themselves. Some suspected that her illness was psychosomatic. Then an internist determined the actual cause: She had fibrous tumors in her uterus. A hysterectomy would be needed.

Mabel decided to go back to Buffalo for the operation, where she could be close to her son and mother. She would be gone at least a month. In the meantime, she insisted that her visitors stay on at Los Gallos. Tony would remain behind to oversee everything. Before leaving, Mabel pulled Georgia O'Keeffe aside. She explained that Tony didn't read or write. She asked the artist to take dictation from him so they could exchange letters while she was gone. O'Keeffe readily agreed.

The surgery was a success. While Mabel convalesced in Buffalo, O'Keeffe worked long hours in her Taos studio. She also made time to go touring with Tony, always sitting in the front seat next to him. On the Fourth of July holiday, he drove her and Beck Strand over the mountains to see a rodeo in Las Vegas, New Mexico. Four Taos men joined them for the trip, riding together in the back and singing along the way. Then Tony took O'Keeffe and Beck out to Mesa Verde to visit the ancient cliff dwellings. Tony and the two women slept out under the stars. On the way home, the travelers drank too much bootleg whiskey and got lost in a mountain forest. "We finally slept in the car and on the ground with a fire when we got too cold," O'Keeffe reported to her husband. "We had nothing for supper and breakfast but oranges and whiskey."[25]

Alfred Stieglitz preferred to think of his wife as weak and dependent on him. But a new woman was being born in Taos. She made long horseback journeys into the highest reaches of the Taos Mountains. She kept up with the men, dodging lightning and hiking through knee-high snow. Stieglitz had never wanted his wife to drive a car. But in Taos, O'Keeffe bought herself a black Model A and learned how to operate it.

When Mabel returned from Buffalo, she instantly saw the new intimacy between O'Keeffe and her husband. Worse, the painter flaunted her conquest, insisting on sitting next to Tony and fluttering over him in Mabel's presence. Mabel soon made it clear that O'Keeffe's visit was over. The painter departed Taos in her Model A. She knew she would never again be welcomed at Mabel's, but she would definitely return to New Mexico.

As Ansel Adams finished making his pictures at Taos Pueblo, he realized, "something has clicked inside me." He told his wife, "I have an entirely new perspective."[26] He now recognized that, as much as he loved playing the piano, photography was his true calling.

When Mary Austin wrote the text for *Taos Pueblo*, she didn't even bother to look at Adams's photographs. She assumed they would be merely decorative. She expected to publish a mass-market book that would inform the world about the Taos Peoples' age-old wisdom.

Ansel Adams remained politely deferential to Austin while simultaneously outflanking her to pursue his own vision: a specialty publication aimed at the collector's market, the patron class. With the support of his wealthy benefactor in San Francisco, Adams pursued a high-end, fine-press volume limited to just a hundred copies. Each book would sell for seventy-five dollars (over $1,000 today). Special paper was made to order, as was the hand-finished leather for the cover. Adams selected his twelve favorite images, including a portrait of Tony Luján, wrapped in a blanket and gazing out with the dignity of an Egyptian pharaoh. Adams then spent thc fall of 1929 making original photographic prints for each volume, some 1,200 in all.

Mary Austin understood her young friend's desire to showcase his photographs. But she also demanded they publish an inexpensive mass-market edition so that everyday people could read her writing about Taos Pueblo. But Adams, now securely in command of the project, explained that would be impossible. He and Albert Bender, who was bankrolling the project, both agreed that a standard book would fail to adequately present the photographic images. Adams also assured Austin that the beauty of her writing deserved "a fine typographic treatment."[27] At long last, Austin understood the reality. *Taos Pueblo* was Adams's project, *his* book. It was her contribution, not his, that was merely "decorative."

She doubted Adams would find enough buyers for his book, especially at such a steep price. Yet *Taos Pueblo* soon sold out, even as the stock market crashed and the Great Depression took hold. Its resounding success marked Adams's arrival as an up-and-coming photographer. Soon, he was able to meet his heroes, including O'Keeffe's husband Alfred Stieglitz. Adams was welcomed into the fold and celebrated with a one-man show at Stieglitz's gallery in New York. Georgia O'Keeffe warmed up, becoming a treasured friend. Even amid the plummeting Depression, Adams's patron in San Francisco, Albert Bender, was able to joke: “I note the Stock Market reports only Ansel Adams's photographs as the sole commodity that is on the rise.”[28]

In late January 1930, Mabel received a new letter from D. H. Lawrence. “The doctor from England came on Monday,” he informed her. “The bronchitis is acute, and aggravated by the lung. I must lie still for two months.” He told Mabel that “with absolute care for two months, absolute rest from everything, I ought to be well enough to come to New Mexico and there get quite strong.” He ended, “Love from us both.”[29]

That was the final letter she received from him. A month later, Lawrence was dead.

CHAPTER 22

AN EXPERIMENT WORTH TRYING

1931–1933

FEBRUARY 11, 1931

At precisely 7:45 a.m., the long, lonesome wail of the westbound Chief could be heard as it rounded a final bend and approached the station outside Santa Fe. The train eased to a stop and a bundled-up H. J. Hagerman stepped out into the frosty morning. The Indian Bureau's Special Commissioner looked out to see something odd. Nearly fifty automobiles had converged around the building. At his appearance, the cars began honking.

Hagerman had spent much of the previous month in Washington, DC, battling for his political life. John Collier's American Indian Defense Association had led a charge to oust Hagerman from the Indian Bureau. Collier accused Hagerman of cheating the Natives while running the Pueblo Lands Board. He also denounced Hagerman as corrupt, pointing out that he had granted close friends bargain-priced oil leases on Navajo lands that were later resold for millions of dollars.[1]

Collier's campaign against Hagerman signaled his complete break with the Hoover administration, which he realized would never adequately reform Native affairs. The nation's new Indian Commissioner, Charles Rhoads, had simply continued the Dawes Act's ruinous policies of assimilation and breaking apart Native lands. Rhoads did little to ease the starvation rations for Indigenous children at government boarding schools, nor did he stop the violent beatings of students by school administrators. And then there was the personal matter of H. J. Hagerman, a man who had double-crossed Taos Pueblo yet remained prominently on the Bureau's payroll.

President Hoover's Interior Secretary, Ray Wilbur, denounced Collier's attacks against Hagerman as "a series of misrepresentations almost approaching blackmail."[2] Yet US Senators were listening. During a series of fiery hearings on Capitol Hill, Collier's forces persuaded the Senate to strip Hagerman's salary from the federal budget and eliminate his position. But Collier fell short of victory when the House of Representatives, after arm-twisting from the Hoover administration, voted to restore Hagerman.

The ex-governor had survived, but the ordeal took its toll. He became ill, diagnosed with depression and nervous exhaustion. His supporters blamed Collier. Now, Hagerman was returning home to Santa Fe to recuperate. He had as many friends in the city as John Collier had enemies.

At the train station, the chorus of blaring horns signaled a hero's welcome. Many of the automobiles were bedecked with placards praising Hagerman and vilifying Collier. The lively reception had been organized by poet Witter Bynner. Nearly every artist and writer in Santa Fe had followed Bynner to this early morning rally. Joining them were anti-Collier forces from the New Mexico Association on Indian Affairs, including the former Pueblo attorney, Francis Wilson.

As the crowd cheered for Hagerman, one man, wrapped in a tribal blanket and perched atop the hood of his car, furiously beat a native drum. This was the painter Willard Nash. Nearby, the artist Will Shuster sported a huge grin as he showed off the life-size puppet he'd created. The straw-filled figure was outfitted in a man's clothes, complete with slacks, shoes, and a jacket. With its sandy hair and round eyeglasses, it bore a remarkable resemblance to John Collier. A sign was attached to the puppet's chest: WANTED—MORE INDIANS FOR MY COUNCIL—DEMIJOHN COLLIER.

The gratified Hagerman waved, and the crowd shouted for him to make a speech. Despite his exhaustion, he said a few words, expressing his appreciation: "This is not a question of my vindication. This reception is vindication enough." He spoke of how those gathered were the Pueblos' true friends. Then he concluded to rousing applause, "It is imperative that the Indians be saved from John Collier."[3]

The parade of honking cars led Hagerman into Santa Fe. The automobiles circled the main plaza, drawing curious onlookers from surrounding hotels and businesses. A few Pueblo people watched from a careful distance. At the Museum of Fine Art, the demonstrators spilled from cars and gathered under a large cottonwood tree. Shuster carried the life-size Collier effigy. Someone else had thought to bring along a rope. In a few moments, the body was hanging from the tree's bare branches. The artists and writers laughed and cheered. The Pueblo onlookers observed quietly from across the plaza. None moved to join the puppet lynch mob.

Witter Bynner stepped forth. He had composed a bit of doggerel in honor of the occasion. Affecting the voice of John Collier, Bynner recited:

> Praise God from whom all blessings flow; praise God for Indians here below; no matter who pay the cost without the Indians I'd be lost. Whoever really helps the tribes receives my curses and my jibes; and there, for Mr. Hagerman, I try to hurt you all I can. If there were many more like you I should have nothing left to do. Love for the Indians is my boast and yet I love John Collier the most.[4]

When Collier heard about the mock lynching party, he shrugged it off. "Their action hugely increased my popularity among the Indian tribes," he maintained. Indeed, the All Pueblo Council soon sent a sharply worded letter to Interior Secretary Wilbur: "John Collier is a friend of the Pueblo Indians and he is recognized as such by us. It certainly is not to the credit of the Indian Bureau that a sense of justice compels him to fight constantly for decent treatment for the Pueblo Indians."[5]

In Santa Fe, Mary Austin had remained aloof from the anti-Collier demonstration. She told the press, "Mr. Collier is young and his zeal outruns his experience, in comparison with the forty years I have spent in the work, but we appreciate it." Privately, Austin counseled Collier, "John, use your charm on those Santa Fe wretches!" He responded that he was "too busy to use my charm on anyone."[6]

Collier kept up his campaign to oust Hagerman. He urged the Senate to conduct a formal investigation, which brought legislators to New

Mexico for government hearings. Taos Pueblo's Antonio Mirabal testified about Hagerman's treachery as chairman of the Pueblo Lands Board. "We do not know what he has ever done for us," Mirabal said, "not a single thing."[7]

Damning evidence against Hagerman piled up. He'd not only double-crossed Taos Pueblo, but he'd also compiled a long record of lies and misdealings. Ultimately, the inquiry revealed the truth: Hagerman's command of the Pueblo Lands Board had caused the Pueblo People to lose more than 44,000 acres of precious irrigated lands—while receiving only a pittance of compensation in return. The results were nearly as ruinous for the Pueblos as the original Bursum Bill had it passed. The Senate condemned him for "serious injury to the property and tribal interests of the Indians."[8] Armed with the indisputable facts, the entire congress voted overwhelmingly to remove Hagerman from office.

Collier's zealotry may have offended the Santa Fe crowd, but he'd proved to everyone, even those who'd lynched him in effigy, that he'd been right about Hagerman's chicanery all along.

As the nation sank into the Great Depression, President Hoover took to the radio to assure the country that "the present adversity is but a passing phase." Yet conditions worsened throughout 1932. Unemployment reached 25 percent in the cities, farms were failing, and families were starving. Hoover dismissed calls for federal intervention as "the rosy path of panacea." He counseled, "The way to the nation's greatness is the path of self-reliance, independence, and steadfastness."[9]

Despite the deepening gloom, the aura of Taos—and New Mexico's Pueblos—glowed as brightly as ever. Seemingly every major newspaper dispatched a writer to Taos for a report on "America's leading artist colony." A new play opened on Broadway called "Night Over Taos." Exhibitions of Native art went up at New York galleries, and Taos dancers won applause in touring performances. Americans who could still afford vacations were avoiding Europe and traveling west instead, making a point to see Taos. Hopes for the burgeoning New Mexico literary scene were lifted when a young Harvard-educated anthropologist, Oliver La Farge, published his first novel, *Laughing Boy*, set in New Mexico's Navajo country. The novel became a bestseller, and La Farge won the Pulitzer Prize for fiction, beating out William Faulkner and F. Scott Fitzgerald.

In early 1932, Mabel Dodge Luhan published her first book, an account of her complicated relationship with D. H. Lawrence. Titled *Lorenzo in Taos*, it was composed as an appeal to California poet Robinson Jeffers, who Mabel hoped to lure to New Mexico. She described, with brutal candor, the many ways she and Lawrence had sparred. In a modernist twist, she represented Lawrence's voice by including his letters to her, some ninety in all.

Many critics, especially women writers, applauded Mabel's literary debut. "Done in sharp, clear, brilliant lines," observed Fanny Butcher in the *Chicago Tribune*, "it is one of the most interesting literary portraits ever to be published." But several male reviewers dissented. In New York, William Soskin complained that "Mrs. Luhan has no literary record of importance to justify her part in the drama." In San Francisco, Charles Hanson Towne sneered at her writing, comparing it to "a child practicing at the piano." Closer to home, a disaffected Santa Fe writer, Philip Stevenson, denounced Mabel as an "unhappy, rootless, inert, willful female." He castigated her book as "formless with the pathetic formlessness of cultish intellectual processes."[10]

Despite the carping, *Lorenzo in Taos* became a solid success. Mabel, who'd long been considered little more than a high-profile hostess, had at last arrived as a literary artist in her own right.

America's Great Depression and the nation's unraveling self-confidence reinforced Mabel's belief that Taos Pueblo offered a better way of life. "No one in the east is any nearer the cure or the salvation," she told an interviewer. "Everything is crumbling. People are in despair." She praised the Taos People's enduring spirit. "Their mode of life is as strong and as sweet as ever," she said. "Their values are not changing, except very imperceptibly. In the main the Indians still like their mystical inner life, valuing the earth, the sun and the streams for what they are worth to them, which is life itself."[11]

Mabel had originally come to Taos to "save the Indians." But as she looked back on her life, she now realized that the opposite had occurred. "I feel saved by something I have learned from the Indians," she confessed. "It is a secret of being, I suppose. If I can ever 'put it over' to my own people, they will be able to benefit by it as much as I."[12]

In June 1932, John Collier left Washington for a summer visit to Taos. With his family and their dog in tow, he drove along the patchwork of dirt and gravel roads known as Route 66. On a muddy stretch outside Oklahoma City, he swerved to avoid a culvert and his car spun out of control. The vehicle flipped, landing on its roof. His wife, Lucy, their boys, and the family dog, Angus, escaped with only minor wounds. But Collier suffered severe chest and back injuries along with broken ribs. Press reports described his condition as grave.

Collier spent the next three weeks in a hospital bed. Finally, in mid-July, he and the family resumed their journey to Mabel's, where he would spend the rest of the summer recuperating. There, they joined the usual collection of high-profile visitors: famed conductor Leopold Stokowski, poet Robinson Jeffers—who Mabel had successfully drawn from California, and the social activist and writer, Fritz Kunz, who gave several lectures on Buddhism.

For the hard-charging Collier, the long convalescence proved frustrating. But hope was on the horizon. Franklin D. Roosevelt was running for president against Herbert Hoover. Mabel was busy organizing support for FDR in New Mexico. Collier's American Indian Defense Association was officially nonpartisan, and he counted many Republicans among its backers. But Hoover had proved as incapable at reforming Native affairs as he'd been at dealing with the Great Depression. Franklin Roosevelt said little about Native policy, but Collier—like Mabel and so many others—saw strength in Roosevelt's jaunty confidence. Collier began tilting toward Roosevelt, hoping that doing so might help him gain a voice in selecting the next Indian Commissioner.

In January 1933, two months after Roosevelt's landslide election, Tony Luján and Antonio Mirabal traveled to New York to meet with the president-elect. Of all the sophisticated diplomacy Taos Puebloans had engaged in over the previous decades, this would be their highest-stakes mission yet.

Antonio Mirabal, who had earlier debated with Carl Jung, had no problem making himself very clear to Roosevelt. "We have had politicians for commissioners before this time," Mirabal said. "We do not want any more of them." He argued for "an Indian commissioner who really will be helpful to the Indians." He told the incoming president that John Collier "is the only man we can say who knows our problem."[13]

The conference between the Taos Pueblo men and President-Elect Roosevelt drew national press coverage. When the Hoover administration learned of the encounter, it publicly offered Mirabal and Luján their own meeting with Hoover at the White House. Mirabal, in a cutting dismissal that must have delighted Roosevelt, waved off the suggestion. "I do not want to meet him."[14]

As Mirabal and Luján were leaving New York, the All Pueblo Council in New Mexico adopted a resolution that it sent to Roosevelt: "We want a new deal. We feel we are entitled to it. Our hope for that new deal is John Collier."[15]

A few weeks later, Roosevelt summoned Harold Ickes, a progressive Republican from Chicago who'd broken with Hoover to campaign for Roosevelt. Ickes had a long-standing interest in Indigenous affairs and had been an early ally of John Collier. The two had split after Collier sacked the attorney Francis Wilson, who was an old friend of Ickes's. In the years since, Collier and Ickes had gradually patched up their differences, though they were not particularly close.

If Collier was regarded as a radical extremist, Ickes was considered a curmudgeon, a man known for speaking his mind. He had emerged as the favorite for the post of Indian Commissioner, a prospect that left Collier unenthusiastic. He judged that Ickes's "personal idiosyncrasies unfit him for the task which requires considerateness of co-workers, subordinates, cooperation with Congress and subordination of egoism."[16]

Roosevelt had never met Ickes, but knew of his reputation as an efficient and honest administrator. Within a few moments of their introduction, Roosevelt became charmed by Ickes's blunt candor. He decided against offering him the Indian Commissioner post and instead asked Ickes to become his Interior Secretary.

FDR's adviser Raymond Moley was stunned. He described it as "one of the most casual appointments to a Cabinet position in American history." Roosevelt explained his choice by saying of Ickes, "I liked the cut of his jib."[17]

For Indian Commissioner, the leading candidate became E. B. Meritt, who'd been Assistant Commissioner during the Burke years. Meritt was anathema to Collier and other reformers, but he was strongly favored by the incoming Senate Majority Leader, Joe Robinson of Arkansas. The political trade-off was obvious. Roosevelt needed to keep Senator Robinson happy to ensure passage of his ambitious New Deal legislation.

Yet Roosevelt dallied on the Indian Commissioner appointment while the new congress swiftly passed bill after bill. By April 1933, he still hadn't named anyone. Senator Robinson kept pressuring him to choose Meritt. Finally, Roosevelt invited the senator to join him and his new Interior Secretary at the White House. There, Ickes curtly informed the Majority Leader his man was unacceptable. Roosevelt turned to Senator Robinson, "Well, Joe, you know what I am up against. Every highbrow organization in the country is opposed to Meritt, and Secretary Ickes, under whom he would have to work, doesn't want him."[18]

Several other candidates emerged, including John Collier. A fierce "Stop Collier" campaign erupted, spurred by the many enemies he had made over the years. Interior Secretary Ickes even heard from an old friend in Santa Fe, the attorney Francis Wilson, who advised: Collier "is by nature a promoter and a propagandist and not an executive or administrator. He is consistently unable to hold even-balanced views on any subject. He must be an extremist or nothing."[19]

Yet Ickes also knew that many Natives strongly favored Collier. With Roosevelt's blessing, Ickes made his choice. He replied to Wilson: "I think you know that I have had serious differences of opinion with John Collier, the principal one of which in the old days revolved about yourself. I do believe, however, that no one exceeds him in knowledge of Indian matters or his sympathy with the point of view of the Indians themselves. I want someone in that office who is the advocate of the Indians. The whites can take care of themselves, but the Indians need someone to protect them from exploitation. I want a man who will respect their customs and have a sympathetic point of view with reference to their culture. I want the Indians to be helped to help themselves. John Collier, with whatever faults of temperament he may have, has to a higher degree than any one available for that office, the point of view toward the Indians that I want in a commissioner of Indian Affairs."

Ickes concluded, "At any rate I think the experiment is worth trying."[20]

CHAPTER 23

THE COMMISSIONER

1933–1934

APRIL 21, 1933

After his swearing in, John Collier obligingly posed for press photographs inside his new office at the Indian Bureau. Though he'd only been commissioner a few hours, his desk was already cluttered with papers. Flowers and telegrams from well-wishers filled the room. His dog, Angus, who'd earlier survived the wreck on Route 66, lay curled up in a corner, oblivious to the commotion.

Collier wore his best suit and took a moment to carefully comb his usually tousled hair. Then the flashbulbs popped. At age fifty, he looked like a man carrying an enormous burden on his slight, stooped shoulders. He'd gone from a gadfly to suddenly assuming responsibility for hundreds of tribes representing 300,000 people.

"The Indians themselves expect great things of me," he told the press. "I hope they will not be too greatly disappointed."[1]

His confirmation had not come easily. Some senators objected that he was a "fanatic" and "hopelessly idealistic." One political observer noted, "All the winds of patronage were dead set against him. . . . Land, oil and water companies did everything but offer a bounty for his skin." Yet Interior Secretary Harold Ickes held firm, and Roosevelt's landslide victory ensured that the holdouts fell in line. "GLORY BE," read the congratulatory telegram from Mabel Dodge Luhan. "START A NEW ERA NOW."[2]

After the photographers left, Collier removed his suit jacket and slipped on his favorite green sweater. He reached for his corncob pipe. Then he got to work. It was day forty-eight of FDR's First Hundred Days and there was little time to lose.

First on the legislative front was rectifying the tragedy visited upon the Pueblo People by H. J. Hagerman's Pueblo Lands Board. Collier knew that getting those 44,000 acres back for the Pueblos would be impossible, but he damn well intended to ensure they at least received fair compensation—and a fighting chance to acquire comparable lands. During the previous session of Congress, he'd spurred the filing of a "Pueblo Relief Act" to make the payments commensurate with what whites had received. Hoover's Indian Bureau, allied with Hagerman, had refused to support the measure and it died.

Within days of taking office. Collier had a new version of the bill introduced. The Pueblo Relief Act provided New Mexico's Pueblos $761,954 ($18 million today) to acquire additional lands along with water rights. Significantly, the Pueblos would also gain an important new power: the right to approve all land purchases, rather than being dependent on the Interior Department's selections. The bill breezed through Congress and was signed into law by President Roosevelt on day ninety. Collier hailed the achievement as "a long step in the right direction."[3]

Then Collier turned his attention to government boarding schools. By the time President Roosevelt completed his First Hundred Days, his new Indian Commissioner had already closed six campuses and was in the process of shuttering several more. Meanwhile, FDR's Works Progress Administration (WPA) got busy constructing more than a hundred new local schools for Natives, including one at Taos Pueblo.

Collier was determined to break the missionaries' hold over Native education. In the past, religious groups had essentially comanaged the campuses, making Christian worship mandatory. As part of the curriculum, Native children were required to sing a self-loathing hymn:

> Let the Indian. . . . Let the rude barbarian hear,
> Of the glories of the kingdom . . .[4]

Now Collier ordered that all religious services were to become optional. He also mandated that "the cultural liberty of Indians is in all respects to be considered equal to that of any non-Indian group."[5] Never again, after Collier, would Indigenous children be forced to mouth such soul-erasing propaganda.

Collier also lifted the prohibition on speaking Native languages at schools. "It is desirable that Indians be bilingual," he declared. "Fluent and literate in the English language and fluent in their vital, beautiful, and efficient native languages." The new commissioner also reversed long-standing bans on tribal artistic expression. He announced a new policy: "The Indian arts and crafts are to be prized, nourished, and honored."[6]

One boarding school student, Floyd O'Neil, later recalled how his missionary teachers "despised Collier almost beyond belief," adding, "I had never heard anyone accused of being in league with the devil until I heard a school teacher claim that Collier was."[7]

The missionaries and assimilationists howled about Collier's changes, but the commissioner found a way to cut off their oxygen. For years, a missionary-dominated advisory board had held sway over the Indian Bureau, stalling the pace of reforms. Collier and Interior Secretary Ickes persuaded President Roosevelt to issue an executive order abolishing the board. The president claimed it was for budgetary reasons, yet the annual expenditure had amounted to only $13,000. Everyone knew the real reason. The missionaries fumed but were now shut out of influencing Bureau policy.

For years, Collier had been viewed as an incendiary zealot, even by his supporters. Few expected him to be able to actually govern, and many of his opponents hoped that his tenure as Indian Commissioner would soon self-destruct. But once Collier was on the inside, with his hands on the levers of power, the burden of responsibility seemed to transform him. He became the consummate team player within the Roosevelt administration. He built bridges and fostered positive relations with others, all in pursuit of a single overarching goal: to improve the lives of Indigenous people. That the new president, along with Interior Secretary Ickes, both supported that same cause made Collier's path significantly smoother.

Collier was able to ensure that Native peoples substantially benefitted from FDR's landmark relief programs, including the WPA and the Civilian Conservation Corps (CCC). The WPA employed over 10,000 Indigenous people to help build the new schools on reservations, along with roads and hospitals. The CCC found jobs for some 85,000 young Native people, who engaged in soil conservation and reforestation efforts to rehabilitate tribal lands. The Civil Works Association employed another 4,000 people to renovate government and tribal buildings. In recognition of Indigenous artistry, Native painters were hired by various agencies to create murals in public buildings. For a population that had a per capita income of about $100 per year, these new wage-earning opportunities, many of which were designed to improve their own communities, proved transformative.

To the surprise of everyone who knew both men, Collier and Interior Secretary Harold Ickes developed a warm, close partnership. Collier often sprinted up two flights of stairs for impromptu meetings with his boss. Together, the two allies found creative solutions to vexing problems. For years, Collier had railed against the federal practice of charging Native tribes for public works projects that mostly benefited neighboring whites. He had battled unsuccessfully to stop this abusive practice. By the time he became Indian Commissioner, tribal nations had amassed $12 million of burdensome debt for such dubious "improvements." Working with Ickes, the two men hatched an elegantly simple administrative remedy: The Interior Secretary simply canceled the Natives' debt.

Ickes and Collier both understood that the most devastating impact on Indigenous sovereignty was the longtime federal policy of reallocating Indian lands to whites, as mandated by the 1887 Dawes Act. "The cumulative loss of land brought about by the allotment system," Collier reported, totaled ninety million acres—"two-thirds of the land heritage of the Indian race." The results, he charged, caused Natives to be "ruined economically and pauperized spiritually."[8]

Neither Collier nor Ickes had the power to overturn federal law, but the Interior Secretary found a way to throw a wrench into the machinery. On August 12, 1933, Ickes imposed a freeze on further allotments of Native lands, citing "existing economic conditions and the very poor market." To Indian superintendents across the country, the Secretary ordered "no more trust or restricted Indian lands, allotted or inherited, shall be offered for sale."[9]

Collier and his family moved into a red brick colonial townhome with a view of the Potomac, but he spent most of his time at the Indian Bureau working long into the night. His wife, Lucy, reported to Mabel that her husband sometimes put in twenty-four-hour days. Rumors abounded about the often-rumpled Collier. Some claimed that he kept a pet frog in a pants pocket. Others swore that he cared for a family of mice living in one of his desk drawers. One of his chief assistants admitted that Collier was "really a poet, not an administrator."[10]

But administrate he did. He issued a directive requiring all Bureau staff to maintain "an affirmative, appreciative attitude toward Indian cultural values." He knew many longtime employees were resistant to his ideas. "The system—any system—is a hard thing to beat," he warned his supporters. "There is no system here or elsewhere in the world that is more strongly entrenched, more firmly settled or more ramifying and complex than the Indian Bureau. It will be difficult to loosen this bureaucratic grip; difficult to diminish and distribute its powers."[11]

He had a network of spies everywhere, including Mabel Dodge Luhan in Taos, who alerted him to disloyal Bureau employees. Collier worked every angle he could to reshape the agency to become more responsive to Native people. Observing that only 25 percent of the Bureau's staff were Natives and that most of them held only menial jobs, he complained, "Our Indian Bureau has operated as the white man's agency for employing white men." He decided "a radical change is essential."[12] He abolished six hundred positions held by whites and made it a policy to hire Indigenous people whenever possible, including as reservation superintendents. Under his tenure, the Bureau's staff would become completely transformed, rising to 65 percent Native American.

By the time he was appointed Indian Commissioner, Collier realized that

Taos Pueblo's 1927 Cooperative Agreement with the US Forest Service had become as worthless as a broken treaty. The agency had promptly ignored the Pueblo's right to regulate outside visitors, instead allowing unfettered access while promoting Blue Lake as "great natural playground."[13] It continued stocking the waters with fish over the Taos People's objections and even built a ranger cabin on Blue Lake's shores, complete with a garbage pit and outhouse. When Pueblo leaders protested, the agency responded that these "improvements" had been made for their own good, to better regulate the increasing tourist traffic. The agency also threatened the Pueblo by noting that it could terminate the Cooperative Agreement at any time.

Soon after taking office, Collier pushed for Taos Pueblo to regain sovereignty over the Blue Lake watershed. He tried to expand the Pueblo's reservation, but the Forest Service fought back, arguing that it had successfully balanced national forest management with being "consistently regardful of the Indians in this watershed and [making] the most complete provision for their protection practicable under the circumstances."[14]

Ultimately, Roosevelt's cabinet decided that the best compromise would be a new cooperative agreement, a fifty-year "Special Use Permit" for Taos Pueblo. This new arrangement would be codified by law, meaning its provisions would presumably be more enforceable. While the Forest Service still owned the land, the Taos People were promised "free and exclusive use of the Blue Lake watershed."[15] Logging would be banned in 30,000 acres of the 48,000-acre area. To prevent outsiders from interrupting religious rituals, the Forest Service was required to secure Taos Pueblo's written permission before allowing any tourists into the area. This arrangement was not the perfect solution, Collier realized, but it was the best he could do—and clearly represented a significant improvement over the previous agreement.

Beyond Taos, Collier sought to restore tribal connections to nature wherever possible. His Chief Forester at the Indian Bureau, thirty-two-year-old Bob Marshall, had noted with alarm that roadless areas were rapidly vanishing from the United States. Marshall and Collier knew that the US Forest Service, encouraged by Aldo Leopold, had earlier begun preserving broad tracts of land as "wilderness" areas. Soon Marshall developed a plan to prohibit road construction in remote stretches of a dozen reservations, an area totaling nearly five million acres. Collier then issued an executive order designating the regions as permanent roadless wilderness. This new directive, he believed, would "permit the Indian to follow his own way of life."[16]

As the American bison began to recover from the brink of extinction, Collier worked to reconnect the buffalo to Native American communities as part of his campaign for "spiritual rehabilitation." In early 1934, four surplus bison were harvested from Yellowstone National Park and their carcasses shipped by refrigerated rail to New Mexico. At the Santa Fe Indian School, a huge festival was staged, drawing two thousand Pueblo People including Tony Luján from Taos. Amid celebratory dances and the somber distribution of the animals' hides, heads, and horns, heaping platefuls of roasted bison were served to everyone. Many of the older people had not eaten buffalo meat in decades, while younger ones had never before consumed the revered animal.

But the big barbecue was just the beginning. Collier wanted to restore living bison to as many Native People as possible. "We believe that small herds may be put on certain reservations and under the care of Indians prosper," he said. Soon, seventy-seven bison were shipped to the Crow Reservation in Montana, followed by another fifty-four arriving at the Sioux's Pine Ridge Reservation in South Dakota. "Even if the experiment has chiefly a sentimental value," Collier said, "it will be worth undertaking. And it may have a practical value far greater than can now be foreseen."[17] As the stocks grew, bison were distributed to several more tribes, including Taos and other Pueblos in New Mexico.

Collier's sweeping changes at the Indian Bureau were cheered by many Native Americans. One tribal leader paid Collier the ultimate compliment, praising the commissioner as a "white man with a red man's heart."[18]

Although gratified by his early successes, Collier realized that many of his reforms were just a start—and could easily be overturned by a new Indian Commissioner, just as he had reversed the policies of his predecessors. The only way to truly break the fever of white conquest and restore Indigenous societies would be through legislation, which would enshrine even bigger, truly transformative changes into federal law.

Ten years earlier, Collier had laid out his vision for the future in a letter to Mabel Dodge Luhan. The first step was "to establish our right to dictate Indian policy," he'd said. Next came the matter of getting "ourselves strongly on top politically." Finally, "*After* our power is established, then we can get the fundamental changes needed."[19]

Now that Collier was "on top," the time had come at last to make those fundamental changes. This, he knew, would be the most difficult challenge of all. "The next session of Congress," he prophesied, "will be for the Indians and the Indian Service a fateful time."[20]

CHAPTER 24

THE INDIAN NEW DEAL

1933–1945

Mabel Dodge Luhan cherished her friend John Collier's revolutionary fervor even as she worried about his punishing workload. On a rare trip away from Washington, Collier only managed a brief stop in Taos before speeding off to his next appointment. Knowing he was extraordinarily busy, she wrote to him, "I have to hold on to myself not to deluge you with letters. . . . But I will try not to because the work is so massive all the details will sink you if you're not careful."[1]

Nevertheless, Mabel proved an energetic correspondent. From troubles over Tony's personal land allotment[2] at Taos Pueblo to complaints about local Indian Bureau officials, her letters soon piled up on Collier's desk. She fired off several dispatches about the inadequacy of the new school building at Taos, which was not large enough to allow the students to play basketball indoors. She also sent Collier a telegram about an older Taos Pueblo man who needed to get his teeth fixed.

Mabel was just one of hundreds of people appealing to Collier with reports and complaints and demands. Meanwhile, the new commissioner was trying to reform a creaky bureaucracy of six thousand employees spread across the country. Many longtime Bureau staff opposed the new regime, and Collier had to personally intervene in dozens of instances. He was known to pen harsh letters castigating those "unwisely persuading the Indians to stultify their traditions." Resistance to Collier's reforms was so pervasive that Interior Secretary Ickes sent his own missive to all staff.

Those who opposed the new policies, Ickes wrote, "should do so honestly and openly from outside of the service." Those who didn't resign voluntarily, he warned, "will be summarily eliminated, wherever found, by dismissal."[3]

Even as Collier was swamped by daunting administrative challenges, he kept his eyes on the biggest prize of all—the grand culmination of the revolutionary dream he and Mabel had shared ever since he got turned on by Taos Pueblo. Collier planned to create what he called an "Indian New Deal," a monumental legislative program that would roll back four hundred years of conquest and revitalize Indigenous America. He envisioned the ascendant tribes serving as shining examples of communal living and natural harmony for all Americans, inspiring a new, more sustainable path for the country as a whole.

Fundamental to Collier's plan was toppling the 1887 Dawes Act, which had broken so many tribes through forced assimilation and dispossession. Manifesting centuries of Native policy, the Dawes Act's brutal objectives had been endorsed by generations of political leaders. A handful of reformers had criticized its methods, but few dared to question its premise. Now Collier aimed to tear the entire thing down.

He would seek to repeal the Dawes Act and pass new federal laws ensuring the rights of Indigenous people to maintain their own traditions and cultures. He would grant each tribe the right of self-government and allow each to have its own courts and constitutions. New government financing would help Native People break free of outside domination and gain economic self-sufficiency. The new statutes would protect Indigenous languages, religions and cultures from any further attacks. Simultaneously, Collier would expand educational opportunities to send more Native Americans to college and develop Indigenous professional expertise.

Above all, Collier knew that power flowed from land ownership. He believed that substantial reparations were necessary to reverse centuries of dispossession. "It is now the moral duty of the government to supply land," he argued. "What we have got to do now is get the Indian back on his own land."[4] He recognized that a big part of the problem was that so many reservations had become "checkerboarded" with privately owned parcels. He envisioned vast government funding to purchase at least twenty-five million acres and consolidate broken lands into contiguous, communal holdings for Native people.

Collier began referring to his collective vision as the Natives' "Magna Carta," their "Emancipation Proclamation."

But the clock was ticking. The seventy-third Congress, which had already passed a tidal wave of New Deal legislation, was entering its final months. President Roosevelt remained enormously popular and the Democrats controlled the House and Senate, but midterm elections loomed in 1934. The time to act was now.

Even as he worked around the clock, Collier could not personally craft his groundbreaking legislation while also directing the Indian Bureau. So he turned to outside help. The expert he came to rely on was Felix S. Cohen, a twenty-six-year-old assistant solicitor who earned a PhD from Harvard and a law degree from Columbia. Cohen possessed a dazzling legal mind, but he knew practically nothing about Indigenous people. Collier sought to rectify that by dispatching the young attorney on a whirlwind tour of Native reservations in November 1933. Cohen was just three weeks into his trip when Collier sent a telegram recalling him to Washington. The timeline for the Indian New Deal had been moved up.

Over the next six weeks, Cohen worked long nights and weekends to write the various bills. He met regularly with Collier and other top Indian Bureau officials, all white men. No Natives were consulted. Even as Collier plotted for Indigenous people to gain greater control over their own affairs, he gave them no voice in developing the proposed laws to do so. In part this was because of the tremendous rush to get the bills filed. Collier also knew he had the trust of his most important constituency, the Pueblo People of New Mexico. Yet excluding Native input reflected Collier at his worst—the domineering paternalist who believed he already possessed all the right answers.

It wasn't just Native leaders shut out of Collier's conferences. He also ignored powerful members of Congress. This was no mere oversight but, rather, a calculated strategy. Collier had allies in Congress who were sympathetic to reforming Native affairs, but he knew that his proposed legislation—which amounted to the most radical change in federal Indigenous policy in US history—went far beyond what many of these senators and congressmen would tolerate. He anticipated that the bills might encounter stiff resistance. So he decided it was best to keep Congress in the dark about the details—and then leverage FDR's groundswell of popular momentum to get everything passed.

By the end of January, the bills were nearly ready. At this pivotal moment, Collier decided to consolidate everything into a single package, calling it the Indian Reorganization Act. At a lengthy fifty-two pages, it would be one of the largest bills Congress had ever seen. Collier understood that such a document, "would have a massive and dramatic nature, commanding the imagination of Indians and Congressmen alike."[5]

He shared a copy of the bulky text with Mabel Dodge Luhan. She responded with one word: "masterly." When President Roosevelt saw the plan, endorsed by Interior Secretary Ickes, he heartily approved, scrawling on his copy, "Great Stuff."[6]

On Lincoln's birthday, February 12, 1934, Collier carried the thick sheaf of papers to Capitol Hill, marking up last-minute edits on the way. He presented the document to Senator Burton K. Wheeler of Montana, a progressive ally for Native reform who now chaired the Committee on Indian Affairs. Wheeler promptly introduced the bill without even bothering to read it. A cosponsor in the House, Edgar Howard, quickly signed on.

Collier's public announcement of an Indian New Deal was greeted with effusive support, and the press showered him with praise: "The bill is really his," a typical article read. "It is born of his long service among the Indians, of his burning sense of the wrongs that have been done to the tribes, individually and collectively."[7]

But once the actual text of the Wheeler-Howard Bill began to circulate, it became clear there was a problem. While Felix Cohen was undeniably brilliant, the bill's daunting length and abstruse language sowed widespread confusion and suspicion. Describing the structure of the new tribal governments, Cohen's text read:

> An Indian community chartered under this act shall be recognized

> as successor to any existing political powers heretofore exercised over the members of such community by any tribal, or other native political organizations comprised within the said community, not withheld by such tribal or other native political organizations, and shall, subject to the terms of said charter, further be recognized as successor to all rights, interest, and title to all funds, property, choices in action, and claims against the United States heretofore held by the tribes or other native political organizations comprised within the community.[8]

Few could make sense of that passage, nor many others in the bill. Making matters worse for Collier was his disregard of Congress while drafting the bill. The Senate may have confirmed his appointment as Indian Commissioner, but that didn't mean he'd gained its trust. Many suspected that the bill's inscrutability might be deliberate, as a means of disguising its radical intent.

When Senator Wheeler finally read the bill introduced under his name he was appalled: "I will swear that it is impossible for me to understand some of the provisions," he told Collier. An experienced attorney, Wheeler noted that several of his senate colleagues, all lawyers, "cannot themselves tell exactly what you are going to do."[9]

Collier sought to allay concerns, pointing out that the bill's length was necessary because it would replace "several thousand pages of Indian law." Its complexity owed to the fact that "the situation itself is exceedingly complicated."[10] Few were convinced by these excuses.

At the first Senate hearing on February 17, the reception for Collier was anything but warm. He tried to explain the bill but was repeatedly interrupted with hostile questions. Collier finally invoked Franklin Roosevelt, saying that the president "has indicated his personal enthusiasm"[11] for the measure. Chairman Burton Wheeler and the other senators remained skeptical. Wheeler adjourned the committee without taking any action on the bill.

As momentum stalled, missionary leaders rushed to condemn the Wheeler-Howard Bill. One former member of the now-defunct Indian Bureau Advisory Board, G. E. E. Lindquist, charged that Collier's "anti-Christian scheme" encouraged paganism and would destroy "most of the gains of the last fifty years." Another ex-board member, Flora Warren

Seymour, denounced the legislation as a move "toward a Communist experiment."[12]

Collier was ready for these attacks. He leapt into battle, blaming "special interests" and their "audacious attempt to seize Indian properties." He charged that "those attacking the bill are threatening the very lives and existence of the Indians."[13]

But what he didn't count on was a storm of dissent from many Natives. These were people from across the country who had acclimated to modern American life. Many were Christians and quite comfortable in their faith. They saw in Collier's plan a reactionary, segregationist impulse to force them back to a tribal era that had long since passed.

A Crow woman named Mary Riley Small eloquently skewered Collier before the US Senate: "Despite Mr. Collier's reputed knowledge of the Indian, he seems to have overlooked the fact that most of the old-time Indians who might have been interested in his plan 50 years ago have long since passed on to the Happy Hunting Grounds."[14]

She pointed out that people of her own generation "do not know a great deal about the old customs and we are more interested in this good old modern time of ours, we enjoy our good books, magazines, music, contract bridge, our homes. . . . Most of us have never had a blanket to which we yearn to return."[15]

Collier, who for years had been obsessed by Taos Pueblo's stubborn fight to preserve its traditional way of life, had assumed that all Native people shared the same goal. He had failed to adequately consider the cumulative effects of generations of assimilation on many diverse Indigenous populations across America.

He would soon learn, as the Senate was bombarded with protests. A Blackfoot woman appealed to legislators: "Why belong to a separate little community when we already are a part of the biggest and best nation on earth?" An Ogalala Sioux man testified, "I am sincerely interested in . . . working and living as the white man, and having an interest in life's achievements."[16]

Many of these people, who'd acquired their 160-acre allotments as the result of the Dawes Act, found that they *enjoyed* individual land ownership. They denounced Collier's plan to restore communally held lands. Mary

Riley Small told the senate: "I have inherited the 'white man's way' to such an extent that somehow I have no desire to share my land with others." A Christianized Native from California complained, "I am one hundred percent American. I tell you this bill preaches communism and socialism." The chair of the Crow Creek delegation warned that if Collier's legislation passed, "We might just as well live in Russia."[17]

As criticisms raged, the press turned against Collier, lashing out at his attempt to "convert the red men into the type of red men found in Moscow."[18]

To have any chance of saving his bill, Collier would have to shore up rapidly dissipating Native support. In a move born of desperation, he decided to barnstorm the country and sell his plan in person. The Bureau quickly set up a series of ten "Indian Congresses," which would allow him to speak to nearly all affected tribes. For someone who'd been too rushed to engage with Native leaders while creating the bill, Collier would now have to spend weeks traveling the nation in order to sell that same legislation to thousands of Indigenous people in person.

On March 1, Collier arrived in Rapid City, South Dakota, for the first gathering. The next morning some three hundred delegates assembled, representing the Blackfeet, Crow, Sioux, Dakota, Chippewa, Flathead, and Shoshone People.

The mood in the crowd was uneasy. The tribal delegates, just like members of Congress, hadn't been able to make sense of the bill, but what they'd heard made them suspicious. Many were landowners and had been warned that Collier intended to confiscate their personal property and convert it to communal tribal lands.

Collier took the stage and sought to be reassuring, pointing to his long record fighting on behalf of Indigenous people. He explained that the new measure was intended to replace the old laws that sought to "crush" Native Americans. "I believe most of you will want the bill when you understand it thoroughly," he said. "It takes nothing from you, but gives you many things you want."[19]

Figure 35. John Collier poses with members of the Blackfoot Nation, 1934. Library of Congress, Prints & Photographs Division, LC-USZ62-114913.

For three long days and nights, the earnest, often charming Collier was at his best. He spoke from his heart about his desire to improve Native lives and he explained the Wheeler-Howard bill as clearly as possible. He answered questions with candor and listened carefully to objections. In response to concerns about forced transfers of inherited lands to communal tribal status, Collier declared that the bill would be amended to make that provision voluntary, drawing thunderous applause.

On the final day, members of the Blackfeet Nation came forward to announce that they now supported Collier—and furthermore, they were adopting him into their tribe. In a brief ceremony, they presented the commissioner with a headdress and christened him "Spotted Eagle." That name, their spokesman said, "represents the Indian Reservations, the way they are all checkerboarded. We hope that those spots will be rubbed off so that every Indian Reservation will all be in one spot."[20]

As the first congress came to an end, Collier's voice had grown hoarse, but he'd succeeded in turning most of the skeptics around. One admiring delegate told reporters that the commissioner's Native name should be "Iron Man." John Collier, the man said, "has worn out all our interpreters."[21]

On and on the Indian congresses went—to Oregon, Arizona, California, Oklahoma, Wisconsin. Collier's allies also fanned out to build support. From Taos, Tony Luján and Antonio Mirabal lobbied the other Pueblos, some of which had become anxious after hearing alarming rumors about the new law. "We have got a real friend in John Collier," Luján reminded the Pueblos. "He is putting a wall around us to protect us—and this Wheeler-Howard Bill is this wall. And no white man or grafter can come inside and take away our land or our religion." Antonio Mirabal addressed the All Pueblo Council: "We are not going to fight against ourselves," he implored. "We are in favor of this bill."[22]

After several weeks on the road, Collier returned to Washington exhausted, but he'd gained the clear approval of the majority of America's Native People. He was able to report to Congress that 55 tribes comprising 141,881 people had voted in favor of the bill while only 12 tribes with 15,106 had voted against it.[23]

But the bill's sponsor, Burton Wheeler, was in no mood to be receptive. The senator considered himself a far better-informed authority on Indigenous people than the headline-grabbing, know-it-all John Collier. Wheeler staged more than a dozen Senate hearings, allowing critics to fulminate against the Wheeler-Howard Bill. Then he adjourned his committee without taking action, saying that the bill needed more study.

Behind the scenes, the increasingly frantic Collier worked to secure Franklin Roosevelt's support. He told Interior Secretary Ickes, "Unquestionably we greatly need a formal statement from the President on the Indian bill and self-government bill . . . without a definite expression from the President, I do not believe we will get the bill across at the present session."[24]

With time running out, the most powerful man in America came to the rescue. On April 28, 1934, Roosevelt issued a public appeal, calling the Wheeler-Howard Bill "a measure of justice that is long overdue." The president expressed his support in the strongest possible terms: "We can and

Figure 36. President Franklin Roosevelt greets Pueblo representatives while Indian Commissioner John Collier smiles at left, 1936. Glasshouse Images/Alamy Stock Photo.

should, without further delay, extend to the Indian the fundamental rights of political liberty and local self-government and the opportunities of education and economic assistance that they require to obtain a wholesome American life. This is but the obligation of honor of a powerful nation toward a people living among us and dependent on our protection."[25]

Roosevelt also sent a gracious private note to Senator Wheeler, commending him for his leadership on such important legislation. Two days later, Wheeler reconvened his committee in a new spirit, observing that the president was "very anxious that the bill should be passed at this session of congress."[26]

Wheeler devoted himself to "improving" the bill, rewriting major portions and stripping away objectionable provisions as the marginalized Collier watched helplessly from the sidelines. Plans for communal lands were scaled back drastically, and the Oklahoma nations were exempted from portions of the act. Wheeler called the idea of a separate Indigenous court system "crazy," and yanked it out of the bill. He also had little patience for Collier's proposal to provide $103 million for tribal nations to acquire twenty-five million acres of land. Instead, he cut the funding to $5 million. Finally, all tribes' participation in the new law was made voluntary, and subject to the results of binding tribal elections. As Wheeler wrapped up his work, the original sixty sections in the act were trimmed to nineteen and the bill's length was reduced from fifty-two pages to five.

Yet front and center remained the most important component of all: repealing the 1887 Dawes Act and ending forced assimilation and dispossession. Existing tribal lands and Indigenous cultures would be protected while granting new rights of self-government.

On May 17, Wheeler introduced a new draft of the bill, which he fast-tracked through the senate. The House readily followed. On June 18, 1934, Franklin D. Roosevelt signed the Indian Reorganization Act into law.

John Collier had fallen short of his grand vision. "Perhaps never in American history has any legislation been written and enacted so completely in a goldfish bowl,"[27] he complained. His Indian Reorganization Act would not be a Magna Carta or an Emancipation Proclamation. Yet even in its diminished form, the new law became a landmark turning point in the long crusade for Indigenous justice. White America's long-raging fever for conquest had finally been tempered. The crushing machinery of dispossession and cultural extinction had been dismantled.

Collier would go on to serve nearly twelve years as Commissioner of Indian Affairs, the longest tenure in US history. His time in office was hardly placid, and he was battered by repeated attacks against the Indian New Deal. Montana Senator Burton Wheeler became an enemy and tried to repeal the Indian Reorganization Act he had earlier cosponsored. An increasingly conservative Congress cut funding for the Indian Bureau, forcing Collier to scale back his ambitious plans. Still, the new law survived, and a majority of tribes voted to embrace it, seeing it as the best pathway to gain federally recognized self-determination. In the years since its passage, Indigenous land holdings in the United States have increased some three million acres. While that growth is modest, it stands in stark contrast to the ninety million acres lost in the fifty-year period before the Indian Reorganization Act became law.

Collier's efforts to gain further reforms were mostly thwarted. Among his most disappointing failures was Congress's refusal to establish an Indian Claims Commission, which he envisioned as a means to restore stolen land—most prominently Taos Pueblo's Blue Lake. The outbreak of World War II soon relegated Native affairs to the margins. Congress slashed the agency's budget nearly in half, and Collier's staff resigned in droves, many of them leaving to join the armed services. No longer expanding his fight for reform, Collier scrambled to simply maintain basic services.

Still, despite the many setbacks and disappointments, the Indian New Deal remained largely intact when Collier retired in January 1945. President Roosevelt saluted him: "One achievement of my administration in which I shall always take the deepest pride has been the progress that has been made in connection with our first Americans . . . In encouraging him to pursue his own life and revive and continue his own culture, we have added to his worth and dignity." He told Collier, "All of these things have been done under your leadership because of your wisdom and courage."[28]

While the Indian New Deal was the culmination of Collier's reform efforts, the law represented only part of a broader revolution. From a small group of cross-cultural rebels in Taos came a transformative change far more profound than anything that could be codified in legislation. America's Native People were no longer regarded by the white majority as a defeated enemy, a "vanishing race" destined for assimilation and extinction. Instead, for the first time since European conquest, Indigenous cultures became valued as national assets deserving respect and protection. This profound shift not only reset the basic calculus of the US government's approach to Native affairs; it also helped empower the resilient native societies that had survived centuries of darkness. A new era dawned as life began flowing back in the direction of Indigenous America.

John Collier had emerged as the movement's political leader, but he was hardly its creator, or its energizing force. The Pueblo People, who had earlier staged a formidable revolt in 1680 that humbled the Spanish Empire, continued to resist the forces of conquest in the twentieth century. Facing an overwhelming military power, they adapted by targeting the soft underbelly of American democracy: enlisting prominent allies in a peaceful campaign to amass broad public support. None of the Pueblos' white allies were perfect, and many were deeply flawed. Yet in large part they served their purposes by advancing the Pueblos' resistance. In the end, John Collier became their most powerful advocate. Cultivated from the beginning by Tony Luján and others, Collier became inspired to devote his abundant energies and talents to justice for Native people. In doing so, he found his life's mission. Yet Collier was as much a creation of the Pueblos as he was their champion.

Despite the Indian New Deal's achievements, latter-day academics have picked apart Collier's record and trumpeted his flaws—particularly his tendency toward paternalism. Many have blamed Collier for the ugly resurgence of "Termination" in the 1950s, when the US government pivoted back towards assimilation and targeting tribal lands.

Scholarly pundits have offered varying explanations for Termination's onset: Collier's policies were flawed, his reforms were too timid, or maybe his reforms had gone too far, or maybe his contentious personality had left Native peoples more vulnerable to attack. Few of the critics seem to have considered the obvious historic context: the push for Termination was part of a wider conservative backlash against Franklin Roosevelt's New Deal, accelerated by a national mania for conformity as the Cold War began. While Collier's reforms were sorely tested during those bleak years, they largely endured. Support for Termination collapsed in the 1960s and was finally renounced as government policy in 1970 by Richard Nixon—during a historic White House meeting with Taos Pueblo leaders.

Ultimately, the most generous assessments of Collier's Indian New Deal have often come from Indigenous voices. Alfonso Ortiz, the prominent anthropologist from Ohkay Owingeh Pueblo in New Mexico, remarked, "There are many, including me, who believe the most enduring contribution that the Collier policies made to Indian life, especially after a half a century, was to encourage traditional cultural expression." John Echohawk, founder and executive director of the Native American Rights Fund, noted: "The Indian New Deal wasn't perfect, but its results were fundamentally beneficial for Indian people." The legendary Standing Rock Sioux scholar Vine Deloria, writing with Clifford Lytle, observed, "Collier was not the first non-Indian to appreciate the Indian tradition. He certainly became the first to understand, appreciate, articulate, and fight zealously for it." Deloria and Lytle concluded, "The fact remains that the man engineered a complete revolution in Indian affairs."[29]

Joseph W. Hayes, a Chickasaw leader, spoke for many when he said that, thanks to the Indian New Deal, "Every morning our children will be Indians."[30]

EPILOGUE

JULY 8, 1970
WASHINGTON, DC

Sixty-four years into the Pueblo's unbroken quest to recover its sacred Blue Lake, a delegation of Taos men arrived at the White House. The group was led by Paul Bernal, a one-time schoolteacher who'd volunteered for the US Navy when World War II broke out. Bernal had served aboard the USS *Ticonderoga*, where he fought off waves of kamikaze attacks that killed 143 of his crewmates and nearly sunk the ship. After the war, Bernal returned home with a single mission—to help his people regain Blue Lake. Over the past twenty years he'd become the Pueblo's chief strategist and spokesperson.

Accompanying Bernal was the Taos People's ninety-year-old spiritual leader, Juan de Jesús Romero. The cacique had been a young man in 1906 when Teddy Roosevelt appropriated Taos Pueblo's land for a national forest. Later, in the 1920s, Romero had been among those jailed in the US government's drive to destroy his people's religion. For more than half a century, he'd spent every morning and evening praying for Blue Lake. "If our land is not returned to us," he said, "then it is the end of Indian life."[1] The elderly cacique had climbed into an airplane for the first time in his life to make this trip to Washington, DC.

Bernal and Romero wore traditional tribal blankets and beaded deerskin moccasins, just as Tony Luján and Antonio Mirabal in 1933 when they met with Franklin D. Roosevelt. Other Taos elders accompanying Bernal and Romero were similarly dressed. Yet one man stood apart, outfitted in a conservative business suit and tie. This was fifty-seven-year-old John

Rainer, the first person from Taos Pueblo to secure a college education. Rainer had gone on to become a national voice for Native justice, described by a wary US senator as "one of the most aggressive Indian leaders in America."[2] Rainer was intimately connected to the Blue Lake battle. It had been his uncle, Sun Elk, who had first recruited the painter Bert Phillips to help protect Taos Pueblo's lands from white encroachment.

Sun Elk was now gone, as were so many of those who'd advocated for Blue Lake—among them John Collier, Bert Phillips, Mabel Dodge Luhan and Tony Luján. Yet the movement lived on, renewed by fresh generations. As John Rainer bluntly informed a group of senators at a hearing: "A good number of the old people of Taos Pueblo, and my father was among these, hoped for, but did not live to realize the cherished dream that this Government would return the ill-gotten lands. Today my father is appearing before you through me and if I too should leave in disappointment my sons shall appear here for both of us, and they shall have sons who will continue to haunt these halls until a final and just settlement is reached."[3]

Just as from the very beginning of this battle, Taos leaders strategically recruited outside supporters, building an increasingly broad and diverse constituency. By the time these Taos men arrived at the White House, the Pueblo's advocates had come to include writers and artists, the National Council of Churches and the American Civil Liberties Union, tribal leaders from across the nation, politicians from both parties, university presidents, business executives, environmentalists, movie stars, hippies, and girl scouts.

And then there was the weirdest, most improbable ally of all: Richard M. Nixon.

Soon after Nixon took office, Sun Elk's nephew John Rainer gained access to the White House upon his appointment to new a cabinet-level council on Indigenous affairs. Chairing the body was Vice President Spiro Agnew. Rainer and another Native councilor, Comanche activist LaDonna Harris, brought the Blue Lake issue to the attention of Agnew and other key officials. They soon gained enthusiastic support.

A cadre of White House insiders worked for months to convert President Nixon to Taos Pueblo's cause. There were political calculations in addition to moral considerations, though Nixon was not easily convinced of either. Presidential counselor Leonard Garment argued that Blue Lake "has snowballed and is now the single specific Indian issue . . . strong on the merits, and powerfully symbolic." Nixon's close adviser, John Ehrlichman, told him, "It was cowboys and Indians and that we were on the side of the Indians." Nixon thought that over a moment, then responded that he was "more of a John Wayne man."[4]

While Nixon hedged, popular support for Taos Pueblo continued to swell. A new generation was rising, sparked by a growing environmental movement. The Taos People, always wise stewards of their homeland, now became revered for their ecological prescience. As the prominent conservationist and former Interior Secretary Stewart Udall put it, "These are Indians who happen to have the same attitude toward nature that we are coming around to today rather belatedly."[5]

In the spring of 1970, as the nation celebrated its first Earth Day, Taos Pueblo's long battle to recover Blue Lake gained fresh momentum as young people flocked to its cause. Pueblo supporters even came to include Kim Agnew, the fourteen-year-old daughter of Vice President Spiro Agnew.

The vice president was among those who pressed Nixon to claim the Taos issue as his own. Supporting the Pueblo, Agnew and others argued, would make Nixon seem statesmanlike. It would also help bolster his anemic polling among younger voters, which had plummeted after the Kent State shootings. There was also a real concern that the Democrats would claim all the credit if the Taos People prevailed. Finally, Nixon was converted. He agreed to invite a group of Taos leaders to the White House.

The Taos men were ushered into the Cabinet Room, where a brooding portrait of Dwight Eisenhower, who had presided over the Termination era, stared from above the fireplace. Outside the French doors, the White House's Rose Garden bloomed in the steamy heat. Then Nixon strolled in, joined by Vice President Agnew, Interior Secretary Walter Hickel, and various staffers.

The visitors from Taos had been promised fifteen minutes with the president. They were told that Nixon would read a statement endorsing their cause and pose for photographs. Instead, something astonishing happened, an event so rare that it caught the president's staff off guard. The introverted Nixon, normally ill-at-ease in social settings, soon began smiling and chatting easily with fellow World War II Navy veteran Paul Bernal and the others. Time slipped by, and still the president hadn't read his statement. After fifteen minutes, an aide rushed forward with what Nixon's people called an "escape note"—a blank piece of paper purporting to carry an important message. This would allow the president to gracefully excuse himself. Instead, Nixon waved the aide off. He and the Taos leaders kept up their lively conversation.

Figure 37. President Richard Nixon meets with Taos Pueblo leaders in the White House. Pictured here are Governor Quirino Romero, left, and Paul Bernal, right. Richard M. Nixon Presidential Library and Museum/National Archives and Records Administration.

Nixon appeared to be enjoying himself immensely. Thirty minutes passed. The aide returned with another escape note. Again, Nixon dismissed the man. Finally, after an enchanting morning with his guests, Nixon read his presidential statement. He praised America's Native peoples and he forcefully repudiated the old policy of Termination, calling it "morally and legally unacceptable." The president then brought up Taos Pueblo's long campaign for Blue Lake, calling it "an issue of unique and critical importance to Indians throughout the country." He called for restoring the Pueblo's sacred land.[6]

The Taos leaders left the White House heartened by the president's endorsement, yet they faced a sobering reality. They knew that even support from the most powerful man in the world might not be enough to win back Blue Lake.

In 1946, the year after John Collier left office, Congress finally established the Indian Claims Commission he'd long advocated for. Yet the entity was set up in a very different manner than Collier had proposed. The three-person tribunal would not include any Indigenous representatives. Nor were there any provisions for returning stolen tribal lands. Instead, the Indian Claims Commission would limit all compensation to cash settlements.

Still, Taos leaders and their allies—who by now included Pulitzer Prize–winning novelist Oliver La Farge—saw a potential path to justice. If the Pueblo could win a favorable judgment, it might have leverage to persuade the US government to return Blue Lake. It was a long shot, but few other options existed.

As Taos Pueblo prepared its case, the artist Bert Phillips again provided crucial support. At age eighty, Phillips provided first-hand testimony that fully backed the Pueblo's claim. He described how Teddy Roosevelt's Chief Naturalist Vernon Bailey had pledged to help, and Phillips explained that the rationale for government intervention was "to protect the entire watershed for the exclusive Indian use as always in the past."[7]

Phillips's detailed account, valuable on its own merits, also helped

Pueblo allies pinpoint key documents in government archives. For tribal leader Paul Bernal, Phillips's latest contribution absolved the artist of his previous sins. Bernal began referring to Phillips as "a great friend to the Indians."[8]

It would take the slow-walking, Termination-minded Indian Claims Commission fourteen agonizing years to finally rule on the case, but in 1965 its decision was announced—and Taos Pueblo won an emphatic victory. Taos leaders refused to accept money, instead insisting on Blue Lake's return.

This uncompromising position was denounced as unrealistic, even fanatical, for the US government had never before agreed to restore stolen Indigenous land. But effective lobbying by Paul Bernal, John Rainer, and their allies led to positive action in the House of Representatives—which passed bills to return Blue Lake in 1967 and 1968.

Yet each of those bills got crushed in the Senate, where Taos was opposed by Clinton P. Anderson, one of the most powerful men on Capitol Hill. Tall and flinty-eyed, Anderson was New Mexico's most dominant politician since Albert B. Fall. He'd been the first since Fall to win a cabinet post, serving as Harry Truman's Agriculture Secretary in the 1940s, where he'd overseen the US Forest Service. Now a four-term US senator, Anderson remained the Forest Service's most zealous proponent in Congress. He vowed that the only way Taos Pueblo would get Blue Lake back would be "over my dead body."[9]

On July 9, 1970, the morning after Nixon's White House blessing, the Taos delegation arrived at the US Capitol for Senate hearings on a House-passed bill to restore Blue Lake. The timing of Richard Nixon's White House endorsement the day before was no coincidence. It was designed to pressure Clinton Anderson and the Senate to approve the measure.

Buoying the men's spirits were the morning newspapers. Their meeting with President Nixon made the front pages and included a photo of the smiling president seated between Paul Bernal and Taos Pueblo Governor Quirino Romero. The *New York Times* suggested that Nixon's enthusiastic backing might finally break the Senate blockade over Blue Lake.

The elderly cacique, Juan de Jesús Romero, brought the Pueblo's two ceremonial silver-tipped canes—one from the king of Spain and the other given by Abraham Lincoln. Each symbolized the Taos People's sovereignty over their ancestral lands.

The cavernous hearing room overflowed with spectators. A seat had been reserved up front for the Pueblo's teenaged devotee, vice presidential daughter Kim Agnew. On the raised dais at the head of the room was Clinton Anderson and five other men, all members of the Senate's Subcommittee on Indian Affairs.

Several Pueblo advocates were on hand to testify, including a progressive young senator from Oklahoma named Fred Harris. He was married to LaDonna Harris—the Comanche leader who'd worked with John Rainer to gain White House support. Senator Harris had met with Taos Pueblo leaders earlier in the year and became an instant convert, telling one of his staffers, "If we don't do another damn thing while we're here in the Senate, let's help these people get back their land."[10]

The Senate's Indian subcommittee, under Anderson's grip, had delayed hearings on the House-passed bill for ten long months. A frustrated Fred Harris had publicly called on his colleagues to act. This drew the ire of New Mexico's senior senator. Clinton Anderson confronted Harris on the Senate floor, telling him, "Fred, I don't mess with your Indians in Oklahoma and you don't mess with my Indians in New Mexico." Harris was momentarily stunned. Then he responded, "Senator, they aren't our Indians."[11]

For decades Anderson had opposed every effort by Taos Pueblo to regain Blue Lake. In previous Senate hearings, he had bullied Pueblo supporters while openly favoring their opponents. He'd even indulged a "witness" who resurrected charges from the Secret Dance File days, claiming that the Pueblo's religion was "immoral and obscene."[12] Most ignominiously, in 1968 the senator endorsed a dirty tricks operation: Anderson operatives, in cahoots with the Forest Service, planted empty beer bottles and other trash at Blue Lake, then presented photographic "evidence" at a Senate hearing to discredit Taos Pueblo's religious claims.

The senator took every opportunity to belittle the Taos People's land management practices, which he regarded as primitive and unscientific. Anderson relentlessly pushed to "harvest" the Pueblo's old-growth forests, which he described as "over-mature timber." Thirty thousand acres of the Blue Lake watershed were protected from logging thanks to the Pueblo's Special Use Permit from John Collier's era. But the remaining 18,000 acres were at the mercy of Forest Service technocrats. Blitzkrieg clearcuts buzzed across the Taos mountains, where logging rights to 400-year-old trees were sold for fifty cents each.

Over time, the agency's insistence on destroying complex ecosystems in favor of single-crop lumber farms made the entire region vulnerable to pest infestation. The Forest Service responded by turning to chemical warfare. With funding secured by Senator Anderson, the agency doused the mountains above Taos with DDT, assuring everyone the compound was perfectly safe. When Pueblo leaders objected to the spraying, Senator Anderson highlighted their resistance as further proof the Natives were incapable of properly managing the watershed.

For years, Taos leader Paul Bernal had challenged these Forest Service practices, to no avail. In a 1969 congressional hearing, Bernal eloquently summarized the difference between US Forest Service management and Taos Pueblo's environmental ethos:

> In all of its programs the Forest Service proclaims the supremacy of man over nature; we find this viewpoint contrary to the realities of the natural world and to the nature of conservation. Our tradition and our religion require our people to adapt their lives and activities to our natural surroundings so that men and nature mutually support the life common to both. The idea that man must subdue nature and bend its processes to his purposes is repugnant to our people.[13]

By the time of the 1970 Senate hearings, growing environmental awareness had put the Forest Service on defense over its DDT bombardments and clearcuts of old-growth forests. So Clinton Anderson pivoted to a new line of attack. He railed about "a disturbing precedent with national implications." If Taos Pueblo prevailed in regaining 48,000 acres, Anderson warned, the American people could count on losing Yellowstone, the Grand Canyon—and much more. In a heated confrontation with the Pueblo's attorney, William Schaab, Anderson claimed that Native Americans regarded 477 million acres of public domain as "their promised land." Raising his voice at Schaab, Anderson barked: "477 million acres! You wouldn't settle for the possession of that? Will you settle for 477 million acres?"[14]

Taos Pueblo's capable attorney had meticulously prepared for the hearing, but nothing could have readied him for this paranoic reasoning. Gaping at Anderson, he could only respond: "Do you intend the question seriously, or rhetorically, Senator?"[15]

While Anderson dominated the committee, it was his close ally, Lee Metcalf of Montana, who chaired the proceedings. Where Anderson was sarcastic and rude, Metcalf conducted himself with exaggerated civility—which all too often came across as mocking condescension. Both Anderson and Metcalf cast doubt on Taos Pueblo's religious appeals, insinuating that the Natives secretly planned to make money off Blue Lake, perhaps through timber sales.

A skeptical Senator Metcalf mused, "Maybe passage of this bill would be an encouragement and inspiration for a whole lot of Indian religions—and medicine men would spring up all over the country." Pueblo leader Paul Bernal rose to challenge Metcalf, and the two sparred for a couple of moments. Then Bernal asked the senator: "Do you believe in religion?" The chairman was unbowed. "Monetary compensation," Metcalf brayed to the stunned audience. "That is my own religion."[16]

The dismal Indian subcommittee hearings adjourned with no action on the House bill. The deflated Pueblo delegation returned to Taos having again been denied justice. But they were hardly finished fighting. Taos leaders kept the pressure on, announcing a "Justice Day" gathering at the Pueblo and inviting Richard Nixon to join them. The president was intrigued, but his schedule was already packed. Still, the administration wanted to send *someone* to Taos, if only to carry the Blue Lake fight to Senator Anderson's backyard. Then came an inspired idea of political jiujitsu: Nixon would hit Clinton Anderson right between the eyes with a hardball-disguised-as-a-softball—by sending an emissary no one could resist.

Two weeks after the Senate hearings, Air Force Two was on its way to New Mexico. Aboard were White House officials, Secret Service agents, and jaded Washington journalists. But there was no sign of Richard Nixon's blustery vice president, Spiro Agnew. Instead, this delegation was led by fourteen-year-old girl.

Kim Agnew had clashed with her father over rock and roll and the Vietnam War, but they had found common cause in Taos Pueblo's battle for Blue Lake. The Vice President, as the son of Greek immigrants, viewed the matter as justice for an embattled minority community. His daughter was also passionate about Native justice, but she also realized—like young people everywhere—that the Taos area exuded a deep cosmic vibe, that it was "the new hippie mecca."[17] Many young Americans had gotten turned on to Taos by the blockbuster 1969 film *Easy Rider*, made by Dennis Hopper. In the movie, two hippie motorcyclists on a cross-country trip enjoyed a blissful detour in Taos. They visited an area commune and rode their Harleys into Taos Pueblo, puttering alongside the sacred blue stream as the peaceful, tolerant Natives went about their daily business. While antiwar demonstrations and protests ripped American society apart, Taos represented a paradisical antidote. As Hopper's character says in the film: "Taos, man . . . Taos, New Mexico. There's freedom there. They don't mind long hair. The herds mingle." Not since the days of the old Santa Fe Railway propaganda paintings had Taos been depicted in such idyllic terms for the broad mass of American people.[18]

When Kim Agnew arrived at Taos Pueblo, she was given a gentle horse to ride for the next stage of her journey. Just as Taos People had earlier guided Bert Phillips, Mabel Dodge Luhan, and John Collier to their most sacred shrine, now it was time to lead the vice president's daughter. She set out with a dozen Pueblo men, Nixon aides, and Secret Service men. Under heavy clouds, the group rode past towering forests and alongside steep cañons, stopping for lunch in a meadow bursting with wildflowers. When they finally reached the lake, the clouds parted and the sun lit up the entire world. "It truly is a most beautiful and inspirational place," Kim told John Rainer. She now realized, firsthand, "how much the return of this sacred land means."[19]

The next morning, hundreds of visitors crowded into the Pueblo for Justice Day. After two hours of speeches and tribal dances, Kim Agnew stepped on to the wooden stage. There, the beaming young woman presented a gift to the Taos People from President Nixon. It was a teakwood cane, capped with a silver head inscribed with Nixon's name and the date of the Taos leaders' White House visit. The cane, she told Governor Quirino Romero, is a "symbol of the continuing integrity of the ancient kingdom of the Taos."[20] In return, Kim and the White House officials were showered with gifts—including a drum to take back to President Nixon.

Then it was time for one last dance. The drums began beating and a circle formed "with men carrying eagle feathers and corn rattles and women wearing buckskin, long silk dresses and bright blankets. Bells chinked, bone whistles tooted, chanters and drummers kept up a hypnotic tempo."[21] This was the Round Dance—the same one Tony Luján had orchestrated at Mabel's fifty years earlier—a dance symbolizing unity and communion. Kim Agnew joined the circle next to John Rainer, the nephew of Sun Elk. She held the Taos man's hand as everyone came together in rhythm.

Rhapsodic press coverage of the charming teenager's visit to Taos upped the pressure on the Senate to act. The *New York Times*, *Washington Post*, and other major newspapers published editorials endorsing Taos Pueblo—and blasting Senate opponents. A new pro-Taos documentary aired on public television and tribal leader Paul Bernal made the rounds of daytime talk shows. Taos Pueblo and its allies distributed thousands of mimeographed information sheets about Blue Lake, calling on people to send messages of support to congress. The Nixon White House also organized its own letter-writing campaign.

Letters and telegrams flooded the Senate. Yet a handful of powerful insiders—Clinton Anderson and his cabal of anti-Native Westerners—remained unmoved by public pressure. Instead, they quietly proceeded with a backroom deal. The Senate's Interior Committee, headed by an old Anderson pal, Henry "Scoop" Jackson of Washington, rejected the House-passed bill for Taos Pueblo. Instead, it approved a substitute measure, a "compromise" authored by Anderson. This new bill offered the Taos People nominal concessions while retaining Forest Service ownership.

With Senator Anderson's committee-approved bill headed for a vote on the floor, veteran Washington correspondent Seth Kantor declared victory. "Anderson will win this one in the Senate arena," Kantor told newspaper readers. "And look for Indian leaders to charge that the senate has given them a scalping."[22]

The pro-Taos forces refused to concede. The young Oklahoma Senator, Fred Harris, notified Anderson that he would fight his bill on the Senate floor and introduce the House bill in its place. Such guerilla tactics were nearly unheard of in the genteel chamber, and Harris's older colleagues called a closed-door meeting to rebuke him. Clinton Anderson got in Harris's face and told him, *If you don't agree to my bill, there won't be any bill.*[23]

On December 1, Pueblo partisans filled the Senate gallery. John Rainer was given a seat in the row reserved for the vice president's guests. A small delegation from Taos Pueblo—the elderly cacique Juan de Jesús Romero, strategist Paul Bernal, Governor Quirino Romero, and Councilman James Mirabal—joined Fred Harris's wife, LaDonna, in the area reserved for Senate families. The cacique had brought the Pueblo's ceremonial canes, including the new one from Richard Nixon.

Fred Harris stood to remind his colleagues of the stakes: "Support for the Taos Indians in their struggle to reclaim Blue Lake and the surrounding land has spread far beyond the Taos Pueblo. Millions await our decision."[24] Nixon's White House had done its part, joining Harris in vigorously lobbying against Anderson's bill. The president, upon learning that two key Republican senators were away from Washington, dispatched a jet to fly them back for the vote. He also personally called for a police escort to bring another senate straggler in from western Maryland.

As the proceedings began, it was clear that few of Anderson's colleagues dared openly oppose him. New Mexico's junior senator Joseph Montoya, who'd privately professed sympathy for Taos Pueblo, decided to skip the proceedings entirely. It was up to Fred Harris to lead the resistance.

For two days debates raged as the scrappy Harris went toe to toe with Anderson and his allies. Dismissing fears of a "dangerous precedent," Harris countered, "We have set plenty of precedents for injustice. . . . It is that long history of doing the wrong things that I am against. I want to do the right thing for once."[25]

Harris had built a bipartisan alliance of younger senators that included Democrat Ted Kennedy and Republican Robert Griffin. Still, no one was betting against Clinton Anderson. Then, late on the second day, just before the scheduled vote, Senator Barry Goldwater asked for the floor. This arch-conservative from Arizona wasn't always in political harmony with his colleagues, but he was widely regarded as the Senate's leading expert on Native Americans. Nixon's people had tried to lobby Goldwater, but the Republican had kept his own counsel. No one knew what he would do.

Now Goldwater looked out at his fellow senators and declared of Anderson's bill, "I cannot support his approach." He then forcefully defended Taos Pueblo, its religion, and its land rights. He urged his colleagues to "vote today for these Indians."[26]

With the Senate's most conservative voice now endorsing the liberal Harris, the dam broke. In a stunning rebuke to Anderson, the body voted 56–21 to kill his bill. Immediately, Fred Harris moved to replace that defeated measure with the House bill, which would restore Blue Lake. This vote was even more overwhelming—70 to 12 in favor of Taos Pueblo.

Cheers erupted in the gallery as the spectators rose to applaud, defying Senate rules for silence. Juan de Jesús Romero, the ninety-year-old cacique, stood and raised the ceremonial canes in triumph. The roars even grew louder. The Senate's presiding officer gaveled for quiet, but already dozens of senators on the floor were rising to their feet, turning to face the Taos delegation and joining the applause as tears of joy flowed at last.

Figure 38. President Nixon signs into law legislation restoring Taos Pueblo's sovereignty over Blue Lake. Looking on is Paul Bernal, left and Cacique Juan de Jesús Romero. December 15, 1970. Richard M. Nixon Presidential Library and Museum/ National Archives and Records Administration.

Two weeks later, at the White House signing ceremony, Paul Bernal and Cacique Romero stood by Richard Nixon's side. In the front row of the audience sat John Rainer, wearing a feathered headdress to symbolize this important victory for all Native peoples.

As Nixon prepared to sign the Blue Lake bill into law, he hailed Taos Pueblo's long fight for justice and he told the audience, "Our Indian people, who are a small part of America in numbers, have made an enormous contribution because they have given great character to so many parts of our country. We are grateful for that. . . . We restore this place of worship to them for all the years to come."[27] Finally, after nearly seventy years of struggle, Taos Pueblo regained sovereignty over its sacred "beating heart of the world."

Cacique Romero followed with his own remarks: "A new day begins not only for the American Indians, but for all the Americans in this country. . . . I do believe there is peace within and among ourselves and we have to find that peace."

The cacique continued with a prayer: "My dear sons and daughters, we are a foundation with Mother Nature. Mother Nature gives us the opportunity to walk on her blanket, a beautiful blanket that is spread for us to walk in front of destiny, and the sun gives us the light that we will be able to find our destiny when we walk with Mother Nature, and all the great ecology that we have in this country is meant for you and I to enjoy. And that is the way I feel and that is the way I do and that is the way I consider you and include you in my daily prayers."[28]

Just as opponents feared, Taos Pueblo's recovery of Blue Lake opened the door for other tribes to win long-delayed justice—including the return of stolen lands. The Taos People's inspiring victory is widely regarded as one of the greatest Native triumphs of the twentieth century. Pueblo leader Paul Bernal summed it up this way: "A long time ago the Indians had won a battle from General Custer. This is the second victory."[29]

Acknowledgments

So many generous people have helped make this book possible. I'd like to thank Stephen Harrigan and Joe Holley for inspiring me to set me on this journey, and also Marcia Hatfield Daudistel and Jim James for helping to carry me across the finish line. I'm indebted to Lauren Sharp, the smart and talented literary agent who opened my eyes to the best possible vision for this book. I'm also grateful to Wes Ferguson, Frances Hatfield, and W. K. "Kip" Stratton for advice and support. Several manuscript readers offered generous encouragement and helpful critiques: Bryan Burrough, Sandra Cisneros, Hampton Sides, Sherry L. Smith, Diane Reyna, William Broyles, Tom Zigal, Stephen Harrigan, Joe Holly, Jim James, Marcia Hatfield Daudistel, Becky Duval Reese, Sam Pfiester, Ricardo Romo, Susannah Broyles, and Ron Querry. Gratitude also to my literary compadre Bill Minutaglio, who partnered with me on two earlier books and taught me so much about writing.

In researching this book, I was fortunate to receive assistance from top-notch archivists and Special Collections directors who provided extraordinarily capable reference and access services, helping me navigate sometimes uncharted papers. I salute Senior Archivist Dena Hunt at the New Mexico State Records Center and Archives. Thanks also to Amanda Ferrara and Dan Linke at Princeton University's Seeley G. Mudd Manuscript Library; Nik Kendziorski at Fort Lewis College's Center for Southwest Studies; the staff at the University of New Mexico's Center for Southwest Research; Dennis Dailey and Teddie Moreno at New Mexico State University's Archives and Special Collections; Lorna K. Kirwan and Susan McElrath at the University of California-Berkeley's Bancroft Library; June Can and Melissa Barton at Yale University's Beinecke Library; Catie Carl at the Palace of the Governors Photo Archives; Karen Hinchcliffe at the San Diego Museum of Art; Logan Esdale of the Carl Van Vechten Trust;

Marissa Hendricks at the Lunder Research Center; Eric C. Stoykovich at the University of Maryland College Park's Special Collections; Viki Lynne Glantz at the University of Wyoming's American Heritage Center; Carla Braswell at the Richard Nixon Presidential Library and Museum; Dave Stack at the Forest Service Museum; George Fuller and Cody White at the National Archives and Records Administration; and Michele Williams at Texas State University's Alkek Library.

I'm grateful to University of New Mexico Press Director Stephen Hull along with the excellent staff at the Press, including Assistant Director James Ayers, Sales and Marketing Manager Don Redpath, Editor Anna Pohlod, Acquisitions Editor Sonia Dickey, Data and Digital Publishing Manager Brenton Woodward, Publicists Mary Bisbee-Birk and Sarena Ulibarri, and book designers Felicia Cedillos and Isaac Morris. Thanks also to copyeditor Zubin Meer for help whipping the final manuscript into shape.

With love and thanks to my supportive family: daughters Lucia and Natalie, most excellent dog Ralfred, and my wife, Georgia Ruiz Davis, to whom this book is dedicated.

Notes

Prologue

1. Rodney Dutcher, "No Crime, No Graft and Selfishness Is the Greatest Disgrace Among Ancient Pueblos Living in Their Quaint Adobe Villages," *Victoria Daily Times* (British Columbia), May 6, 1933.

2. Rodney Dutcher, "Pueblo Indians: Ancient 'Communists' Fight Encroachment on their Tribal Lands," *Salisbury Post* (NC), Jan. 29, 1933.

3. "Indian Help Bill Will Not Pass at Present Session," *Las Vegas Daily Optic* (NM), Jan. 14, 1933. "Representatives of Pueblo Indians Stop Here Following Conferences with Nation's Chiefs," *Dayton Daily News*, Jan. 18, 1933.

Chapter 1

1. "Taos Society of Artists July 15, 1915, 100 Year Anniversary, Membership Who's Who (Part 2 of 6)," Two Graces Taos, Jan. 12, 2015, https://twograces.blogspot.com/2015/01/.

2. Schimmel and White, *Bert Geer Phillips*, 309.

3. Phillips to Blumenschein, Dec. 14, 1898. Bert G. Phillips Papers, Huntington Library, San Marino, California.

4. Schimmel and White, *Bert Geer Phillips*, 279–80. Phillips to Blumenschein, Dec. 14, 1898, Bert G. Phillips Papers.

5. William McKinley, "Message to Congress Requesting a Declaration of War with Spain," The American Presidency Project, accessed May 17, 2024, www.presidency.ucsb.edu/node/304972.

6. Schimmel and White, *Bert Geer Phillips*, 326.

7. Schimmel and White.

8. Larson and Larson, *Ernest Blumenschein*, 97.

9. Schimmel and White, *Bert Geer Phillips*, 162. Florence Merriam Bailey Papers, box 1, folder 8, Bancroft Library, University of California, Berkeley.

10. Phillips to Blumenschein, Dec. 14, 1898, Bert G. Phillips Papers.

11. Schimmel and White, *Bert Geer Phillips*, 309.

12. Richard Melzer and Phyllis Ann Mingus, "Wild to Fight: The New Mexico Rough Riders in the Spanish-American War," *New Mexico Historical Review* 59, no. 2 (1984):

109–36, https://digitalrepository.unm.edu/nmhr/vol59/iss2/1. "Topics of the Times," *New York Times*, Aug. 24, 1898.

13. Schimmel and White, *Bert Geer Phillips*, 285.

14. James Howard Bridge, "The Collapse of Spain and the Rise of the Anglo-Saxon," *Overland Monthly and Out West Magazine*, July 1898.

15. Phillips to Blumenschein, Dec. 14, 1898, Bert G. Phillips Papers.

16. Phillips to Blumenschein, Dec. 14, 1898, Bert G. Phillips Papers. Schimmel and White, *Bert Geer Phillips*, 280.

17. This account of the 1898 "Taos riot" is woven from several sources, including Bert Phillips's correspondence as cited earlier, newspaper accounts, various issues of *El Palacio* and *New Mexico* magazines, as well as Grant's *When Old Trails Were New*, Evans's *Long John Dunn of Taos*, and Anderson's *History of New Mexico*.

Chapter 2

1. Malaquias Martínez's father was Santiago Valdéz, considered the putative son of Padre Martínez and recognized by the priest in his will as his primary heir, which also instructed that Valdéz and his children "share and take my surname in the future." While some reject any possibility that the famous priest might have fathered children, Santiago Valdéz Martinez's descendants have proudly asserted their Martínez lineage.

2. Sun Elk told Anglos of this history, but surprisingly, Martínez's land holdings have received little attention from historians. A notable exception is Myra Ellen Jenkins, "Taos Pueblo and Its Neighbors," *New Mexico Historical Review*, 41, no. 2 (1966): 85–114, which describes how Martínez acquired land from Taos Pueblo leaders under duress after the 1847 revolt. Pueblo historian Joe S. Sando also mentions this in his book *Pueblo Profiles*.

3. Lorraine Carr, "It Happened in Santa Fe," *Albuquerque Journal*, June 24, 1968.

4. Schimmel and White, *Bert Geer Phillips*, 58.

5. Schimmel and White, 310.

6. "Art," *Chicago Tribune*, Sept. 10, 1899.

7. Schimmel and White, *Bert Geer Phillips*, 65.

8. See vols. 5–8 of *El Palacio*, from 1918, the magazine of the Museum of New Mexico (available online via Google Books).

9. "The New Indian Policy," *Los Angeles Times*, Feb. 3, 1887.

10. Dunbar-Ortiz, *Indigenous People's History*, 212.

Chapter 3

1. Theodore Roosevelt, "Remarks in Santa Fe, New Mexico," May 5, 1903, The American Presidency Project, accessed September 16, 2025, www.presidency.ucsb.edu/node/343443.

2. Scurlock, *From the Rio to the Sierra*, 366.

3. Roosevelt, "Remarks in Santa Fe."

4. Kofalk, *No Woman Tenderfoot*, 81.

5. Vernon Bailey, "Field Notes, New Mexico, May 16–October 14, 1903" (unpublished journal), Smithsonian Institution.

6. Florence Merriam Bailey Papers, New Mexico Journal, 1903–1904, box 4, Bancroft Library, University of California, Berkeley.

7. Florence Merriam Bailey, "In the Land of the Red Willow People" (unpublished typescript), Florence Merriam Bailey Papers, box 11, Bancroft Library, University of California, Berkeley.

8. Bailey, "In the Land of the Red Willow People."

9. Bailey, "Field Notes."

10. Florence Merriam Bailey Papers, New Mexico Journal, 1903–1904, box 4, Bancroft Library, University of California, Berkeley.

11. Forwood, *Bert Geer Phillips.*

12. In her 1903 New Mexico journal, Florence Merriam Bailey reports that the interpreter "asked if we could help them hold this land—that they were afraid they would lose it."

13. Vernon Bailey, "Taos Mountains, New Mexico," September 1903, Taos Blue Lake Collection, Rufus G. Poole Papers, 1903–1959, box 16, Princeton University Special Collections, Mudd Manuscript Library.

14. Nov. 23, 1903, Taos Blue Lake Collection, Rufus G. Poole Papers, 1903–1959, box 16, Princeton University Special Collections, Mudd Manuscript Library.

15. Nov. 23, 1903, Taos Blue Lake Collection, Rufus G. Poole Papers, 1903–1959, box 16, Princeton University Special Collections, Mudd Manuscript Library.

16. Theodore Roosevelt, "Second Annual Message," The American Presidency Project, Dec. 2, 1902, accessed May 17, 2024, www.presidency.ucsb.edu/node/206194. Theodore Roosevelt, "First Annual Message," The American Presidency Project, Dec. 1, 1901, accessed May 17, 2024, www.presidency.ucsb.edu/node/206187.

17. C. Hart. Merriam, "The Indian Population of California," *American Anthropologist*, n.s., 7, no. 4 (1905): 594–606.

18. Merriam to Roosevelt, Mar. 19, 1904, Theodore Roosevelt Papers, Library of Congress.

19. Merriam to Roosevelt, Mar. 26, 1904, Theodore Roosevelt Papers, Library of Congress.

20. Roosevelt, *Winning of the West*, 119.

21. Theodore F. Rixon, "Report on an Examination of the Taos Forest Reserve Territory of New Mexico," (unpublished typescript), US Geological Survey, 1905, Taos Blue Lake Collection, Rufus G. Poole Papers, 1903–1959, box 16, Princeton University Special Collections, Mudd Manuscript Library.

22. Rixon, "Report on an Examination."

23. Vernon O. Bailey, "Memorandum Respecting the (Taos) Forest Reservation," Taos Blue Lake Collection, Rufus G. Poole Papers, 1903–1959, box 16, Princeton University Special Collections, Mudd Manuscript Library.

24. Oct. 21, 1904, from Taos Pueblo to Sec. of Interior, Taos Blue Lake Collection, Rufus G. Poole Papers, 1903–1959, box 16, Princeton University Special Collections, Mudd Manuscript Library.

Chapter 4

1. DeBuys, *Enchantment and Exploitation*, 161.

2. Brinkley, *Wilderness Warrior*, 665–66.

3. Ross McMillan to Cruz Suazo, Mar. 31, 1909, Taos Blue Lake Collection, Rufus G. Poole Papers, 1903–1959, box 16, Princeton University Special Collections, Mudd Manuscript Library.

4. Steen, *US Forest Service*, 100.

5. C. J. Crandall, "Letter to the Commissioner of Indian Affairs Regarding the Survey of Land near the Santa Clara Canyon and the Santa Clara Reservation," December 25, 1903, National Archives and Records Administration, Denver, Colorado, 1903.

6. Crandall to Myers, Apr. 22, 1908, Francis C. Wilson Papers, box 42, folder 45, New Mexico State Records Center and Archives, Santa Fe.

7. Florence Merriam Bailey Papers, box 1, folder 8, Bancroft Library, University of California, Berkeley.

8. Francis Cushman Wilson Papers on Pueblo Legal Issues, Center for Southwest Research and Special Collections, University of New Mexico Libraries. B. Alan. Dickson, "The Professional Life of Francis C. Wilson of Santa Fe: A Preliminary Sketch," *New Mexico Historical Review* 51, no. 1 (1976): 35–55.

9. Hoxie, "Beyond Savagery," 419.

10. "New Indian Commissioner," *Elgin Register* (NE), Jan. 5, 1905.

11. Crandall to Leupp, July 31, 1908, Myra Ellen Jenkins Papers, box 25, folder 4, Reed Library, Fort Lewis College.

12. Crandall to Leupp, July 31, 1908, Myra Ellen Jenkins Papers, box 25, folder 4, Reed Library, Fort Lewis College.

13. Harry Hall to Myers, June 18, 1909, Francis C. Wilson Papers, box 42, folder 45, New Mexico State Records Center and Archives, Santa Fe. McMillan to Myers, May 17, 1909, Francis C. Wilson Papers, box 42, folder 45, New Mexico State Records Center and Archives, Santa Fe.

14. Crandall to Leupp, Dec. 4, 1908, Myra Ellen Jenkins Papers, box 25, folder 4, Reed Library, Fort Lewis College.

Chapter 5

1. Crandall to Leupp, May 16, 1908, Myra Ellen Jenkins Papers, box 25, folder 4, Reed Library, Fort Lewis College.

2. Hoxie, "Beyond Savagery," 419. Crandall to Leupp, Mar. 31, 1909, Myra Ellen Jenkins Papers, box 25, folder 4, Reed Library, Fort Lewis College.

3. "Notice," *Santa Fe New Mexican*, May 29, 1909.

4. Crandall to Leupp, Nov. 3, 1909, Myra Ellen Jenkins Papers, box 25, folder 4, Reed Library, Fort Lewis College.

5. *Taos Valley News* clipping, Myra Ellen Jenkins Papers, box 25, folder 4, Reed Library, Fort Lewis College.

6. Crandall to Wilson, Apr. 10, 1910, Francis Cushman Wilson Papers on Pueblo Legal Issues, Center for Southwest Research and Special Collections, University of New Mexico Libraries.

7. Robert Tórrez, "The Taos 'Revolt' of 1910," *Ayer y hoy en Taos* (Newsletter of the Taos County Historical Society), Spring 2000.

8. Tórrez, "The Taos 'Revolt' of 1910."

9. "Pueblo Indians on Rampage," *Santa Fe New Mexican*, May 13, 1910.

10. "Pueblo Indians Raid Cattle Ranches," *San Francisco Chronicle*, May 14, 1910. "Pueblo Indians Ugly; Troops "Called Out," *Idaho Statesman*, May 14, 1910. Tórrez, "Taos 'Revolt' of 1910."

11. "Truce Is Declared: Trouble Happily Ended," *Los Angeles Times*, May 15, 1910. "Taos Indians Rise: Troops March to Prevent New Mexico Massacre," *Washington Post*, May 14, 1910.

12. "Militia To Quell Indian Uprising," *New York Times*, May 14, 1910.

13. "El Levantamiento de los Indios de Taos," *Revista de Taos*, May 20, 1910.

14. "Bears Kill Cattle in Taos County, New Mexico," *Tucumcari News and Tucumcari Times* (NM), July 1, 1910.

Chapter 6

1. Bailey, *Wolves in Relation to Stock*, 24–25.

2. Leopold, *Sand County Almanac*, 11.

3. Montgomery, *Spanish Redemption Heritage*, 75, 93. Robert W. Larson, "Statehood for New Mexico, 1888–1912," *New Mexico Historical Review* 37, no. 3 (1962): 161–200. https://digitalrepository.unm.edu/nmhr/vol37/iss3/2. "In Hotel Lobbies," *Washington Post*, July 4, 1900.

4. Linda C. Noel, "'I am an American': Anglos, Mexicans, *Nativos*, and the National Debate over Arizona and New Mexico Statehood," *Pacific Historical Review* 80, no. 3 (2011): 430–67.

5. Frank Clifford, "Albert Fall, New Mexico's Dark Knight," *El Palacio*, Spring 2012.

6. Arthur Clarence Probert once opened a hospital in Michigan, posing as a medical doctor. He founded banks and siphoned off deposits in Wisconsin, Michigan, Colorado, Oregon, and California. He'd escaped from several cities as the banks began to fail, but in Wisconsin, he was apprehended and sentenced to thirty months in the state penitentiary. After being paroled, he moved to Redding, California and used the name Clarence P. Davis. There he'd established a bank, a newspaper, and a mercantile business. He also married a wealthy socialite from Oakland in an elaborate church wedding. But soon he was recognized by a traveler as the same man wanted on mail fraud charges in Chicago. He managed to escape, and his wife had the marriage annulled. Needing a fresh start where no one knew him, he moved to Taos in 1909 and opened the State Savings Bank of Taos. He quickly ingratiated himself with Malaquias Martínez and soon became a close business associate, serving as the secretary-treasurer of the local newspaper, operated by Martínez's son-in-law. Probert, long active in Republican politics, had earlier been a delegate at the convention that

nominated McKinley for president. Just a few weeks after nominating Martínez for lieutenant governor in 1911, he was arrested for embezzlement and the bank in Taos was shut down. After his conviction, he was sentenced to six to eight years in the New Mexico State Penitentiary.

7. "Statehood Proclamation Signed," *Santa Fe New Mexican*, Jan. 6, 1912.

8. *Congressional Record*, May 15, 1912.

9. Ebright et al. *Four Square Leagues*, 256.

10. Much of this is well-covered in Baca, "Somos Indígena."

11. *Pine Cone* newsletter, Carson National Forest, Apr. 1912.

12. Perry, *Walt Perry*, 72–73.

13. Perry, 72. Perry was a young man at the time, and in his memoir, completed late in his life, he expressed sympathy for the Taos People's religion.

14. *Congressional Record*, May 15, 1912.

15. *Pine Cone* (Official Bulletin of the Albuquerque Game Protective Association), Christmas, 1915. Aldo Leopold papers, University of Wisconsin–Madison. (Note that this *Pine Cone* differs from the earlier newsletter that Leopold published for Carson National Forest.)

16. *Pine Cone* (Official Bulletin of the Albuquerque Game Protective Association), 1915. Aldo Leopold, "Stockmen and Sportsmen of New Mexico Pay $100 a Minute to Feed Predatory Animals on Range," *Santa Fe New Mexican*, Mar. 21, 1917.

17. Leopold, who died in 1948, later became regarded as a patron saint of American environmentalism for championing a holistic approach to nature. His eloquent and influential book, *A Sand County Almanac*, sold millions and inspired generations of environmentalists. Leopold never directly acknowledged his leading role in extirpating New Mexico's wolf population, nor did he ever acknowledge that Taos Puebloans and other Indigenous people had long understood and practiced the very same holistic principles he eventually came to embrace.

18. United States Supreme Court, *US v. SANDOVAL* (1913), No. 352. Argued: Feb. 27, 1913. Decided: Oct. 20, 1913.

19. Francis C. Wilson memorandum, Dec. 5, 1911. Taos Blue Lake Collection, Rufus G. Poole Papers, 1903–1959, box 16, Princeton University Special Collections, Mudd Manuscript Library.

Chapter 7

1. Fenn, *Beat of the Drum*, 215.

2. "Art: Fifty Years in Front," *Time*, Nov. 18, 1946.

3. "Unmindful of the Present," *Boston Globe*, Mar. 6, 1913.

4. "Will Live with Indian Friends," *Santa Fe New Mexican*, Feb. 8, 1906.

5. Johnson, "Secretsharers," 156.

6. "Human Sacrifices by Indians," *Washington Post*, Apr. 17, 1915. "Human Sacrifices, She Says, Are Still Offered by Tewa Indians," *Washington Post*, Jan. 18, 1915.

7. Frederick Hodge to Stevenson, Jan. 27, 1915, Darlis Miller Papers, Matilda Coxe Stevenson Correspondence, New Mexico State University.

8. "Investigation Will Be Asked of Pueblo Human Sacrifice Charges," *Santa Fe New Mexican*, Apr. 23, 1915. Frederic J. Haskin, "The Pueblo Indians," *Pittsburgh Post-Gazette*, Jan. 25, 1915.

9. For more, see Fenton, *Factionalism at Taos Pueblo*, and Stewart, *Peyote Religion*.

10. "Kindred Spirits and The Adobe Connection: E. I. Couse And J. H. Sharp," Antiques and the Arts Weekly, July 28, 2009, www.antiquesandthearts.com/kindred-spirits-and-the-adobe-connection-ei-couse-and-jh-sharp/.

11. As Frank Waters noted in his 1951 essay, "Indian Influence on Taos Art," *New Mexico Quarterly* 21, no. 2 (1951), 173–80. https://digitalrepository.unm.edu/nmq/vol21/iss2/11: "Every painter had his favorite models who also patched his roof, planted his garden, and cut his firewood."

12. Fenn, *Beat of the Drum*, 239. Taggett and Schwarz, *Paintbrushes and Pistols*, 170.

13. Ernest L Blumenschein, "The Painting of To-morrow," *Century Magazine*, Apr. 1914.

14. James Moore, "Ernest Blumenschein's Long Journey with Star Road," *American Art*, Autumn, 1995.

15. Ernest L. Blumenschein, "The Taos Society of Artists" *Magazine of American Art*, Sept. 1917.

16. "New Mexico Artists Take Issue with Commissioners Over U.S. Indian Policy," *Albuquerque Tribune*, Apr. 30, 1919.

17. Forwood, *Bert Geer Phillips*.

18. "New Mexico Artists."

19. "New Mexico Artists."

Chapter 8

1. Sterne, *Shadow and Light*, 114.

2. Steffens, *Autobiography of Lincoln Steffens*, 654. Rudnick, *Mabel Dodge Luhan and Company*, 23. Patricia Leigh Brown, "The Muse of Taos, Stirring Still," *New York Times*, Jan. 16, 1997.

3. Luhan, *Edge of the Taos Desert*, 4.

4. Chris Elcock, "Mabel Dodge Luhan's First Peyote Trip," Oct. 11, 2018, www.pointshistory.org/post/mabel-dodge-luhan-s-first-peyote-trip.

5. Elcock, "Mabel Dodge Luhan's First Peyote Trip."

6. "Art Notes: First Exhibition of the Taos Society of Artists," *New York Times*, Nov. 24, 1917.

7. Mabel's initial reaction to the show was negative, as described in a letter to her husband, Maurice Sterne. "My dear! It's—terrible!" she wrote to him on November 28, 1917. Yet the paintings clearly put some kind of spell on her, and she later credited the Couse painting for helping draw her to Taos.

8. Hassrick and Cunningham, *In Contemporary Rhythm*, 100.

9. Rudnick, *Mabel Dodge Luhan*, 142.

10. Luhan, *Edge of the Taos Desert*, 23.

11. Burke, *From Greenwich Village to Taos*, 34.

12. Luhan, *Edge of the Taos Desert*, 39.
13. Luhan, 53.
14. Luhan, 44.
15. Dean, *Travel Narratives from New Mexico*, 77.
16. Mabel to Maurice Sterne, Nov. 28, 1917. Maurice Sterne Papers, Yale Collection of American Literature, Beinecke Rare Book and Manuscript Library.
17. D'Emilio and Campbell, *Visions and Visionaries*, 76.
18. Frazer, *Mabel Dodge Luhan*, 71.
19. Wetzsteon, *Republic of Dreams*, 45.

Chapter 9

1. Sterne, *Shadow and Light*, 137.
2. Auerbach, *Explorers in Eden*, 99. Rudnick, *Mabel Dodge Luhan*, 150. Goodman and Dawson, *Mary Austin and the American West*, 195.
3. Wenger, *We Have a Religion*, 87.
4. Wenger, 86.
5. Luhan, *Edge of the Taos Desert*, 111.
6. Luhan, 140.
7. Rudnick, *Mabel Dodge Luhan*, 148.
8. Luhan, *Edge of the Taos Desert*, 131.
9. Smith, *Reimagining Indians*, 191.
10. Luhan, *Edge of the Taos Desert*, 192.
11. Hahn, *Mabel*, 133.
12. Everett, *Corresponding Lives*, 67.
13. Luhan, *Winter in Taos*, 203.
14. Luhan, *Edge of the Taos Desert*, 318.
15. While Pueblo land was technically held in common, tribal members received individual plots to work.
16. Luhan, *Edge of the Taos Desert*, 148.
17. Stephen May, "Marsden Hartley: Searching for the Sublime," southwest art, Jan. 1, 1999. www.southwestart.com/articles-interviews/featured-artists/marsden_hartley.
18. Jonathan Kantrowitz, "Georgia O'Keeffe, Marsden Hartley & The American Southwest," Art History News, May 22, 2017, http://arthistorynewsreport.blogspot.com/2017/05/sothebys-american-art-23-may.html.
19. Luhan, *Edge of the Taos Desert*, 66.
20. Luhan, 158.
21. Hahn, *Mabel*, 147.

Chapter 10

1. Rudnick, *Suppressed Memoirs of Mabel Dodge Luhan*, 140.
2. Luhan, *Edge of the Taos Desert*, 332.

3. Rudnick, *Mabel Dodge Luhan,* 165.

4. Rudnick.

5. Cronyn, *Path on the Rainbow,* xxxii. Rhonda Packer and Tamar Frankiel, "Anglo Women and Indians in the West, 1895–1920," *International Social Science Review* 70, nos. 3–4 (1995): 73.

6. Austin, *Earth Horizons,* 354. Jacobs, "Uplifting Cultures," 124.

7. Erna Fergusson, "Crusade from Santa Fe," *North American Review* 242, no. 2 (1936–1937): 376–87.

8. Luhan, *Edge of the Taos Desert,* 292.

Chapter 11

1. Collier, *From Every Zenith,* 126.

2. Morgan, *Heritage of Community,* 30

3. Collier, *Entry to the Desert,* 12.

4. Collier, *From Every Zenith,* 126. Collier, "Plundering the Pueblo Indians," *Sunset Magazine,* Jan. 1923, 25. Collier, "The Red Atlantis," *The Survey,* Oct. 1922.

5. Collier, "Red Atlantis."

6. Collier.

7. Collier.

8. Stratton, *Tempest over Teapot Dome,* 188. "Fall Received with Doubt," *Indianapolis Star,* Mar. 5, 1921. Stratton, 202.

9. Rusco, Elmer R. *A Fateful Time,* 1815.

10. "Story of Indian Is Story of Unparalleled Progress Upward," *Santa Fe New Mexican,* Sept. 5, 1922.

11. Russell, *Shadow of Blooming Grove,* 491.

12. "Secretary Fall Asserts that National Resources Cannot be Exhausted in U.S.," *El Paso Herald,* Jan. 21, 1922.

13. *Congressional Record,* Senate. Aug. 7, 1922. "Indians of America are Not Decreasing," *Missoula Sentinel* (MT), June 16, 1921.

14. *Santa Fe New Mexican* clipping, Myra Ellen Jenkins Papers, box 25, folder 4, Reed Library, Fort Lewis College.

15. Twitchell, *Leading Facts of New Mexico History,* viii.

Chapter 12

1. Bachrach, *D. H. Lawrence in New Mexico,* 3.

2. Luhan, *Lorenzo in Taos,* 3.

3. Patricia Leigh Brown, "The Muse of Taos, Stirring Still," *New York Times,* Jan. 16, 1997.

4. Luhan, *Lorenzo in Taos,* 5.

5. Lawrence to S. S. Koteliansky, Dec. 26, 1921, in Lawrence, *Letters of D. H. Lawrence,* 151. Luhan, *Lorenzo in Taos,* 35.

6. Stratton, *Tempest over Teapot Dome*, 210. Steen, *US Forest Service*, 150.

7. "Col. Twitchell to Have Charge of All Controversies Over Pueblos," *Santa Fe New Mexican*, June 8, 1921.

8. Long, "To the Edge of the World," 241, 217, 238.

9. Long, 257.

10. Long.

11. "Col. Twitchell," *Santa Fe New Mexican*, June 8, 1921.

12. Crane, *Desert Drums*, 302.

13. Kelly, *Assault on Assimilation*, 214.

14. *Congressional Record*, Senate, Sept. 11, 1922.

15. "Bill Proposed to Give Relief to Buyers of Indian Lands," *Santa Fe New Mexican*, July 22, 1922.

16. Wenger, *We Have a Religion*, 105.

17. Wenger.

18. In *Assault on Assimilation*, Kelly indicates that Albert B. Fall told Lenroot that attorney A. B. Renehan had represented the Pueblos "by their own choice" (214). This seems doubtful, for Renehan was notoriously well known for representing white settlers. It is much more likely that Fall claimed Twitchell had been the Pueblos' own choice, for Twitchell's appointed position was ostensibly intended to represent the Pueblos' interests.

19. Collier, *From Every Zenith*, 128.

20. *The Clubwoman*, California Federation of Women's Clubs, June 1922, accessed Aug. 23, 2020, https://archive.org/stream/clubwoman14cali/clubwoman14cali_djvu.txt.

21. *The Clubwoman*.

22. Kelly, *Assault on Assimilation*, 218.

23. Collier, *From Every Zenith*, 132. Leech would soon find himself transferred out of New Mexico.

24. John Collier, "American Congo," *The Survey*, Aug. 1, 1923. Kelly, *Assault on Assimilation*, 250, 216.

Chapter 13

1. Luhan, *Lorenzo in Taos*, 19.

2. Luhan, *Lorenzo in Taos*, 36.

3. Collier, *From Every Zenith*, 132.

4. Jones, "'Hope for the Race of Man,'" 195.

5. Mayhew, "New Mexico Association on Indian Affairs," 8.

6. Luhan, *Lorenzo in Taos*, 59.

7. Bachrach, *D. H. Lawrence in New Mexico*, 13.

8. D. H. Lawrence, "New Mexico," *The Survey*, May 1, 1931.

9. Lawrence.

10. "Protest 'Wrong' Against Indians," *Cleveland Plain Dealer*, Nov. 20, 1922.

11. Taos Blue Lake Collection, Rufus G. Poole Papers, 1903–1959, box 16, Princeton University Special Collections, Mudd Manuscript Library.

12. Kelly, *Assault on Assimilation*, 221.

13. Bachrach, *D. H. Lawrence in New Mexico*, 16. D. H. Lawrence, "Certain Americans and an Englishman," *New York Times*, Dec. 24, 1922.

14. United States Congress, *Pueblo Indian Lands: Hearings Before a Subcommittee on S. 3865 and S. 4223* (Government Printing Office, 1923).

15. "Messrs. Burke and Bursum Still Disagree with U. S. Senate on Indian Bill," *Santa Fe New Mexican*, Dec. 13, 1922.

16. *Current Opinion*, vol. 74, Feb. 1923, 213–14.

17. Mabel to Mary Hunter Austin, "Sunday," 1922. Mary Hunter Austin Papers, Huntington Library, San Marino, California.

Chapter 14

1. United States Congress, *Pueblo Indian Lands: Hearings Before a Subcommittee on S. 3865 and S. 4223* (Government Printing Office, 1923).

2. United States Congress, *Pueblo Indian Lands*.

3. *Congressional Record*, Senate, 1922, p. 809. Kelly, *Assault on Assimilation*, 235.

4. Collier to Mabel, Jan. 2, 1923, John Collier Papers, Yale Collection of American Literature, Beinecke Rare Book and Manuscript Library, microfilm reel 4.

5. Kelly, *Assault on Assimilation*, 224.

6. "Teapot Dome Oil Fight," *New York Times*, May 7, 1922. McCartney, *Teapot Dome Scandal*, 114.

7. Chamberlain, "Controversial Term of Albert Bacon Fall," 25.

8. Kelly, *Assault on Assimilation*, 232–33. Stratton, *Tempest over Teapot Dome*, 228.

9. Jones, "'Hope for the Race of Man,'" 208.

10. Scott, *Strange Mixture*, 94.

11. Lanigan, *Mary Austin*, 175. Ruderman, "Lawrence as Ethnographer and Artist," 41.

12. Reed, *Woman's Place*, 46.

13. Luhan, *Lorenzo in Taos*, 122. D. H. Lawrence, Sept. 22, 1922, in Lawrence. *Letters of D. H. Lawrence*, 305. Lawrence, 234. Luhan, *Lorenzo in Taos*, 72.

14. Luhan, 120.

15. "Pueblos Menaced by Land Grabbers, Mary Austin Says," *Brooklyn Eagle*, Jan. 17, 1923.

16. "No Place in New York to Look But Up, Pueblo Tony Says," *Santa Fe New Mexican*, Jan. 19, 1923.

17. Austin to Mabel, Jan. 27, 1923. Mabel Dodge Luhan Papers, Yale Collection of American Literature, Beinecke Rare Book and Manuscript Library.

Chapter 15

1. "*The Rescue* (sculpture)," Wikipedia, last modified Mar. 8, 2025, https://en.wikipedia.org/wiki/The_Rescue_(sculpture).

2. All quotations from the senate hearing come from *Pueblo Indian Lands: Hearings*

Before a Subcommittee of the Committee on Public Lands and Surveys, United States Senate, Sixty-Seventh Congress, Fourth Sessions, on S. 3865 and S.4223 (Government Printing Office, 1923). Additional details come from correspondence files of Francis C. Wilson and John Collier.

3. The hearing transcript indicates that Abeita said, "which means illegal," but I believe that the eloquent, well-educated Abeita—incorrectly referred to as "Abeyta" in the transcript—more likely would have said "with means illegal," which makes more sense given the context of his statement.

4. Fall managed to postpone several criminal trials by claiming ill health. Finally convicted in 1929, he was sentenced to a year in prison despite pleas from his supporters that it amounted to a death penalty for such an obviously enfeebled man. After his release from the penitentiary, Fall went on to live another fifteen years, dying at age eight-three.

5. Crane, *Desert Drums*, 311.

Chapter 16

1. "Why Bohemia's Queen Married an Indian Chief," *Detroit Free Press*, June 10, 1923.

2. Kelly, *Assault on Assimilation*, 222.

3. Collier to Mabel, Jan. 2, 1923, John Collier Papers, Yale Collection of American Literature, Beinecke Rare Book and Manuscript Library, microfilm reel 4.

4. Richard O. Clemmer, "'A carnival of promiscuous carnal indulgence': Bureaucrats' Ambivalence in Reconciling Capitalist Production with Native American Habitus," *Dialectal Anthropology* 33 (2009): 51–70. See also Jacobs, *Engendered Encounters*, 109.

5. Wenger, *We Have a Religion*, 153.

6. Jacobs, *Engendered Encounters*, 109. Jacobs, "Uplifting Cultures," 207. Clemmer, "'Carnival of promiscuous carnal indulgence.'"

7. Clemmer. Wenger, *We Have a Religion*, 219.

8. Kenneth Philp, "John Collier and the Crusade to Protect Indian Religious Freedom, 1920–1926," *Journal of Ethnic Studies* 1, no. 1 (1973): 23.

9. Department of the Interior Office of Indian Affairs, Supplement to Circular No. 1665, Feb. 14, 1923.

10. Wenger, *We Have a Religion*, 148. Jacobs, *Engendered Encounters*, 79.

11. "Pueblo Indian Tribes Adopt Policy of Non-Resistance," *San Francisco Examiner*, May 25, 1924.

12. Collier to Wilson, Apr. 12, 1923, Francis C. Wilson Papers, box 42, folder 45, New Mexico State Records Center and Archives, Santa Fe.

13. Collier to Wilson, Apr. 17, 1923, Francis C. Wilson Papers, box 42, folder 45, New Mexico State Records Center and Archives, Santa Fe.

14. Philp, *John Collier's Crusade for Indian Reform*, 47.

15. Kelly, *Assault on Assimilation*, 285.

16. Wenger, *We Have a Religion*, 99.

17. Tisa Wenger, "'We Are Guaranteed Freedom': Pueblo Indians and the Category of Religion in the 1920s," *History of Religions*, 45, no. 2. (2005): 103. Wenger, *We Have a*

Religion, 203–4. "Statement of Joe Lejon (Lujan) and Manuel Mondragon, May 15, 1924, microfilm reel 40. Indian Rights Association Papers, Historical Society of Pennsylvania.

18. Wenger, *We Have a Religion*, 194.

19. Wenger, 135.

20. Grant, *Taos Indians*, 103.

21. Kelly, *Assault on Assimilation*, 309. Wenger, *We Have a Religion*, 189.

22. Wegner, 136. Philp, *John Collier's Crusade for Indian Reform*, 59–60. William E. Johnson, "Those Sacred Indian Ceremonials," *Native American* 24 (Sept. 20, 1924): 173–77.

Chapter 17

1. "States·Must Eventually Take Over Indian Affairs," *Santa Fe New Mexican*, Apr. 17, 1924.

2. De Angulo, *Jaime in Taos*, 59.

3. This account draws from several sources, but the most useful is that of Jaime de Angulo, who was visiting Tony and Mabel in Taos at the time and wrote a contemporaneous description based on what he heard soon after the meeting ended. His account is published in de Angulo, *Jaime in Taos*.

4. Wenger, *We Have a Religion*, 191. John Collier, "The Vanquished Indian," *The Nation*, Jan. 11, 1928.

5. Taos Pueblo to Commissioner Burke, May 7, 1924. Taos Blue Lake Collection, Rufus G. Poole Papers, 1903–1959, box 16, Princeton University Special Collections, Mudd Manuscript Library.

6. "Pueblo Indian Tribes Adopt Policy of Non-Resistance," *San Francisco Examiner*, May 25, 1924.

7. Kelly, *Assault on Assimilation*, 311.

8. Kenneth Philp, "John Collier and the Crusade to Protect Indian Religious Freedom, 1920–1926," *Journal of Ethnic Studies* 1, no. 1 (1973): 28. "Preserving Indian Dances," *New York Times*, May 8, 1923.

9. Kelly, *Assault on Assimilation*, 346.

10. Kelly, 321.

11. Everett, *Corresponding Lives*, 83.

12. Hahn, *Mabel*, 188.

13. Everett, *Corresponding Lives*, 88.

14. Zumwalt, *Wealth and Rebellion*, 239–40.

15. The bill was for services rendered to Everett Marcy, a young writer who Mabel was having an affair with. The manuscript was accepted as only a partial payment. Eventually it was sold to the University of California, Berkeley, in 1963 by the psychoanalyst's son.

16. De Angulo, *Jaime in Taos*, 55.

17. Elizabeth Sergeant to Collier, Oct. 9, 1933. John Collier Papers, Yale Collection of American Literature, Beinecke Rare Book and Manuscript Library, microfilm reel 17.

18. De Angulo, *Jaime in Taos*, 87.

19. "Carl Jung and Taos, New Mexico," Beezone Library, accessed Sept. 29, 2025, https://beezone.com/carl-jung/jung/jung_pueblo.html.

20. Jung, *Memories, Dreams, Reflections*, 248-50. See also Timothy Thompson, "Lessons of Jung's Encounter with Native Americans," The Jung Page, last updated Oct. 27, 2013, https://jungpage.org/learn/articles/analytical-psychology/881-lessons-of-jungs-encounter-with-native-americans.

21. Jung, *Memories, Dreams, Reflections*, 250–52.

22. Jung, *Modern Man in Search*, 213.

23. Jung, *Memories, Dreams, Reflections*, 252.

24. Jung, 251.

25. Jung.

26. There is considerable dispute about the number of strokes ordered in this case; some sources claim only a single lash was applied, while others say twenty-five.

27. "Ceremonial Slap of Pueblos Legal," *Hartford Courant*, Aug. 17, 1925. Collier, *From Every Zenith*, 136.

Chapter 18

1. Lawrence, *Woman Who Rode Away*, 51.

2. Lawrence, 88.

3. Smith, *Reimagining Indians*, 198.

4. Marc Simmons, "Englishman D. H. Lawrence Found a Home in Taos," *Santa Fe New Mexican*, Aug. 23, 2013.

5. Mabel Dodge Luhan, "A Bridge Between Cultures," *Theatre Arts Monthly* 9, no. 5 (1925): 297–301.

6. Mabel Dodge Luhan, "Paso Por Aqui," *New Mexico Quarterly* 21, no. 2 (1951): 137–46.

7. De Angulo, *Jaime in Taos*, 55.

8. De Angulo, 54.

9. Rudnick, *Mabel Dodge Luhan*, 228.

10. Lanigan, *Mary Austin*, 164–65. Everett, *Corresponding Lives*, 80.

11. This refers to Everett Marcy, a young writer in New York Mabel was consorting with. It was Marcy's extensive psychoanalysis bill that Mabel would partially "pay" with the D. H. Lawrence manuscript. See Van Vechten, *Splendid Drunken Twenties*, 100.

12. Rudnick, *Suppressed Memoirs of Mabel Dodge Luhan*, 108.

13. "Lovely Taos," *Santa Fe New Mexican*, May 20, 1925.

14. *Life*, Apr. 8, 1926.

15. Marta Weigle, "Exposition and Mediation: Mary Colter, Erna Fergusson, and the Santa Fe/Harvey Popularization of the Native Southwest, 1902–1940." *Frontiers: A Journal of Women Studies* 12, no. 3 (1992): 117–50.

16. Erna Fergusson, "Crusade from Santa Fe" *North American Review* 242, no. 2 (1936–1937): 376–87.

Chapter 19

1. Collier, *From Every Zenith*, 137.

2. Collier, 138.

3. Kenneth Philp, "John Collier and the Crusade to Protect Indian Religious Freedom, 1920–1926," *Journal of Ethnic Studies* 1, no. 1 (1973): 33.

4. Philp, *John Collier's Crusade for Indian Reform*, 81.

5. *The Survey*, Jan. 1, 1927, p. 454.

6. "Records Reveal Shameful Deal the Indians Got," *Helena Daily Independent-Record*, Nov. 20, 1927.

7. Collier, *From Every Zenith*, 55. "Indian's Friends Renew Charges," *Los Angeles Times*, Apr. 25, 1926.

8. Taos Blue Lake Collection, Rufus G. Poole Papers, 1903–1959, box 16, Princeton University Special Collections, Mudd Manuscript Library.

9. "Survey of Conditions of Indians in the United States," United States Senate, Subcommittee of the Committee on Indian Affairs, Feb. 23, 1927, 69 (available online via Google Books). Kelly, *Assault on Assimilation*, 343.

10. Hagerman to Burke, Sept 30, 1926. Taos Blue Lake Collection, Rufus G. Poole Papers, 1903–1959, box 16, Princeton University Special Collections, Mudd Manuscript Library.

11. Transcript, Pueblo Lands Board meeting at Taos Pueblo, Oct. 4, 1926. Taos Blue Lake Collection, Rufus G. Poole Papers, 1903–1959, box 16, Princeton University Special Collections, Mudd Manuscript Library.

12. Transcript, Pueblo Lands Board meeting at Taos Pueblo, October 4, 1926. Taos Blue Lake Collection, Rufus G. Poole Papers, 1903–1959, box 16, Princeton University Special Collections, Mudd Manuscript Library.

13. Hagerman to Burke, October 13, 1926. Taos Blue Lake Collection, Rufus G. Poole Papers, 1903–1959, box 16, Princeton University Special Collections, Mudd Manuscript Library.

14. Hagerman to Burke, October 13, 1926. Taos Blue Lake Collection, Rufus G. Poole Papers, 1903–1959, box 16, Princeton University Special Collections, Mudd Manuscript Library.

Chapter 20

1. "Wild Horses of Taos Are Among Problems of Indians," *Santa Fe New Mexican*, Nov. 16, 1926.

2. "Wild Horses."

3. "Wild Horses."

4. "Wild Horses."

5. Philp, *John Collier's Crusade for Indian Reform*, 69.

6. United States Congress, Senate, Survey of Conditions of the Indians in the United States, *Hearings Before a Subcommittee of the Committee on Indian Affairs Pursuant to S*

Res. 79, a Resolution Directing the Committee on Indian Affairs of the United States Senate to Make a General Survey of the Condition of the Indians of the United States (Government Printing Office, 1932), 109–11 (available online via Google Books).

7. Floyd Beutler to Hubert Work, May 27, 1927. Taos Blue Lake Collection, Rufus G. Poole Papers, 1903–1959. Box 16. Princeton University Special Collections, Mudd Manuscript Library.

8. Floyd Beutler to Hubert Work, May 27, 1927. Taos Blue Lake Collection, Rufus G. Poole Papers, 1903–1959. Box 16. Princeton University Special Collections, Mudd Manuscript Library.

9. Work to Jardine, June 29, 1927. Taos Blue Lake Collection, Rufus G. Poole Papers, 1903–1959, box 16, Princeton University Special Collections, Mudd Manuscript Library.

10. US Forest Service Agreement with Taos Pueblo, May 28, 1927. Taos Blue Lake Collection, Rufus G. Poole Papers, 1903–1959, box 16, Princeton University Special Collections, Mudd Manuscript Library. The entire watershed is about 48,000 acres. This agreement omitted about 21,000 acres, including the 7,000 acres given to Anglo cattle ranchers during World War I. Ultimately, the Pueblo's advocates determined the current deal was the best they could hope for.

11. US Forest Service Agreement with Taos Pueblo, May 28, 1927. Taos Blue Lake Collection, Rufus G. Poole Papers, 1903–1959, box 16, Princeton University Special Collections, Mudd Manuscript Library.

12. "Forget It," *Santa Fe New Mexican*, Apr. 29, 1929. United States Congress, Senate, *Survey of Conditions of the Indians in the United States*. "Jabs in the Solar Plexus," *Santa Fe New Mexican*, Oct. 22, 1925.

13. "Charges Come Thick and Fast at Hearing," *Winston-Salem Journal*, Jan 8, 1929, "Indian Bureau Head Resigns Under Fire," *Grand Rapids Press*, Mar. 13, 1929.

14. Mary Austin, "Why Americanize the Indian?," *The Forum*, Sept. 1929. Baca, "Somos Indígena," 492.

Chapter 21

1. Greenough, *My Faraway One*, 412–13.

2. Mabel Dodge Luhan, "Georgia O'Keeffe in Taos," *Creative Art*, June 1931, 407. Greenough, *My Faraway One*, 416.

3. Greenough, 429.

4. Greenough, 415, 437, 416.

5. Greenough, 416.

6. Greenough, 430.

7. Alinder and Adams, *Ansel Adams* 93–94.

8. Rabb, *Literature and Photography*, 265.

9. Rabb, 266. Lanigan, *Mary Austin*, 189.

10. Lanigan, *Mary Austin*, 190.

11. Katharine Fullerton Gerould, "New Mexico and the Backwash of Spain," *Harper's*, July 1925.

12. "Who is Mary Austin? Most Intelligent Woman in America," *Santa Fe New Mexican*, Jan. 8, 1929.

13. Lanigan, *Mary Austin*, 192–93.

14. Lanigan, 194.

15. Alinder and Stillman, *Ansel Adams*, 39.

16. Spaulding, *Ansel Adams and the American Landscape*, 77.

17. Greenough, *My Faraway One*, 425.

18. Spaulding, *Ansel Adams and the American Landscape*, 76.

19. Greenough, *My Faraway One*, 433.

20. "Taos, a Wonderland in New Mexico," *Albuquerque Journal*, Sept. 15, 1929.

21. "Oral History Interview with Miriam Hapgood DeWitt, 1987–1988," Smithsonian, accessed May 17, 2024, www.aaa.si.edu/collections/interviews/oral-history-interview-miriam-hapgood-dewitt-12941#transcript.

22. Luhan, *Lorenzo in Taos*, 280.

23. Luhan, 296.

24. Luhan, 337, 346, 347.

25. Greenough, *My Faraway One*, 619.

26. Rabb, *Literature and Photography*, 265.

27. Lanigan, *Mary Austin*, 195.

28. Hammond, *Ansel Adams*, 20–22.

29. Luhan, *Lorenzo in Taos*, 351.

Chapter 22

1. See Chamberlain, "Controversial Term of Albert Bacon Fall."

2. Philp, *John Collier's Crusade for Indian Reform*, 112.

3. "Fear Indian Betrayal by John Collier," *Santa Fe New Mexican*, Feb. 11, 1931.

4. "Fear Indian Betrayal."

5. Collier, *From Every Zenith*, 155. "Pueblo Council Challenges Wilbur to Prove Statements," *Santa Fe New Mexican*, Mar. 15, 1932.

6. "Protection of Indian Arts is Discussed," *Albuquerque Journal*, May 8, 1931. Collier, *From Every Zenith*, 155.

7. *Survey of Conditions of the Indians in the United States. Hearings Before a Subcommittee of the Committee on Indian Affairs, United States Senate, Seventieth Congress, Second Session, Pursuant to S. Res. 79, a Resolution Directing the Committee on Indian affairs of the United States Senate to Make a General Survey of the Condition of the Indians of the United States* (Government Printing Office, 1932), http://hdl.handle.net/2027/uiug.30112086382576.

8. 72nd Congress, Senate, Report 25, part 3, Feb. 16, 1932. Taos Blue Lake Collection, Rufus G. Poole Papers, 1903–1959, box 16, Princeton University Special Collections, Mudd Manuscript Library.

9. "Hoover Asks Nation to Emulate Courage of Men at Valley Forge," *Christian Science Monitor*, June 1, 1931.

10. "Woman Pens Intimate Study of Lawrence," *Chicago Tribune*, Feb. 20, 1932. Hahn, *Mabel*, 193. Charles Hanson Towne, "A Number of Things," *San Francisco Examiner*, Feb. 20, 1932. Philip Stevenson, "Dere Mabel," *Southwest Review* 17, no. 3 (1932): xvi–xix.

11. "Society Woman Is Indian's Wife," *Courier-Journal* (Louisville), Aug 14, 1932.

12. "Society Woman."

13. Mabel Dodge Luhan correspondence, May 5, 1936. John Collier Papers, Yale Collection of American Literature, Beinecke Rare Book and Manuscript Library, microfilm reel 15. "Pueblo Indians Ask Roosevelt for a Friendly Chief Official," *Albuquerque Journal*, Jan. 11, 1933. Rodney Dutcher, "Pueblo Indians: Ancient 'Communists' Fight Encroachment on their Tribal Lands," *Salisbury Post* (NC), Jan. 29, 1933.

14. Dutcher, "Pueblo Indians."

15. "Pueblo Leaders See Hope for New Deal in John Collier," *Indianapolis Times*, Apr. 20, 1933.

16. Lawrence C. Kelly, "Choosing the New Deal Indian Commissioner: Ickes vs. Collier." *New Mexico Historical Review* 49, no. 4 (1974): 269–88, https://digitalrepository.unm.edu/nmhr/vol49/iss4/2.

17. Kelly, "Choosing the New Deal Indian Commissioner." Clarke, *Roosevelt's Warrior*, 29.

18. Kelly, "Choosing the New Deal Indian Commissioner."

19. Kelly.

20. Kelly.

Chapter 23

1. Kyle D. Palmer, "We Stand Indicted for What We've Done to the Indian," *Los Angeles Times*, Aug. 6, 1933.

2. "John Collier Fights for Indians' Cause," *Omaha World-Herald*, Apr. 18, 1933. Luhan to Collier, Apr. 13, 1933. John Collier Papers, Yale Collection of American Literature, Beinecke Rare Book and Manuscript Library, microfilm reel 14.

3. Palmer, "We Stand Indicted."

4. O'Neil, "Indian New Deal."

5. US Dept of Interior, Office of Indian Affairs, Jan. 3, 1934, Circular No. 2970.

6. US Dept of Interior, Office of Indian Affairs, Jan. 3, 1934, Circular No. 2970.

7. O'Neil grew up to become a historian. This recollection appears in O'Neil, "Indian New Deal."

8. 1934 Indian Commissioner Report to the Secretary of the Interior.

9. Rusco, *Fateful Time*, 183.

10. Rusco, 181.

11. US Dept of Interior, Office of Indian Affairs, Jan. 3, 1934, Circular No. 2970. Palmer, "We Stand Indicted," *Los Angeles Times*, Aug. 6, 1933.

12. Palmer.

13. Cecil Horne, "There's a Paradise in New Mexico," *Fort Worth Star-Telegram*, Jan. 27, 1929.

14. Acting Forester's letter of Nov. 15, 1928), cited in *Taos Indians, Blue Lake. Hearings, Ninetieth Congress, second session, on H.R. 3306 . . . S. 1624 . . . and S. 1625. . . . September 19 and 20, 1968* (US Government Printing Office, 1968), https://hdl.handle.net/2027/uc1.$b643877.

15. Agreement of Executive Order No. 4929. Taos Blue Lake Collection, Rufus G. Poole Papers, 1903–1959, box 16, Princeton University Special Collections, Mudd Manuscript Library.

16. Krahe, "Last Refuge," 93.

17. "Buffalo, Deer and Antelope are Again to Roam Indian Country, Government Plans," *Santa Fe New Mexican*, Apr. 26, 1934. Frank Ernest Hill, "Back to the Indian Goes the Buffalo," *New York Times*, May 26, 1935.

18. Deloria and Lytle, *Nations Within*, 115.

19. Collier to Mabel, Jan. 2, 1923. John Collier Papers, Yale Collection of American Literature, Beinecke Rare Book and Manuscript Library, microfilm reel 4.

20. Rusco, *Fateful Time*, 188.

Chapter 24

1. Mabel to Collier, May 18, 1933. John Collier Papers, Yale Collection of American Literature, Beinecke Rare Book and Manuscript Library, microfilm reel 15.

2. While most Pueblo land was held in common, individual plots were assigned to each inhabitant to use as their own. Tony, backed by Mabel's money, steadily acquired possession of many of these lands, often at a very low cost. Those left landless often became resentful. In 1933, a challenge erupted over Tony's own plot of land. This was the acreage just across the irrigation ditch from Mabel's main house. On it stood the guest houses where luminaries such as D. H. Lawrence and Georgia O'Keeffe had stayed. A survey had been located indicating that the land was not Tony's, but instead belonged to another Taos man. A movement arose at Taos Pueblo to evict Tony from the property and tear down the guest houses. As the battle lines hardened, Mabel appealed to Indian Commissioner John Collier for help. After several months of quiet maneuvers, Collier was able to smooth things over in Tony's favor. He wrote to Mabel, "Just to let you know that the matter of the boundary of Tony's property has been finally settled and made of record, so that he will never have to worry about it anymore."

3. Collier to Indian school teachers, Aug. 8, 1933. John Collier Papers, Yale Collection of American Literature, Beinecke Rare Book and Manuscript Library, microfilm reel 15. "Not Startling," *Santa Fe New Mexican*, May 21, 1934.

4. "Indians Hear Tribal Plans," *Duluth News Tribune*, Mar. 4, 1934. "Collier is Ready to Give American Indian 'New Deal,'" *Christian Science Monitor*, Apr. 20, 1933.

5. Collier, *From Every Zenith*, 173.

6. Mabel to Collier, Feb. 6, 1934. John Collier Papers, Yale Collection of American Literature, Beinecke Rare Book and Manuscript Library, microfilm reel 14. Philp, *John Collier's Crusade for Indian Reform*, 158.

7. "Justice to the Indians," *El Paso Times*, Mar. 13, 1934.

8. Rusco, *Fateful Time*, 223.

9. Rusco, 234.

10. John Collier, "United States Indian Administration as a Laboratory of Ethnic Relations," *Social Research* 12, no. 3 (1945): 277. Rusco, *Fateful Time*, 208.

11. Rusco, 236.

12. "Defeat Feared for Indians' 'New Deal' Bill," *Washington Post*, Apr. 21, 1934. Philp, *John Collier's Crusade for Indian Reform*, 155.

13. "Says Mine Owners Fight Indian Bill," *New York Times*, June 6, 1934. "Defeat Feared for Indians' 'New Deal' Bill," *Washington Post*, Apr. 21, 1934.

14. *Hearing Before the Committee on Indian Affairs, United States Senate, Seventy-Third Congress, Second Session on S.2755, February 27, 1934* (Government Printing Office, 1934, available online via Google Books).

15. *Hearing Before the Committee on Indian Affairs.*

16. Pfouts, "Senator Burton K. Wheeler," 49. *Washington Post*, letter to the editor from David Buffalo Bear, May 5, 1934.

17. Hearings on S. 2755, Senate Committee on Indian Affairs, Feb 27, 1934. Rosier, *Serving Their Country*, 67–68.

18. "Indians Plan Congress of 55,000 to Decide on Wheeler-Howard Bill," *Salt Lake Tribune*, Feb. 17, 1934.

19. "Parley of Plains Indians Is Closed," *Houston Post*, Mar. 6, 1934.

20. Deloria, *Indian Reorganization Act*, 88.

21. "Elimination of Features Fought by Indians Aids," *Rapid City Journal*, Mar. 5, 1934.

22. Luhan, *Winter in Taos*, 219–21. Walden, "Pueblo Confederation's Political Wing," 72.

23. Rusco, *Fateful Time*, 247.

24. Rusco, 238.

25. *Los Angeles Times*, Apr. 29, 1934.

26. Rusco, *Fateful Time*, 241.

27. Collier, *From Every Zenith*, 175.

28. Roosevelt to Collier, Jan. 22, 1945. John Collier Papers, Yale Collection of American Literature, Beinecke Rare Book and Manuscript Library, microfilm reel 31.

29. Philp, *Indian Self Rule*, 93. Limerick, *Legacy of Conquest*, 209. Deloria and Lytle, *Nations Within*, 41, 188.

30. Philp, *John Collier's Crusade for Indian Reform*, 213.

Epilogue

1. "Lake Fight Continues," *Carlsbad Current-Argus* (NM), June 10, 1970.

2. *Taos Indians—Blue Lake amendments. Hearings, Ninety-First Congress, Second Session, on S. 750 and H.R. 471 July 9 and 10, 1970* (US Government Printing Office, 1970), www.hathitrust.org.

3. *Taos Indians—Blue Lake amendments. Hearings, Ninety-First Congress.*

4. Andrew Graybill, "'Strong on the Merits and Powerfully Symbolic': The Return

of Blue Lake to Taos Pueblo," *New Mexico Historical Review* (2001): 147. Gordon-McCutchan, *Taos Indians and the Battle for Blue Lake*, 177.

5. *Taos Indians, Blue Lake Hearings, Ninetieth Congress, Second Session, on H.R. 3306 . . . S. 1624 . . . and S. 1625 . . . September 19 and 20, 1968* (Government Printing Office, 1968), 61 (available online via Google Books).

6. Richard Nixon, "Special Message to the Congress on Indian Affairs," The American Presidency Project, July 8, 1970, accessed September 5, 2025, www.presidency.ucsb.edu/node/240040.

7. Statement by Bert G. Phillips, Nov 12, 1948. Taos Blue Lake Collection, Rufus G. Poole Papers, 1903–1959, box 16, folder 3, Princeton University Special Collections, Mudd Manuscript Library.

8. Meeting of Pueblo Council with US Forestry Service, Aug. 15, 1961. Frank Waters Papers, MSS 332, box 18, folder 16, Center for Southwest Research, University of New Mexico.

9. Gordon-McCutchan, *Taos Indians and the Battle for Blue Lake*, 204.

10. Harris, *Report from a Last Survivor* 185.

11. Ebright et al. *Four Square Leagues*, 315.

12. *Taos Indians, Blue Lake. Hearings, Ninetieth Congress, Second Session, on H.R. 3306 . . . S. 1624 . . . and S. 1625 . . . September 19 and 20, 1968* (US Government Printing Office, 1968), 148.

13. *Taos Pueblo—Blue Lake: Hearings Before the Subcommittee on Indian Affairs of the Committee on Interior and Insular Affairs, House of Representatives, Ninety-First Congress, First Session, on H.R. 471, to Amend Section 4 of the Act of May 31, 1963* (US Government Printing Office, 1969), 67–68 (available online via Google Books)

14. *Taos Indians—Blue Lake amendments. Hearings, Ninety-First Congress, Second Session, on S. 750 and H.R. 471 July 9 and 10, 1970* (US Government Printing Office, 1970), www.hathitrust.org. *Taos Indians, Blue Lake. Hearings, Ninetieth Congress, Second Session, on H.R. 3306 . . . S. 1624 . . . and S. 1625 . . . September 19 and 20, 1968* (US Government Printing Office, 1968), 162 (available online via Google Books).

15. *Taos Indians, Blue Lake. Hearings, Ninetieth Congress, Second Session, on H.R. 3306 . . . S. 1624 . . . and S. 1625 . . . September 19 and 20, 1968* (US Government Printing Office, 1968), 162 (available online via Google Books).

16. *Taos Indians—Blue Lake amendments. Hearings, Ninety-First Congress, Second Session, on S. 750 and H.R. 471 July 9 and 10, 1970* (US Government Printing Office, 1970), www.hathitrust.org.

17. George Michaelson, "Hippies Head for the Hills," *Parade Magazine*, Dec. 14, 1969.

18. After directing *Easy Rider* (Pando Company, Raybert Productions, 1969), Dennis Hopper moved to Taos and purchased Mabel and Tony Luján's old compound. In the same place where Mabel had once invited the world's artists and intellectuals to gather, Hopper created his own salon of sorts, bringing in Bob Dylan, actor Jack Nicholson, beat poet Allen Ginsberg, and many others. In between the parties, Hopper hoped to turn Taos into a creative nexus, a place that would inspire a new American revolution ordered on hippie principles. He spoke about Blue Lake to anyone who would listen, citing spiritual parallels

between Taos Puebloans and Buddhist monks. He swore, *If you bore a hole through the bottom of Blue Lake, you will land in Tibet.*

19. Kim Agnew to John Rainer, July 30, 1970. UMCP Agnew Papers, box 38, folder: Indian Affairs IN/T [1970–1973] Exec.)

20. "Kim Agnew Joins Indians in Tribal Goodwill Dance," *Santa Barbara News-Press*, July 26, 1970.

21. Edwin Shrake, "The Matter of Indian Giving," *Sports Illustrated*, Aug. 17, 1970.

22. Seth Kantor, "Anderson Pushes Taos Bill Support, Should Win Senate," *Albuquerque Journal*, Nov. 27, 1970.

23. Harris writes, "Anderson looked directly at me and said that if I didn't agree to his bill, there wouldn't be any bill." Harris, *Report from a Last Survivor*, 190.

24. *Congressional Record*, Senate, Dec. 1, 1970, pp. 39328–39329.

25. *Congressional Record*, Senate, Dec. 2, 1970, pp. 39600–39601.

26. *Congressional Record*, Senate, Dec. 2, 1970, p. 39591.

27. Office of the White House Press Secretary, Exchange of Remarks Between the President and Cacique Juan de Jesus Romero, December 15, 1970. Taos Blue Lake Collection, Rufus G. Poole Papers, 1903–1959, box 1, folder 2, Princeton University Special Collections, Mudd Manuscript Library.

28. Office of the White House Press Secretary, Exchange of Remarks.

29. "Taos Indians Return, Pledge Cooperation," *Santa Fe New Mexican*, Dec. 6, 1970.

Bibliography

Archival Sources

Couse-Sharp Historic Site, Taos, Lunder Research Center
  Michael Grauer Papers
  Teresa Hayes Ebie Papers
Fort Lewis College, Durango, Colorado, Reed Library
Myra Ellen Jenkins Papers
  Huntington Library, San Marino, California
  Bert G. Phillips Papers
  Mary Hunter Austin Papers
Library of Congress
  Theodore Roosevelt Papers
National Archives and Records Administration
  Richard M. Nixon Presidential Library and Museum
United States Forest Service Personnel Files
New Mexico State Records Center and Archives
  Francis C. Wilson Papers
  Governor William J. Mills Papers
  New Mexico Wildlife Federation Collection
  Paul J. Bernal Collection
  Records of the United States Territorial and New Mexico District Courts for Taos County
New Mexico State University
Darlis Miller Papers on Matilda Coxe Stevenson
Princeton University, Mudd Manuscript Library
Taos Blue Lake Collection
Smithsonian Institution
  Ernest Blumenschein Papers
  Vernon Orlando Bailey Papers
University of California, Santa Barbara
The American Presidency Project
University of California, Berkeley, Bancroft Library
  C. Hart Merriam Papers

Florence Merriam Bailey Papers
University of Maryland, College Park, Special Collections and Archives
Spiro T. Agnew Papers
University of New Mexico, Center for Southwest Research
Francis Cushman Wilson Papers on Pueblo Legal Issues
Frank Waters Papers
Robert R. White Papers
University of Wisconsin–Madison
Aldo Leopold Papers
University of Wyoming, American Heritage Center
Vernon Bailey Papers
Yale Collection of American Literature, Beinecke Rare Book and Manuscript Library
John Collier Papers
Mabel Dodge Luhan Papers
Maurice Sterne Papers

Book Chapters, Edited Collections, and Monographs

Alinder, Mary Street, and Ansel Adams. *Ansel Adams: An Autobiography*. Little, Brown, 2017.

Anderson, George B. *History of New Mexico: Its Resources and People*, Vol. 2. Pacific States Publishing, 1907.

Auerbach, Jerold S. *Explorers in Eden: Pueblo Indians and the Promised Land*. University of New Mexico Press.

Austin, Mary. *Earth Horizons*. Houghton Mifflin, 1932.

Bachrach, Arthur J. *D. H. Lawrence in New Mexico*. University of New Mexico Press, 2006.

Bailey, Florence Merriam. *Birds of New Mexico*. New Mexico Department of Game and Fish, 1928.

Bailey, Vernon. *Mammals of New Mexico*. North American Fauna No. 53. US Dept. of Agriculture, Washington, DC, 1931.

Bailey, Vernon Orlando. *Wolves in Relation to Stock, Game, and the National Forest Reserves*. US Dept. of Agriculture, Forest Service, 1907.

Baker, Robert D., Robert S. Maxwell, Victor H. Treat, and Henry C. Dethloff. *Timeless Heritage: A History of the Forest Service in the Southwest*. US Department of Agriculture, Forest Service, 1988.

Blumenschein, Helen. *Sounds and Sights of Taos Valley*. Sunstone Press, 2016.

Brinkley, Douglas. *Wilderness Warrior: Theodore Roosevelt and the Crusade for America*. HarperCollins, 2009.

Britten, Thomas A. *National Council on Indian Opportunity: Quiet Champion of Self-Determination*. University of New Mexico Press, 2014.

Broder, Patricia Janis. *Taos: A Painter's Dream*. New York Graphic Society, 1980.

Burke, Flannery. *From Greenwich Village to Taos: Primitivism and Place at Mabel Dodge Luhan's*. University Press of Kansas, 2016.

Burke, Flannery. *A Land Apart: The Southwest and the Nation in the Twentieth Century.* University of Arizona Press, 2017.

Cather, Willa. *Death Comes for the Archbishop.* Introduction by Kali Fajardo-Anstine. Penguin Classics, 2023.

Catton, Theodore. *American Indians and National Forests.* University of Arizona Press, 2016.

Clarke, Jeanne Nienaber. *Roosevelt's Warrior: Harold L. Ickes and the New Deal.* Johns Hopkins University Press, 1996.

Cline, Lynn. *Literary Pilgrims: The Santa Fe and Taos Writers' Colonies, 1917–1950.* University of New Mexico Press, 2007.

Coke, Van Deren. *Taos and Santa Fe: The Artist's Environment, 1882–1942.* University of New Mexico Press, 1963.

Collier, John. *Entry to the Desert.* Stonehouse Press, 1922.

Collier, John. *From Every Zenith: A Memoir; and Some Essays on Life and Thought.* Sage Books, 1963.

Collier, John. *On the Gleaming Way: Navajos, Eastern Pueblos, Zunis, Hopis, Apaches, and Their Land; and Their Meanings to the World.* Sage Books, 1962.

Crane, Leo. *Desert Drums.* Little, Brown, 1928.

Cronyn, George, ed. *The Path on the Rainbow: An Anthology of Songs and Chants from the Indians of North America.* Boni and Liveright, 1918.

Crosswhite, Virginia Hyde, and Earl G. Ingersoll, eds. *Terra Incognita: D. H. Lawrence at the Frontiers.* Fairleigh Dickinson University Press, 2010.

Dean, John Emory. *Travel Narratives from New Mexico: Reconstructing Identity and Truth.* Cambria Press, 2009.

de Angulo, Jaime. *Jaime in Taos: The Taos Papers of Jaime de Angulo.* City Lights Books, 1985.

deBuys, William. *Enchantment and Exploitation: The Life and Hard Times of a New Mexico Mountain Range.* University of New Mexico Press, 2015.

Deloria, Vine, Jr. *The Indian Reorganization Act: Congresses and Bills.* University of Oklahoma Press, 2002.

Deloria, Vine, Jr., and Clifford M. Lytle. *The Nations Within: The Past and Future of American Indian Sovereignty.* University of Texas Press, 1998.

Demark, Judith Boyce. *Essays in 20th Century New Mexico History.* University of New Mexico Press, 1994.

D'Emilio, Sandra, and Suzan Campbell. *Visions and Visionaries: The Art and Artists of the Santa Fe Railway.* Peregrine Smith Books, 1991.

Dippie, Brian W. *The Vanishing American: White Attitudes and US Indian Policy.* University Press of Kanas, 1982.

Dunbar-Ortiz, Roxanne. *An Indigenous People's History of the United States.* Beacon Press, 2014.

Ebright, Malcolm, and Rick Hendricks. *Pueblo Sovereignty: Indian Land and Water in New Mexico and Texas.* University of Oklahoma Press, 2022.

Ebright, Malcolm, Rick Hendricks, and Richard W. Hughes. *Four Square Leagues: Pueblo Indian Land in New Mexico.* University of New Mexico Press, 2014.

Egan, Timothy. *The Big Burn: Teddy Roosevelt and the Fire That Saved America*. Houghton Mifflin Harcourt, 2009

Egan, Timothy. *Short Nights of the Shadow Catcher: The Epic Life and Immortal Photographs of Edward Curtis*. Mariner Books, 2013.

Eldredge, Charles C., and Julie Schimmel. *Art in New Mexico, 1900–1945: Paths to Taos and Santa Fe*. Abbeville Press, 1986.

Ellis, Florence Hawley. "Anthropological Data Pertaining to the Taos Land Claim." In *Pueblo Indians I: American Indian Ethnohistory, Indians of the Southwest*, compiled and edited by David Agee Horr. Garland, 1974.

Ellis, Reuben J., ed. *Beyond Borders: The Selected Essays of Mary Austin*. Southern Illinois University Press, 1996.

Evans, Max. *Long John Dunn of Taos: From Texas Outlaw to New Mexico Hero*. Clear Light Publications, 1992.

Everett, Patricia R. *Corresponding Lives: Mabel Dodge Luhan, A. A. Brill, and the Psychoanalytic Adventure in America*. Routledge, 2019.

Fenn, Forrest. *Beat of the Drum and the Whoop of the Dance: A Study of the Life and Work of Joseph Henry Sharp*. Fenn Galleries, 1983.

Fenton, William N. *Factionalism at Taos Pueblo, New Mexico*. Smithsonian Institution, Bureau of American Ethnology Bulletin 164. Anthropological Papers, No. 56. US Government Printing Office.

Fergusson, Erna. *Dancing Gods: Indian Ceremonials of New Mexico and Arizona*. University of New Mexico Press, 1988.

Fergusson, Erna. *Our Southwest*. Knopf, 1946.

Forwood, Jenny Parks. *Bert Geer Phillips: Trailblazer of Southwestern Art*. Privately printed, n.d.

Frazer, Winifred L. *Mabel Dodge Luhan*. Twayne's United States Authors Series. Twayne. 2008.

Gano, Geneva. *The Little Art Colony and US Modernism: Carmel, Provincetown, Taos*. Edinburgh University Press, 2022.

Gibson, Arrell Morgan. *The Santa Fe and Taos Colonies: Age of the Muses, 1900–1942*. University of Oklahoma Press, 1983.

Goodman, Susan, and Carl Dawson. *Mary Austin and the American West*. University of California Press, 2008.

Gordon-McCutchan, R. C. *The Taos Indians and the Battle for Blue Lake*. Red Crane Books, 1995.

Grant, Blanche. *Taos Indians*. Rio Grande Press, 1976.

Grant, Blanche. *When Old Trails Were New*. Sunstone Press, 2007

Greenough, Sarah, ed. *My Faraway One: Selected Letters of Georgia O'Keeffe and Alfred Stieglitz*. Vol. 1, *1915–1933*. Yale University Press, 2011.

Hahn, Emily. *Mabel: A Biography of Mabel Dodge Luhan*. Houghton Mifflin, 1977.

Hammond, Ann. *Ansel Adams: Divine Performance*. Yale University Press, 2002.

Harris, Fred. *Report from a Last Survivor*. University of New Mexico Press, 2024.

Hassrick, Peter, and Elizabeth Cunningham. *In Contemporary Rhythm: The Art of Ernest L. Blumenschein*. University of Oklahoma Press, 2008.

Hewett, Edgar L., and Bertha P. Dutton Hewett. *The Pueblo Indian World: Studies on the Natural History of the Rio Grande Valley in Relation to Pueblo Indian Culture*. University of New Mexico Press, 1945.

Hutchinson, Elizabeth. *The Indian Craze: Primitivism, Modernism, and Transculturation in American Art, 1890–1915*. Duke University Press, 2009.

Hyde, Virginia Crosswhite, and Earl G. Ingersoll, eds. *Terra Incognita: D. H. Lawrence at the Frontiers*. Fairleigh Dickinson University Press, 2010.

Jacobs, Margaret D. *Engendered Encounters: Feminism and Pueblo Cultures, 1879–1934*. University of Nebraska Press, 1999.

Jenkins, Philip. *Dream Catchers: How Mainstream American Discovered Native Spirituality*. Oxford University Press, 2004.

Jung, Carl G. *Memories, Dreams, Reflections*. Vintage, 1989.

Jung, Carl G. *Modern Man in Search of a Soul*. Harcourt, 1933.

Kelly, Lawrence C. *The Assault on Assimilation: John Collier and the Origins of Indian Policy Reform*. University of New Mexico Press, 1983.

Kofalk, Harriet. *No Woman Tenderfoot: Florence Merriam Bailey, Pioneer Naturalist*. Texas A&M University Press, 2000.

Kosek, Jake. *Understories: The Political Life of Forests in Northern New Mexico*. Duke University Press, 2006.

La Farge, John Pen. *Turn Left at the Sleeping Dog: Scripting the Santa Fe Legend*. University of New Mexico Press, 2001.

Lanigan, Esther F. *Mary Austin: Song of a Maverick*. University of Arizona Press, 1997.

Larson, Robert W., and Carole B. Larson. *Ernest L. Blumenschein: The Life of an American Artist*. University of Oklahoma Press, 2013.

Lawrence, D. H. *The Letters of D. H. Lawrence*. Vol. 4, *June 1921–March 1924*. Edited by Warren Roberts, Jame T. Boulton, and Elizabeth Mansfield. The Cambridge Edition of the Letters of D. H. Lawrence. Cambridge University Press, 1987.

Lawrence, D. H. *The Woman Who Rode Away and Other Stories*. Knopf, 1928.

Lears, T. J. Jackson. *No Place of Grace: Antimodernism and the Transformation of American Culture, 1880–1920*. University of Chicago Press, 2021.

Leopold, Aldo. *A Sand County Almanac*. Oxford University Press, 1949.

Lewis, Edith. *Willa Cather Living: A Personal Record*. University of Nebraska Press, 1953.

Limerick, Patricia Nelson. *The Legacy of Conquest: The Unbroken Past of the American West*. Norton, 1988.

Luhan, Mabel Dodge. *Edge of the Taos Desert: An Escape to Reality*. University of New Mexico Press, 1987.

Luhan, Mabel Dodge. *Lorenzo in Taos*. Knopf, 1933.

Luhan, Mabel Dodge. *Winter in Taos*. Las Palomas de Taos, 1987.

Lujan, Vernon G. "Taos Pueblo Blue Lake: A Legacy of Cultural Perseverance." In

Indigenous Perspectives on Sacred Natural Sites: Culture, Governance and Conservation, edited by Jonathan Liljeblad and Bas Verschuuren. Routledge, 2018.

Matuz, Roger, ed. *St. James Guide to Native North American Artists*. St. James Press, 1998.

McCartney, Laton. *The Teapot Dome Scandal: How Big Oil Bought the Harding White House and Tried to Steal the Country*. Random House, 2008.

Meine, Curt D. *Aldo Leopold: His Life and Work*. University of Wisconsin Press, 1988.

Miller, Darlis A. *Matilda Coxe Stevenson: Pioneering Anthropologist*. University of Oklahoma Press, 2007.

Montgomery, Charles. *The Spanish Redemption Heritage, Power, and Loss on New Mexico's Upper Rio Grande*. University of California Press, 2002.

Morgan, Arthur Ernest, ed. *The Heritage of Community: A Critique of Community Living Based on Great Ways of Life Practiced by Small Communities Over the World*. Community Service, 1956.

Morrill, Claire. *A Taos Mosaic: Portrait of a New Mexico Village*. University of New Mexico Press, 1973.

O'Neil, Floyd A. "The Indian New Deal: An Overview." In *Indian Self Rule: First-Hand Accounts of Indian-White Relations from Roosevelt to Reagan*, edited by Kenneth Philp. Utah State University Press, 1995.

Ortiz, Alfonso. *The Tewa World: Space, Time Being and Becoming in a Pueblo Society*. University of Chicago Press, 1972.

Parsons, Elsie Clews. *Taos Pueblo*. George Banta Publishing, 1936.

Perry, Walter J. *Walt Perry: An Early-Day Forest Ranger in New Mexico and Oregon*. Wilderness Associates, 1999.

Philp, Kenneth, ed. *Indian Self Rule: First-Hand Accounts of Indian-White Relations from Roosevelt to Reagan*. Utah State University Press, 1995.

Philp, Kenneth. *John Collier's Crusade for Indian Reform, 1920–1954*. University of Arizona Press, 1977.

Rabb, Jane M. *Literature and Photography: Interactions, 1840–1990: A Critical Anthology*. University of New Mexico Press, 1995.

Reed, Maureen E. *A Woman's Place: Women Writing New Mexico*. University of New Mexico Press, 2005.

Robertson, Edna, and Sarah Nestor. *Artists of the Canyons and Caminos: Santa Fe: Early Twentieth Century*. Gibbs Smith, 2006.

Roosevelt, Theodore. *The Winning of the West*, Vol. 1. Current Literature Publishing, 1889.

Rosier, Paul C. *Serving Their Country: American Indian Politics and Patriotism in the Twentieth Century*. Harvard University Press, 2012.

Ruderman, Judith. "Lawrence as Ethnographer and Artist: Apprehending 'Culture' in the American Southwest." In *Terra Incognita: D. H. Lawrence at the Frontiers*, edited by Virginia Crosswhite Hyde and Earl G. Ingersoll. Fairleigh Dickinson University Press, 2010.

Rudnick, Lois, ed. *Mabel Dodge Luhan and Company: American Moderns and the West*. Museum of New Mexico Press, 2016.

Rudnick, Lois Palken. *Mabel Dodge Luhan: New Woman, New Worlds*. University of New Mexico Press, 1987.

Rudnick, Lois Palken. *The Suppressed Memoirs of Mabel Dodge Luhan: Sex, Syphilis, and Psychoanalysis in the Making of Modern American Culture*. University of New Mexico Press, 2012.

Rudnick, Lois P., and Jonathan Warm Day Coming. *Eva Mirabal: Three Generations of Tradition and Modernity at Taos Pueblo*. Museum of New Mexico Press, 2021.

Rusco, Elmer R. *A Fateful Time: The Background and Legislative History of the Indian Reorganization Act*. University of Nevada Press, 2000.

Russell, Francis. *The Shadow of Blooming Grove: Warren G. Harding in His Times*. McGraw Hill, 1968.

Sando, Joe S. *Pueblo Nations: Eight Centuries of Pueblo Indian History*. Clear Light, 1992.

Sando, Joe S. *Pueblo Profiles: Cultural Identity Through Centuries of Change*. Clear Light, 1998.

Santistevan, Corina A., and Julia Moore, eds. *Taos: A Topical History*. Museum of New Mexico Press, 2013.

Schimmel, Julie, and Robert Rankin White. *Bert Geer Phillips and the Taos Art Colony*. University of New Mexico Press, 1994.

Scott, Sascha T. *Strange Mixture: The Art and Politics of Painting Pueblo Indians*. University of Oklahoma Press, 2015.

Scurlock, Dan. *From the Rio to the Sierra: An Environmental History of the Middle Rio Grande Basin*. US Dept. of Agriculture, Forest Service, Rocky Mountain Research Station, 1998.

Smith, Sherry Lynn. *Hippies, Indians, Hippies and the Fight for Red Power*. Oxford University Press, 2012.

Smith, Sherry Lynn. *Reimagining Indians: Native Americans Through Anglo Eyes, 1880–1940*. Oxford University Press, 2000.

Spaulding, Jonathan. *Ansel Adams and the American Landscape: A Biography*. University of California Press, 1998.

Steen, Harold K. *The US Forest Service: A Centennial History*. University of Washington Press, 2013.

Steffens, Lincoln. *The Autobiography of Lincoln Steffens*. Harcourt Brace, 1937.

Sterne, Maurice. *Shadow and Light: The Life, Friends and Opinions of Maurice Sterne*. Harcourt Brace, 1965.

Stewart, Omer. *Peyote Religion, a History*. University of Oklahoma Press, 1987.

Stratton, David H. *Tempest over Teapot Dome: The Story of Albert B. Fall*. University of Oklahoma Press, 1998.

Souder, William. *On a Farther Shore: The Life and Legacy of Rachel Carson, Author of Silent Spring*. Crown, 2012.

Swentzell, Rina. "Anglo Artists and the Creation of Pueblo Worlds." In *The Culture of Tourism, the Tourism of Culture*, edited by Hal K. Rothman. University of New Mexico Press, 2003.

Taggett, Sherry Clayton, and Ted Schwarz. *Paintbrushes and Pistols: How the Taos Artists Sold the West.* John Muir, 1990.

Trachtenberg, Alan. *Shades of Hiawatha: Staging Indians, Making Americans, 1880–1930.* Hill and Wang, 2004.

Treuer, David. *The Heartbeat of Wounded Knee: Native America from 1890 to the Present.* Riverhead Books, 2019

Twitchell, Ralph Emerson. *The Leading Facts of New Mexico History*, Vol. 1. Torch Press, 1911.

Udall, Sharyn Rohlfsen. *Modernist Painting in New Mexico, 1913–1935.* University of New Mexico Press, 1984.

Van Vechten, Carl. *The Splendid Drunken Twenties: Selections from the Daybooks, 1922–1930.* University of Illinois Press, 2007.

Waters, Frank. *The Man Who Killed the Deer.* Sage Books, 1942.

Waters, Frank. *Masked Gods: Navaho and Pueblo Ceremonialism.* University of New Mexico Press, 1950.

Weigle, Marta, and Kyle Fiore. *Santa Fe and Taos: The Writer's Era, 1916–1941.* Ancient City Press, 1994

Wenger, Tisa Joy. *We Have a Religion: The 1920s Pueblo Indian Dance Controversy and American Religious Freedom.* University of North Carolina Press, 2009.

Wetzsteon, Ross. *Republic of Dreams: Greenwich Village: The American Bohemia, 1910–1960.* Simon and Schuster, 2007.

Wilkinson, Charles. *Blood Struggle: The Rise of Modern Indian Nations.* Norton, 2005.

Wilson, Chris. *Myth of Santa Fe: Creating a Modern Regional Tradition.* University of New Mexico Press, 1997.

Zumwalt, Rosemary. *Wealth and Rebellion: Elsie Clews Parsons, Anthropologist and Folklorist.* University of Illinois Press, 1992.

Dissertations and Theses

Archibeck, Ronald P. "Taos Indians and the Blue Lake Controversy." Master's thesis, University of New Mexico, 1972.

Baca, Jacobo. "Somos Indígena: Ethnic Politics and Land Tenure in New Mexico, 1694–1965." PhD dissertation, University of New Mexico, 2015.

Black, Dorothy Skousen. "A Study of Taos as an Art Colony and of Representative Taos Painters." Master's thesis, University of New Mexico, 1959.

Bodine, John James. "Attitudes and Institutions of Taos, New Mexico: Variables for Value System Expression." PhD dissertation, Tulane University, 1967.

Chamberlain, Kathleen Patricia. "The Controversial Term of Albert Bacon Fall, Secretary of the Interior, 1921–1923. Master's thesis, Ohio State University, 1969.

Damico, Denise Holladay. "El agua es la vida" (Water Is Life): Water Conflict and Conquest in Nineteenth Century New Mexico." PhD dissertation, Brandeis University, 2008.

Dauber, Kenneth Wayne. "Shaping the Clay: Pueblo Pottery, Cultural Sponsorship and Regional Identity in New Mexico." PhD dissertation, University of Arizona, 1993.

Hoxie, Frederick E. "Beyond Savagery: The Campaign to Assimilate the American Indians, 1880–1920." PhD dissertation, Brandeis University, 1977.

Jacobs, Margaret Davis. "Uplifting Cultures: Encounters Between White Women and Pueblo Indians, 1890–1935." PhD dissertation, University of California-Davis, 1996.

Johnson, Adam Fulton. "Secretsharers: Intersecting Systems of Knowledge and the Politics of Documentation in Southwesternist Anthropology, 1880–1930." PhD dissertation, University of Michigan, 2018.

Jones, Carter. "'Hope for the Race of Man': Indians, Intellectuals and the Regeneration of Modern America, 1917–1934." PhD dissertation, Brown University, 1991.

Gaither, James M. "A Return to the Village: A Study of Santa Fe and Taos, New Mexico, as Cultural Centers, 1900–1934. PhD dissertation, University of Minnesota, 1957.

Keller, Mary Catherine. "Joseph Henry Sharp—Taos Colony." Master's thesis, Ohio State University, 1934.

King, Brian S. "Mystics, Radicals, Sinners, and Saints: Freedom, Rebirth, and the American West." PhD dissertation, University of New Mexico, 2013.

Krahe, Diane L. "Last Refuge: The Uneasy Embrace of Indian Lands by the National Wilderness Movement, 1937–1965." PhD dissertation, Washington State University, 2005.

Long, Thomas Eugene. "To the Edge of the World and Back: Native American Struggles for Sovereignty Seen Through the Investigations of Colonel L. A. Dorrington, Indian Agent, 1913–1923." PhD dissertation, University of California, Riverside, 2006.

Mayhew, Robert William. "The New Mexico Association on Indian Affairs, 1922–1958." Master's thesis, University of New Mexico, 1984.

Miller, Merle. "A Preliminary Study of the Pueblo of Taos, New Mexico." PhD dissertation, University of Chicago, 1898.

Peck, James Frederick. "Intra-Colonial Spaces: Desire and Displacement in Images of Indian Territory, The Hawa'ian Islands, and New Mexico Territory, 1885–1920." PhD dissertation, University of Oklahoma, 2016.

Pfouts, Sarah B. "Senator Burton K. Wheeler and the 1934 Indian Reorganization Act." Master's thesis, University of Montana, 1981.

Reeve, Kay Aiken. "The Making of an American Place: The Development of Santa Fe and Taos, New Mexico, as an American Cultural Center, 1898–1942." PhD dissertation, Texas A&M University, 1977.

Saxton, Russell Steel. "Ethnocentrism in the Historical Literature of Territorial New Mexico." PhD dissertation, University of New Mexico, 1980.

Smith, M. Estellie. "Aspects of Social Control Among the Taos Indians." PhD dissertation, SUNY-Buffalo, 1967.

Smedshammer, Michael Oren. "Modern Writers in New Mexico: Charles Lummis, Oliver La Farge, D. H. Lawrence, Willa Cather, and the Quest for Purpose and Place in the Southwest." PhD dissertation, University of New Mexico, 1998.

Taylor-Montoya, Amanda. "'Under the Same Glorious Flag': Land, Race, and Legitimacy in Territorial New Mexico." PhD dissertation, University of Oklahoma, 2009.

Turner, Molly Lazear. "The Limits of Enchantment: Landscape and Social Conflict in New Mexico." PhD dissertation, University of Virginia, 2000.

Turo, Bryan W. "An Empire of Dust: Thomas Benton Catron and the Age of Capital in the Hispano Borderlands, 1840–1921." PhD dissertation, University of New Mexico, 2015.

Walden, Robin S. "The Pueblo Confederation's Political Wing: The All Indian Pueblo Council, 1920–1975." Master's thesis, University of New Mexico, 2011.

Walters, Jordan Biro. "Uncommon Knowledge: A History of Queer New Mexico, 1920s–1980s." PhD dissertation, University of New Mexico, 2015.

Zeleny, Carolyn. "Relations Between the Spanish-Americans and Anglo-Americans in New Mexico: A Study of Conflict and Accommodation in a Dual-Ethnic Situation." PhD dissertation, Yale University, 1944.

Newspapers, Magazines, and Scholarly Journals

Albuquerque Journal
American Anthropologist
American Art
Ayer y hoy en Taos (Newsletter of the Taos County Historical Society)
Century Magazine
Chicago Tribune
Christian Science Monitor
Congressional Record
Creative Art
Current Opinion
Dialectical Anthropology
El Paso Herald
El Paso Times
The Forum
Frontiers: A Journal of Women Studies
Harper's
History of Religions
Indianapolis Times
International Social Science Review
Journal of Ethnic Studies
Life
Los Angeles Times
Magazine of American Art
Native American
The Nation
New Mexico Historical Review
New York Times
North American Review
Overland Monthly and Out West Magazine
Pacific Historical Review
El Palacio
Revista de Taos
San Francisco Examiner
Santa Fe New Mexican
Social Research
Southwest Review
Sunset Magazine
The Survey
Taos Valley News
Theatre Arts Monthly
Time
Washington Post

Index

Page numbers in italic text indicate illustrations.